GW00393342

THE BLACK HORSE INSIDE COOLMORE

by William Jones

GOLD RUSH PUBLICATIONS LTD

A GOLD RUSH PUBLICATION

First published in 2015
by Gold Rush Publications Ltd.
207 Regent Street
London
W1B 3HH

Email: info@goldrushpublications.com
Web: www.goldrushpublications.com

© William Jones 2015

All rights reserved. No part of this publication may be reproduced or transmitted in any form or by any means, electronic or mechanical, including photocopying, recording or any information storage and retrieval system, without permission in writing from the publisher.

ISBN:978-1782805748

For Emily, Hannah and Ben;
Cassidy and Delilah.

And Aidan

Contents

PART ONE

INTRODUCTION

"Our lives begin to end the day
we become silent about things
that matter."

Martin Luther King

The eighth wonder of the world. That's how I describe the famous Coolmore Stud to anyone who asks me what it's like. I have been in awe of the place ever since my first day of work on 16 January 2006. I went there initially for just five months for the foaling season, but stayed nine years. When I first entered the foaling barn at Fairy King Farm, the first mare I saw was in foal to the legendary Sadler's Wells. Some difference to the hairy-arsed jumping mares I was used to back home in Wales, who would mostly be in foal to a stallion costing a grand or two.

It was a privilege to work at Coolmore with some of the best thoroughbred horses on the planet and in the most stunning of settings, under the gaze of Slievenamon Mountain, probably better than anywhere else in the racehorse world. The farms and barns are immaculate. When the thousands of trees that are planted everywhere blossom in the spring and early summer your breath can be taken away by the beauty of it all, even more so if the sun agrees to put in an appearance.

Coolmore refers to itself as the Home Of Champions, and there are champions everywhere, equine and human. I worked in the stallion yard, where the likes of Sadler's Wells, Galileo and Montjeu ruled like royalty, and with millionaire yearlings like St Nicholas Abbey, Camelot and Australia. Best of all I was part of the foaling team on John Magnier's own farm, and had a hand to

1

play with Classic winners like Gleneagles, Ruler Of The World, Homecoming Queen, Bracelet and many other top racehorses when they opened their eyes for the first time.

Then there are the people. Brilliant people everywhere you look. The Irish are warm, generous and funny. What you see is what you get. Coolmore, though, is now much more than about the Irish. Many of the workforce are from abroad – foreign staff will work for less money. I loved the cosmopolitan atmosphere. Working alongside people from Eastern Europe, France, Germany, New Zealand, Australia, the UK and other countries only ever added to the

DO NOT DISTURB. The author poses while the great Sadler's Wells takes a nap

richness of the experience as far as I was concerned. The outward signs given to the rest of the world point to Coolmore being a perfect place. Read the stallion brochure and it looks like an equestrian paradise. It can, though, be a very tough place to work and bullying rears its ugly head all too often. It was only in late 2014 that managers put in place a policy for dealing with it that was acceptable to the Health and Safety Authority. I forced them to do this.

Staff work long hours and Coolmore doesn't pay overtime. Trade unions or any kind of employee association are banned. There is no worthwhile support system for staff grievances or problems; you are totally on your own. There have been two suicides on the main farm in recent times. Two young men in their twenties hanged themselves. One was Aidan Purcell, who I knew and whose fine family are still haunted four years later by what happened.

Concerns about safety, repeatedly flagged by staff, have been ignored even when there have been some very serious accidents around the farms. I campaigned for nearly 12 months before managers finally accepted that safety procedures for staff working at night, of which I was one, should be completely re-written. It was all about trying to pre-empt the kind of life changing injury endured by stallion man Michael Power, who had to go to the High Court in Dublin to get justice.

When I raised all of these issues throughout 2014, Coolmore had an investigation carried out into my complaints which completely exonerated the stud and said any employer would find my behaviour unacceptable. I was causing them too much trouble, it was time I left. Staff were told I was retiring, even though I wasn't due to retire.

Thanks to the Rights Commissioner to whom I had made a complaint about the way I had been treated, I was able to leave on my own terms. That wasn't the case for two senior and long standing managers. They left shrouded in mystery in a growing scandal which rocked the stud and shocked the wider bloodstock world.

But I was ready to go, even though I loved my job in Magnier's principal foaling barn, which I had hoped to keep doing until I was seventy. I had been diagnosed with prostate cancer in late 2012, which may have been caused by the excessive hours I was working at night, and successfully underwent treatment in May 2013. My recovery was excellent and I was in good shape, but my mental well-being was then put under enormous pressure by the six month investigation I endured as a result of the bullying complaint I had made. I was happy to put my health first and walk away. This is my story. First, though, back to where it all began for Coolmore.

Slievenamon, which means "mountain of women", provides the backdrop to the 5000 acre Coolmore Stud. According to Irish mythology, a local warrior decided to hold a footrace to the top of the mountain for all the potential brides who were pursuing him. He would marry the winner, which was Grainne. The story goes that it was Grainne he wanted anyway, so he told her of a short cut just to make sure.

Chapter 1

IN THE BEGINNING

Tim Vigors

IN THE BEGINNING

"The best time to plant a tree
was twenty years ago. The
second best time is now."

Chinese Proverb

John Magnier is the mastermind who built Coolmore Stud into a world class racing and breeding empire. The Coolmore brand is acknowledged as the global market leader wherever there are thoroughbred horses and the men and women associated with them. He turned a few hundred acres of Ireland into a super power on three continents and which, in 2015, celebrated 40 years of existence.

Magnier's multi-million euro organisation is based near Fethard, which was founded as a fortified village in the early 1200s by a Norman lord, William de Baorse, who had been installed by King John of England as the chief tenant of a substantial territory roughly equivalent to County Tipperary today. Immigrants were enticed from Britain to come and live in the area, particularly from William De Baorse's vast estates in Wales, and Fethard's medieval population was largely made up of rural folk from across the Irish Sea.

Fethard is remarkable for being heavily fortified. It was surrounded by high walls as part of a policy of establishing secure market villages in those early days, thereby increasing the safety of the inhabitants living within against the aggression of the native Irish population. Much of the fortification built then still survives today, making it the most complete walled circuit of its kind in Ireland. Over 400 years later those walls could not stop the infamously destructive armies of Oliver Cromwell as the English slaughtered everything that moved in a bid to keep control of the rebellious Irish.

7

Tim Vigors was a fighter, though of a completely different kind to those of the dark days of Cromwell. A Battle of Britain pilot in the Second World War, he won the Distinguished Flying Cross for his bravery, achieving the rank of Wing Commander in the RAF. Although born in England in 1921, his family had been land owners in County Carlow for centuries. It was Vigors who laid the foundations for Coolmore Stud.

He spent most of his youth in England but never lost his Irish roots. He had his country's tricolour painted on the nose of his Spitfire. Toughness and bravery were ingrained in him from early in life. He was hunting with the Mendip hounds, aged eight, when his pony hit the top of a stone wall and turned a somersault. His face became a bloodied mess when it landed on a jagged stone. He desperately wanted to carry on but his mother dragged him away to be checked over at the nearest hospital.

After finishing his education at Eton, Vigors enrolled as a cadet at RAF Cranwell in January 1939. One year later he was flying Spitfires with 222 Squadron. In May 1940, he received orders to head for Dunkirk and over the coast of France he shot down his first enemy aircraft, a Messerschmitt 109. Two days later he shot down his first Heinkel 111.

Vigors was known throughout his life to live fast and furious - he married four times including to Atalanta Fairey, widow of aircraft pioneer Richard Fairey - and it was no different in war time. On the night of 19 June 1940, be returned to his base in Lincolnshire having had a few drinks on a night out and went to bed. When a loudspeaker message called for a volunteer to intercept German aircraft which had crossed the coast, Vigors took to the air wearing his scarlet pyjamas under a green silk dressing gown. He shot down another Heinkel.

In December 1941, he led his squadron to northern Malaya and came under immediate attack from Japanese aircraft. Vigors shot three bombers down in the ensuing dogfight, but his own plane was also damaged by gunfire and he bad to bail out. Japanese fighter planes continued to fire at him as he parachuted down, but he escaped death by pulling himself up the lines of his parachute. He eventually landed in the mountains near Penang but was badly burned and a bullet had passed straight through his left thigh. Luckily, two Malays found him and carried him down the mountain to safety.

After the war, he set up a photography agency in Ireland and then joined bloodstock auctioneers, Goffs, leaving in 1951 to start his own bloodstock agency. As one of the first people to see a future for private aviation, Vigors set up a company in England in the late 1950s which specialised in executive aircraft. When the company was taken over, he returned to bloodstock and became a significant player. He was one of the first agents with the vision to see thoroughbred breeding as an international industry. When he sold his firm it became known as The British Bloodstock Agency (Ireland).

Vigors' father had returned to Ireland just before the war and bought a farm in Co Tipperary, called Coolmore, where he trained a few racehorses. After inheriting the farm, Vigors moved there in 1968 and it was he who started building it into the famous stud farm it is today. Among the stallions he stood was the Prix de l'Arc de Triomphe winner Rheingold, whom he acquired in 1973 for £1 million.

That same year, Vincent O'Brien bought two thirds of Coolmore Stud from Vigors, who needed money to settle a divorce case. When Vigors also said he didn't want to run the farm anymore, O'Brien needed to find a new manager and he decided to approach John Magnier, who had been running his family's Grange Stud since the early death of his father. The O'Briens and Magniers were well known to each other; they were old Cork families steeped in farming and horses for generations.

The Magniers had kept National Hunt stallions since the 1850s and a hundred years later their Grange Stud was famous for standing Cottage, the leading jumps stallion of his times and the sire of Cottage Rake, who made Vincent O'Brien's name as a trainer when he won three consecutive Cheltenham Gold Cups in 1948-1950. Then there were three consecutive Champion Hurdles with Hatton's Grace and three consecutive Grand Nationals, all with different horses; Early Mist, Royal Tan and Quare Times. Having done it all in the National Hunt game, O'Brien bought the 300 acre Ballydoyle Farm for IR£17,000 in Co Tipperary in 1950 and built a training operation for flat racing from scratch.

In addition to training, he enjoyed considerable success breeding racehorses long before Coolmore Stud came along. The Ballydoyle Stud was established in 1952 and within a few years had bred an Irish Derby winner, Chamier. O'Brien bought and ran Longfield Stud near Cashel and retired Chamier to stand there as a stallion at the end of his racing career. Then, in the 1970s, he set up Lyonstown Stud at Rosegreen, the nearest village to Ballydoyle, where Sadler's Wells, El Gran Senor, El Prado, Glenstal, King's Lake and Dr Devious were either foaled or reared under the ever watchful O'Brien eyes.

Magnier's stud operation also expanded when he bought and set about developing the 200 acre Castlehyde Stud. By 1975, Castlehyde and Grange were standing thirteen stallions including Deep Run, who would go on to win 14 consecutive National Hunt Sires' Championships, and the sprinters Green God and Deep Diver.

O'Brien and Magnier decided to merge Coolmore Stud in Fethard and Grange and Castlehyde in Fermoy under the Coolmore banner. The big picture was starting to take shape. Magnier also become engaged to O'Brien's daughter, Susan.

Bronze of Champion Stallion Deep Run at Coolmore

Magnier had met Robert Sangster, the heir to the Vernon's Pools business, in 1971, and they impressed each other with their desire to make it big in the racing and bloodstock world. With Tim Vigors now wanting to move away to Spain, Sangster joined in the partnership with O'Brien and Magnier and the Coolmore name was on a one way ticket skywards.

The concept was to buy American bred yearlings, the best in the world at that time, turn them into champion racehorses at Ballydoyle and then earn massive profits standing them as stallions at Coolmore. O'Brien was the trainer with the uncanny ability to repeatedly select the right yearlings which he could develop into outstanding racehorses. Sangster had money to spend, which also attracted other investors in to make sure they had the funds to compete at the very top of the yearling sales in America. Magnier provided the business brain which ensured the stallions fulfilled their financial potential in the breeding shed.

O'Brien's younger brother Phonsie was part of the team which worked the sales grounds in America looking for the next champion racehorse. In an interview in 2010, five months after Vincent died, he gave an insight in to Robert Sangster's role.

"He was a great friend. There isn't a day goes by that I don't think of him. He was a good man, a very good man. He never interfered in any way with the training or the racing of the horses, he knew that they were being trained by the best. But the whole operation would not have been possible without Sangster. They were wonderful years. I had shares in stallions with Tim Vigors for a long time.

Then it came about that, the horses we bought in America, I had 1/40th of them. I was racing at the Curragh one day with Robert, and one of his horses won the Beresford. I had no share in him. I turned to Robert. 'I have no share in him Robert,' I said. 'What will you charge me for a share?' 'One hundred and twenty five thousand,' he said. 'Right, I'll take it.' One hundred and twenty five thousand! Do you know what that horse was? Sadler's Wells. Sadler's Wells. That's what kept Phonsie for the rest of his life."

Surrounded by the charisma, inventiveness and vision of people like Vigors, O'Brien and Sangster, it is little wonder the hugely ambitious Magnier picked up the ball and ran with it, eventually owning Coolmore and Ballydoyle outright and becoming fabulously rich and powerful along the way. No one, not even Sheikh Mohammed with all the oil wealth of Dubai, has been able to catch him since.

Magnier has been described by people who knew him well as intense and focused. A brilliant mind, clicking like a computer, and tough with it. He lived his early life at a tremendous pace and was far more the modern tycoon than any traditional Irish horseman.

Also moving fast around that time was a little horse from Canada who was beginning to re-write the history of thoroughbred breeding. Magnier and his team hung on tightly to the coat tails of Northern Dancer and their lives were changed forever too.

Slievenamon Mountain shrouded in early morning cloud

Chapter 2

NORTHERN DANCER

NORTHERN DANCER

"First is first, second is nowhere."

Sebastian Coe

Northern Dancer's stallion sons and grandsons have become synonymous with the rise of Coolmore to its present day status of being the number one stud and racing operation in the world. He was an outstanding racehorse, the Champion Three Year Old colt in the USA in 1964 when he won the first two legs of the Triple Crown, the Kentucky Derby and the Preakness.

He retired to stud in Canada in 1965 before switching to Maryland in the United States in 1969. He finally retired from stud duties in April 1987 at the age of 26. The remarkable success he achieved from those 23 years as a stallion earned him the title of the Sire Of The Century. He was leading sire in North America in 1970 and his many sons, grandsons and great grandsons have added to his unparalleled success story there. His son Northern Taste was leading sire in Japan for ten years and his grandson Danehill has had a similar impact in Australia, where he was champion sire nine times.

Northern Dancer's record in the UK and Ireland is remarkable. In addition to his own four champion sire titles, sons Sadler's Wells was champion 14 times and Be My Guest and Nijinsky once each. His grandsons Caerleon (twice), Danehill (three times) and great grandson Danehill Dancer (in 2009) were also champions. Grandson Galileo won his seventh title in 2015 in a keen duel with Sheikh Mohammed's flagship stallion, Dubawi. Northern Dancer and Nijinsky were at stud in North America, the remainder stood or still stand at Coolmore in Ireland.

Northern Dancer died on 16 November 1990, which has turned out to be a pivotal year for Coolmore. They have the impressive distinction of standing the champion sire in the UK and Ireland in every year in the 25 since 1990. Not even the golden eras of Manchester United Football Club or New Zealand's All Blacks rugby team can get anywhere near a record like that.

In 2015, every single one of the 26 stallions who stood at Coolmore for the breeding season were descended from the great Northern Dancer, 23 of them directly through the sire line and three through the dam line. Fourteen of the 17 National hunt stallions they stood in the same year were from the Northern Dancer sire line. It's a combined roster without match in the thoroughbred world.

Sadler's Wells, more than any other man or beast, is the reason why Coolmore Stud has become the world leader it undoubtedly is. As champion sire 14 times, he propelled John Magnier into the big time and was the foundation on which he became fabulously wealthy. When Sadler's Wells finally retired it was estimated in the Racing Post he had earned Coolmore in excess of €800 million in stud fees. All tax free, thanks to Charlie Haughey's infamous zero tax policy on stallion income when the country's Finance Minister.

From the huge stud fees Sadler's Wells earned over 20 years, Magnier was not only able to build Coolmore into a magnificent stud farm operation of over 5000 acres in Ireland, with satellite operations in America and Australia, but also to invest in many other ventures which today comfortably make the secretive businessman a billionaire several times over. It has been claimed he owns as many as 25,000 acres around the world.

It was said confidently at the height of his powers that the likes of Sadler's Wells, easily the best stallion in Europe, would never be seen again. Yet almost immediately his son Galileo has taken his place and is probably an even better stallion at this stage of their respective careers. Certainly, in 2015, he is universally viewed as the best stallion in the world. In particular, he is building an outstanding record for siring top class race fillies. Sadler's Wells produced some great ones, like Salsabil, Imagine, Islington and Alexandrova, but if he stays healthy Galileo will end up even better than his own sire. Magnier is well on his way to earning another billion.

Galileo is revered in the influential American bloodstock world in a way that Sadler's Wells was never quite able to achieve, even though he was crowned champion stallion there in 1995. Sadler's Wells and Galileo are son and grandson

The look of an eagle. Triple Oaks winner Alexandrova, daughter of Sadler's Wells, grandaughter of Northern Dancer and a broodmare at Coolmore.

respectively of Northern Dancer, the Canadian bred stallion who has transformed thoroughbred breeding on a scale never seen before. When Northern Dancer won the Kentucky Derby in 1964, he also won an award in his homeland no horse has ever won before or since. Canada's hard-nosed editors and journalists overlooked the sports mad country's top athletes and sportsmen, even their gold medalists in an Olympic year, and named Northern Dancer Athlete Of the Year.

Why was Northern Dancer so good as a stallion? He obviously passed on his own outstanding athletic ability to his sons and daughters. They could run like the wind; but other crucial factors were their toughness, heart, courage, their will to win, all attributes associated with Northern Dancer himself as a racehorse and which he freely passed on. The Minstrel, small in stature like his father, displayed that level of courage needed when winning a war of attrition with Hot Grove in the Epsom Derby in 1977 on his way to being crowned Horse of the Year.

A horse has to be particularly tough as well as talented to win the Triple Crown, the American or English version. Northern Dancer's son Nijinsky was the last to achieve this distinction in England, in 1970. That not one has been special enough to do it in the 45 years since says it all. Then there was Nureyev and St Nicholas Abbey, who both epitomized the level of raw courage so associated with Northern Dancer on the racetrack and when they were faced with calamitous injury and illness themselves.

Although he has been dead for 25 years, Northern Dancer line horses have won more Breeders Cup races than any other stallion. Since 1994, the male bloodline of every winner of the Prix de l'Arc de Triomphe goes back to Nearco and his son Nasrullah and grandson Northern Dancer. Galileo won the English Derby in 2001 and from there 13 of the last 15 winners of the Epsom Classic have been won by Northern Dancer line horses. The brilliant European Champion Sea The Stars, World Champion Frankel and the undefeated Australian Champion Black Caviar all descend from Northern Dancer.

While the bloodstock world looks with awe upon Sadler's Wells and Galileo, and the way Coolmore have brilliantly managed them, the story of how their mould-breaking ancestor came into existence and then flourished comprises a chain of events, coincidences, lucky breaks, twists and turns which would defy belief in a novel. The Northern Dancer story is the stuff of legend. It's Clark Kent turning into Superman, because he was a little horse, dismissed time and again because of his size, and to many he appeared the opposite of what any thoroughbred should look like, let alone a champion. Today, however, his descendants dominate racing the world over.

If one link in that precious chain had been broken along the way there would be no Sadler's Wells and Galileo as we now know them. No Nijinsky, Golden Fleece, or The Minstrel. No Nureyev, Storm Cat, El Gran Senor or Caerleon. No Montjeu, Camelot, St Nicholas Abbey. No Danzig sire line which has also had such an influence on the breed. Not even Hurricane Fly, world record holder of 22 Grade 1 wins, or the heroic Istabraq in the jumping game. There would have been no Northern Dancer to start a dynasty never before seen in the proud history of the thoroughbred racehorse.

The amazing story behind Norther Dancer has carried on into the lives of Sadler's Wells and Galileo, who have both benefitted from chance situations which would make you shake your head in disbelief if you read it in a thriller by Dick Francis, who came to know a thing or two about fiction when writing forty international bestsellers.

The Northern Dancer story began when a wealthy brewing magnate decided it was time for a champion racehorse and stallion to be bred and raised in Canada. That idea brought a few laughs in the racing and breeding world around 1950.

There is a lot of snow and ice in Canada and it's climate does not compare with the temperate blue grass of Kentucky or the lush green of Ireland. E P (Eddie) Taylor, creator of Windfields Farm with his wife Winifred, didn't plan on breeding a horse that would change the course of modern thoroughbred history. An ordinary, everyday champion would have been fine. But that's what happened; he bred, raised and raced Northern Dancer and wrote his name forever into racing history. His dream was to win the Kentucky Derby with a home bred horse, and that's what he did.

Taylor's father was a colonel in the Canadian army and was stationed in England during World War 1. The colonel had his family with him but 15 year old Edward kept running off to join the British army, so he was sent home to Canada. He went to live with his grandfather, Charles Magee, a successful entrepreneur who spent the next year teaching his young grandson the blood and guts of corporate dealmaking.

Magee died during the summer of 1918, just before Edward went to university, but his influence was to be life changing. He decided to follow in his grandfather's footsteps. Magee had been the majority shareholder in a small Ottawa brewery and when Edward returned home after university he was appointed a director. Eddie to his friends, he became universally known otherwise as E P Taylor.

Following the repeal of the Temperance Act in 1927, he presented the board of the brewery with a plan for a major expansion. They said no. Instead, in the wake of the 1929 stock market crash, he convinced ten small breweries to merge into the Brewing Corporation of Ontario, with E P Taylor as president and general manager. This was the forerunner of Canadian Breweries, which grew to be the world's largest brewing company.

In 1936, Taylor decided to merge his beer interests with his passion for thoroughbreds. Alcohol was not allowed by law to be advertised, but he could advertise a racing stable even if it just happened to share the same name, Cosgrave, with one of his brands of beer. He was way ahead of his times.

He became heavily involved in the Canadian government's war effort when World War II broke out and was appointed by Winston Churchill to run the British Supply Council in North America. He nearly lost his life in December 1940 when the ship he was on was torpedoed while crossing the Atlantic. Luck came his way when he and others on the sinking ship were rescued by a captain who broke regulations to pick them up.

Through his war time service, Taylor got to know the top businessmen across North America and around the world. Over the years, as his business career flourished, he owned major stakes in many of his country's greatest companies, such as Canadian Food Products, Massey Ferguson, Dominion Stores, Standard Broadcasting and Hollinger Mines. He became one of Canada's wealthiest men.

There are some striking similarities between the lives of E P Taylor and John Magnier. Thirty years after Taylor, Magnier had to end his formal education at Glenstal Abbey, near Limerick, at 15 years of age to take over the running of the family farm on the premature death of his father. Just as Taylor merged his brewing interests to create an industry giant, Magnier merged his farm with one owned by his father-in-law, Vincent O'Brien, and went on to create the world leading Coolmore brand. Magnier, too, was way ahead of his times in Ireland.

E P Taylor also pioneered the concept of luxury communities in exotic places. He founded the highly exclusive Lyford Cay Development Corporation in the Bahamas. The Lyford Cay Club on New Providence Island is home to some of the wealthiest people in the world. Taylor moved permanently to the Bahamas in 1963 to take advantage of its warm climate and inheritance laws. He died there in 1989 at the age of 88.

Magnier is a tax exile, spending over five months of every winter in Barbados, leaving Ireland around the middle of November and returning in time for the first classic of the new racing season the following May, the 2000 Guineas in England. With business partners J P McManus and Dermot Desmond, he spent US$450 million developing the exclusive Sandy Lane Hotel into a leading holiday destination for the world's rich and famous. Tiger Woods married and honeymooned there.

Taylor was a friend of US President John F Kennedy. In December 1962, the President stayed at Taylor's home in Lyford Cay while he held talks with British Prime Minister Harold MacMillan. Magnier was an adviser to Ireland's Taoiseach Charles Haughey, who appointed him to the Irish Senate in 1987. While Taylor clearly had the best political connections, Magnier is out in front as far as royalty is concerned. The Canadian Royal Family often stayed at Taylor's estate when visiting Toronto. In the summer of 1974 Britain's Queen Mother was a guest there and in 1981 it was the turn of Prince Charles and Diana, Princess of Wales.

But Magnier can claim the friendship and patronage of the head of the British Monarchy. Queen Elizabeth II has reputedly stayed at his Sandy Lane

Hotel in Barbados and on her historical state visit to Ireland in May 2011, she paid a private visit to Coolmore Stud following an official engagement at the nearby Rock Of Cashel in Co Tipperary, lunching in Magnier's mansion on the stud. The Queen has sent mares from her Royal Studs to board at Coolmore and be mated with its stallions.

Taylor and Magnier became directly connected in the late 1960s, when the names of Vincent O'Brien, Robert Sangster and Magnier were added to the Northern Dancer story. They played a huge part in the horse's second career as a stallion, spending the kind of money never seen before in the bloodstock world when buying his yearlings.

Let's now go back even further, to the early journey which led to the birth of the great Northern Dancer, because looking back at how the story evolves it becomes crystal clear fate plays the decisive hand on so many occasions.

Born in Turin in 1869, Federico Tesio was orphaned when he was six years old. He obtained a degree from the University of Florence, was a cavalry officer in the Italian Army in World War 1 and was appointed to the Italian Senate in 1939. However, his place in history is owed to the thoroughbred horse. He is still hugely respected long after his death as one of the world's foremost authorities on breeding thoroughbreds and is celebrated as the breeder of Nearco, paternal grandsire of Northern Dancer.

Tesio bred three exceptional racehorses who became hugely influential stallions, Donatello, Ribot and Nearco. He bred, owned and trained a total of 22 Italian Derby winners and is remembered for his meticulous planning of every stage in the process. Yet if everything had gone according to Tesio's plans, Nearco would never have been born. Tesio was much like Agatha Christie's Hercule Poirot in appearance, character and methodology.

When selecting stallions for his small band of broodmares, he would carefully examine every possible detail, not just the obvious attributes of the prospective stallion. The effects of the mare's long journey from his Dormello Stud in northern Italy to the physical qualities, failings, character and peculiarities of the stallion and his ancestors, they were all painstakingly considered. He would even examine the lay out of the stallion stud and the competence of its staff.

When considering a stallion for Nogara, one of his favourite mares, Tesio was even more thorough than usual. A classic winner in Italy, her conformation was ideal in Tesio's opinion, being small and compact. He had high hopes for her if he chose the right stallion. After much deliberation, he settled on Lord Derby's Fairway, winner of the English St Leger, as perfect for Nogara. They complemented each other in every way and he wanted to add stamina to the mating.

But Tesio had taken too long coming to his decision. By the time he contacted Lord Derby's stud manager to make the necessary arrangements, Fairway's book of mares for the season, restricted without exception in those long gone breeding days, was full. In desperation, Tesio reluctantly decided to send Nogara to France to be bred to Fairway's full brother, Pharos. Compact, muscular and with doubts over his stamina, Pharos was the opposite of Fairway in almost every way. Tesio had no great hopes for the mating.

Nogara's colt foal by Pharos was born on 24 January 1935 and Tesio didn't show much interest in him. That year he started to travel all his weanlings south to spend the winter grazing and growing at Oligiata, the estate of the Marchese Incisa. Running free in the Oligiata paddocks in the milder winter of the south of Italy, Nogara's foal called Nearco blossomed into a beautiful and athletic young horse and was the leader of the gang of Tesio's yearlings.

The two horses who made Tesio's name; Ribot (left) and Nearco.

Now impressed with his attitude and appearance, the Italian began to believe this colt could make a racehorse. When he started to train him, he found the youngster had speed to spare. No matter what he asked of him, Nearco did it with ease, even indifference. Tesio's training methods were gruelling. He believed that a horse should race only if it was at peak fitness and it was preferable to lose a race because of over conditioning than under conditioning. Tesio worked Nearco even harder than usual, yet in morning gallops or in the big races themselves, Nearco did exactly what was required of him. He was never bad tempered or difficult, but always unflinching and completely professional.

He won 14 races from 5 furlongs to 1 mile 7 furlongs in an unbeaten career which included the Italian Derby. His final race was the only time he raced outside Italy. At Longchamps, on Sunday 26 June 1938, he annihilated the field in the Grand Prix de Paris. Well behind him were the English and French Derby winners. Less than a week later, with war looming over Europe and North Americans like E P Taylor not yet involved, Tesio sold Nearco to Martin Benson, an English stud owner, for the then record price for a thoroughbred of £60,000. Nearco was immediately shipped to Benson's Beech House Stud in Newmarket.

When German bombing raids began to threaten Newmarket, Nearco was moved to Wales for two months. As the bombing spread throughout the UK, he was repatriated to Newmarket, where a special air-raid shelter had been built for him in his paddock. He went on to sire many top class racehorses, including English Derby winners Dante and Nimbus.

In North America, two of his sons were responsible for creating breed changing new bloodlines. Nasrullah, the sire of Bold Ruler and grandsire of the great Secretariat, became the ancestor of many outstanding US champions. Best of all, Nearco got Nearctic, sire of Northern Dancer. It was now E P Taylor's turn to play an improbable hand in the mystical creation of Northern Dancer. Pursuing his passion to breed a horse good enough to win the Kentucky Derby, he looked towards England for help. He requested George Blackwell of the British Bloodstock Agency to purchase the best broodmare to be offered at the 1952 December Sales at Tattersalls in Newmarket.

Blackwell recommended the Hyperion mare Lady Angela. She was eight years old and both her dam and sire traced back to some of the greatest horses in British racing history. Hyperion was small but that didn't stop him becoming an outstanding racehorse and now, as a stallion, he was beginning to emerge as a promising sire of broodmares. Crucially, Lady Angela was in foal to the brilliant champion Nearco. Taylor agreed with the choice on one condition; he wanted her to remain in England to foal and then be bred back to Nearco before shipping to Canada.

Stud owner Martin Benson, who had bought Nearco from Tesio, was also the owner of Lady Angela, but for some reason he refused Taylor's request to breed the mare back to his stallion. Taylor said that was the deal, take it or leave it. Blackwell eventually persuaded Benson to think again, telling him that Taylor was a wealthy Canadian and there might be further business to be had down the line.

The deciding factor turned out to be British currency restrictions when travelling abroad. Benson, a wealthy bookmaker in addition to his stud operation, liked to escape the cold and wet British winters by holidaying in Florida. However, he was severely restricted by how much money he could take out of the UK. So he finally agreed to Lady Angela being bred back to Nearco if Taylor would supply him with $3000 in American currency on Benson's next Florida holiday.

Lady Angela was duly sold to Taylor when she appeared at the Newmarket sale. She made £35,000, a huge sum for a broodmare in the 1950s. Although she descended from a blue chip family, which included the brilliant Pretty Polly who won 22 of 24 races at the turn of the century, Lady Angela herself won only one minor race and was yet to supply anything of note in her breeding career. She foaled a colt back at Benson's stud, named Empire Day, and she was then successfully covered again by Nearco.

Lady Angela had already produced two foals by Nearco which caused no excitement as racehorses. The first was a temperamental filly and the next a colt who was soon gelded. Between them they won only one poor race, so while she had claims to be the best mare in the sale, Lady Angela was far from perfect.

Empire Day was also destined to give the Taylors little cause to celebrate. He raced 36 times and won just three minor races. Yet Taylor had stubbornly insisted on breeding the mare back to Nearco before he would buy her. It didn't make much sense at the time and after Empire Day turned out a flop it made no sense at all. Safely inside Lady Angela as she sailed from England to Canada in the summer of 1953 was the foal from that return mating. It was Nearctic, the sire of Northern Dancer.

Disaster, though, was only a heartbeat away as Harry Green, stallion manager at E P Taylor's National Stud, waited on the quay at Montreal Docks for the horses from England to be unloaded. The first one off was a gift from Lord Derby to Taylor, which Harry was able to load in his horsebox without fuss. The wait for Lady Angela and her foal was getting longer and longer when Harry was urgently summoned aboard the ship. They had a problem with one of the horses. Looking over the hatch into the vast hold, Harry saw the mare was severely distressed, shaking in fear and rage, saturated in sweat. He shouted to put her back in her stall and ran down into the hold.

There was not enough room to put the mare and foal together in the crate used to take them off the ship and the deckhands had been trying to offload the mare first, leaving the foal waiting in the hold. Understandably, the mare was having none of it, she wouldn't go anywhere without her foal. Harry stayed close to the frantic mare soothing and calming her. Eventually, when she had quietened down and he had regained her trust, he walked the foal into the unloading crate, leaving the mare behind for as short a time as possible as he rode up with foal.

Harry and the foal were hoisted up high out of the hold and swung over onto the side of the quay. It wasn't a pleasant experience at all. He was able to put the foal into the horsebox, where he had the company of the first horse they had unloaded. He quickly went back into the hold for Lady Angela and with him by her side in the crate she, too, was hoisted out of the depths of the ship, onto the quay and reunited with her foal in the horsebox.

When Harry first went into the hold and found the mare in such an agitated state any thing could have happened. She could have fatally injured herself or Nearctic, the foal inside her. Nearctic could easily have been aborted as Lady Angela was only halfway through gestation. Not necessarily then but hours, days or even weeks later. In my time working at Coolmore, I was once keeping watch at night over the in-foal mare Denebola, a former champion two year old filly by Storm Cat, for a few weeks when she suffered from travel sickness after flying into Shannon Airport from America.

She was particularly sick for the first week, looking more dead than alive, and was treated with intravenous fluids and antibiotics, but with round the clock care from the vets and staff at Drumdeel Farm she slowly pulled through and went on the make a full recovery. For her the problem was just the routine stress, strain and changing temperatures of a long journey, with a trip in a horsebox at

High Chapparal winning Epsom Derby

both ends. For Lady Angela, the journey by boat was infinitely longer and more stressful.

The Sadlers Wells stallion, High Chaparral, had been a regular shuttler to Australia and New Zealand for years, but at Christmas 2014 the stress of long distance travel appears to have caught up with him and, sadly, the outcome was altogether different. He started to show signs of colic only hours after returning to Ireland from Australia, where he had covered close to 200 mares in the southern hemisphere breeding season. He was operated on at Fethard Equine Hospital but had to be euthanised because of the severity of his condition. This was a tragic loss for Coolmore and his handlers because not only was he an outstanding and brave racehorse, winner of the English Derby and two Breeders Cups, he was developing into a top class stallion and there was a lot more to come from him in his second career.

Coolmore, understandably, go to great lengths to do all they can to safeguard their horses' welfare when travelling abroad. For the last seven years of my employment there I looked after the night quarantine for the stallions for the month of July before they headed off to Australia for the southern hemisphere breeding season.

I have seen at first hand the exhaustive detail head stallion man Gerry St John puts into ensuring, as best he possibly can, the stallions arrive at their destination safe and well after a journey which lasts nearly 24 hours door to door. It's a logistical nightmare which includes almost routine flight delays, two stops to refuel and reams of paperwork. Many of the stallions spend five months of the year in South America or Australasia and they handle the long haul travel remarkably well. A vet accompanies every journey.

While High Chaparral had no luck, Lady Angela came through her unloading ordeal unscathed and she gave birth to Nearctic at Taylor's National Stud on 11

February 1954. He grew to over 16 hands high with an almost black coat, a handsome head typical of Nearco's offspring and two white socks on his hind legs. When no one wanted to buy him for $35,000 at the annual sale of yearlings held at Windfields Farm, Taylor put him into training with Pete McCann.

Like his sire Nearco, Nearctic was tough. Unlike Nearco, he was extremely difficult to train, fighting his jockeys and exercise riders almost every stride of the way. McCann would ride him most of the time and his dedication, patience and strength in the saddle eventually paid off. At the end of his first season of racing, Nearctic had won seven races and was Canada's best two year old.

Taylor believed Nearctic had the potential to be a Kentucky Derby horse so he sent him to be trained by famed Argentinian Horatio Luro in California for his three year old season. He was training well when he developed a quarter crack problem and the Kentucky Derby went out of the window. He did eventually race that year, winning four of 13 starts, but it wasn't until Nearctic's fourth year that he started to mature into a powerful and confident champion again.

His biggest win was the Michigan Mile in Detroit in 1958, victory bringing the richest prize ever won by a Canadian horse, $40,000. In the spring of the following year, Nearctic equaled the track record when winning the Vigil Handicap at Woodbine, a six furlong sprint, but two races later his racing days were over. He finished sixth and lame on his last run, his legs no longer able to match his will to win. He had started 47 times, winning 21, was second five times and third in three. Nearctic was retired to the Taylors' National Stud Farm in Ontario and began his stallion duties in the spring of 1960. How times have changed. A prospective stallion racing 47 times is unheard of today, most being retired as three year olds. Racing horses at the highest level is all about big business and maximising

Nearctic

potential income from stud fees now decides when a stallion will be retired. Get everything right and the financial returns are massive.

Sadler's Wells ran 11 times, Galileo 8 times and Montjeu, that other brilliant racehorse and sire at Coolmore in recent years, 16 times. Nearctic faced the starter 12 times more than all of these great horses put together. His ability and toughness were plain to see over four seasons of racing, now he had to prove himself at stud. History shows what he achieved himself and through his son Northern Dancer, from whom Sadler's Wells, Galileo and Montjeu all descend. In Nearctic, E P Taylor had the sire of Northern Dancer, now he had to find his dam.

He had decided to re-invest his record prize money won in the Michigan Mile in a yearling filly at the Saratoga Sales in New York. It was August 1958. He wanted to buy something special with the long term aim of upgrading his band of broodmares. The dream to breed and raise a Kentucky Derby winner in Canada was still very much alive.

The special yearling he finally settled on was a bay filly by Native Dancer who descended from an outstanding family. She cost $35,000 and the Taylors named her Natalma. She was the third foal out of Almahmoud, a high class daughter of English Derby hero Mahmoud. Natalma's sire, Native Dancer, had burst on to the racing scene just as television began to cover major races in North America. Standing an imposing 16.3 hands, the steel grey colt won all his nine starts as a two year old in 1952 and became an instant television star.

At three he emerged bigger and stronger than ever and could run with ease over any distance. He won the Triple Crown races the Belmont and Preakness, every one of his 22 career races bar one. The one that got away was the Kentucky Derby, still considered the greatest upset in the long and proud history of the race. He was beaten into second by rank outsider Dark Star.

Interestingly, Native Dancer didn't much like humans. He enjoyed picking up grooms in his teeth and flinging them through the air. He hated the whip and didn't take orders from the little generals on his back, sometimes swinging his mighty head around, clamping his jaws on a boot and pulling the rider out of the saddle. Much has been said over the years about the varied distances Northern Dancer racehorses excelled over, for example how the Danzig line are mostly sprinter/milers but the Sadler's Wells line are known more for their stamina. The same applies to their temperament.

Sadler's Wells and his son Galileo are revered for their mostly faultless manners whereas Montjeu could be a handful. His trainer John Hammond called him an eccentric genius. These traits usually follow through to their offspring. I know from my own experiences at Coolmore that many Montjeu weanlings and yearlings had that little bit extra attitude which always made you careful when handling or working with them. They could be difficult to train, too. Danehill's yearlings were the same, whereas in most cases Sadler's Wells and Galileo passed on their own wonderful temperaments to their offspring.

Nijinsky was viewed as highly intelligent but also highly strung and it was the latter "quality" which mostly went through to his son Caerleon. Nijinsky's three parts brother The Minstrel was small in stature but as tough as they come. He was thoroughly genuine, but still nearly killed his stallion manager in Canada when he once turned on him unexpectedly. Danehill Dancer was naturally aggressive and you wouldn't want to wander into his paddock and forget where you were, as Gerry St John once did in Australia when working the southern hemisphere covering season.

He had gone in to clean the water trough when he suddenly remembered it was Danehill Dancer staring at him from the far end of the paddock. As a man who likes to keep fit with plenty of road running, Gerry turned quickly and sprinted for the nearest fence and as he jumped up to make his escape Danehill Dancer grabbed his trailing ankle in his jaws as he was half over the fence. Maybe the stallion, who could roar like a rock band at the Aviva when in the mood, was only being playful on that occasion, because Gerry managed to pull himself free.

Perhaps this aggressive trait was handed down to some of Northern Dancer's stock from his dam sire, Native Dancer. As if to prove the point, his daughter Natalma turned out to have a mind of her own too. She showed a lot of promise early on in her two year old season, winning her first two races at Belmont Park, New York. Unfortunately, she was disqualified for interference on the second run. Jockey Bobby Ussery had cracked her with the whip in the closing stages and she shied away from it, pushing another filly into the inside rail.

Worse was to follow. It seemed she equated the racetrack with Ussery's whipping and she wanted nothing more to do with it. Every morning she was fed, watered and groomed. Every morning she was saddled and bridled. Every morning an exercise rider was legged up. And every morning Natalma refused to go near the track to train. So trainer Luro would go for a gentle hack on his pony, everywhere but to the racetrack, and he slowly coaxed her into following. It was a long drawn out process but the filly eventually consented to resume training. She again began to show lots of ability but twice broke down, so the Taylors finally accepted defeat and her racing days were over. She was bred to Nearctic

Early morning at Godfrey's F[redacted] where John Magniers best mares and foals are kept

late in the covering season of 1960 and, unlike on the racetrack, there were no hitches. Her soon-to-be famous broodmare career was up and running.

Northern Dancer was born at 12.15am on 27 May 1961 at the National Stud Farm, Oshawa, Ontario. He was just like every other newborn foal, with disproportionately long legs going everywhere except the right direction. Two days later Natalma and her lively foal were turned out in a small paddock close to the foaling barn. This is a magical time for those who work on thoroughbred studs, as you watch these beautiful foals grow and develop on a daily basis right before your very eyes.

At Coolmore, the same as most studs in Europe, newborn foals are likely to be stabled at night for the first month or so, to protect them from the cold and wet late winter and early spring nights. To get them used to being handled, to be led to and from their paddocks, to learn some basic discipline.

As the summer comes you see sights that make your heart sing. The best times are as the sun sets in the evening and as it starts to appear again early in the morning. That's when the foals are at their most energetic, jumping over each other, racing around madly, generally acting the fool.

Sometimes, when I was checking the paddocks at these times, I would just pull the jeep up and watch them mesmerized. Most of them where I worked were descendants of the great Northern Dancer.

Back in Canada, in 1962, Northern Dancer the yearling was anything but great. Yearling manager Andre Blaettler remembered him as a real devil. "Especially when it came time to come into the barn. He'd be flying around the paddock with that choppy gait of his - I thought he looked like a hackney pony - and then he'd come skidding to a halt at the gate. He'd rear. No one wanted to bring him in on their own." Every autumn at Windfields Farm, E P Taylor would hold a sale of all his yearlings. He would put a price on all of them and invite Canadian thoroughbred experts, whether they be trainers, owners or agents, to come and view them on one particular day. He would keep any which didn't find a buyer and put them into training himself.

Taylor put a price tag of $25,000 on Northern Dancer. Staff on the farm couldn't understood why he was valued so highly, he certainly didn't look the part. He was one of Taylor's personal favourites, it was as simple as that. Maybe, without realising the implications at the time, Taylor was tempting fate to get involved again. On 16 September 1962, a good crowd turned up at Windfields and turned down the greatest horse deal in history.

Taylor, now 63 years old, looked on as each yearling was walked in front of the assembled crowd, with manager Joe Thomas giving a commentary. Northern Dancer was easily recognisable. He didn't look much like the other yearlings. He was the shortest, standing a fraction over 14 hands 2 nches tall, and he weighed about 40lbs less than the average. He looked more like an American quarter horse than a thoroughbred. He was a bundle of anxious and nervous energy, constantly on his toes.

Horses born and bred at Windfields were easily the best racehorses in Canada. Four winners of the countries most prestigious race, the Queen's Plate, had been offered as yearlings at the Windfields' annual sale and been overlooked or rejected by the invited buyers. Flaming Page was actually bought but returned to the farm because she had a mildly inflamed fetlock.

Taylor replaced her with another filly and put Flaming Page into training himself. She won the Queen's Plate in 1962 and was voted Canadian Horse Of The Year. When she retired to the paddocks she was mated with Northern Dancer and produced Nijinsky, the first British Triple Crown winner in 35 years and the last since. This time around Taylor sold 15 of the 33 yearlings he offered for sale. No one wanted Northern Dancer.

When Taylor put him into training he was a nightmare, no one volunteered to ride him. He wouldn't settle; when asked to trot and eventually canter he would go a couple of strides and explode. Powerful and agile, he could stop, turn and fly off in another direction in a breath. Yet, in the end, when they got him to the racecourse and later to the breeding shed, all these characteristics were vital ingredients which contributed to his extraordinary success.

Bizarrely by modern day standards, Northern Dancer was ridden by a young apprentice in his first race. It was 2 August 1963 at Fort Erie Racetrack in Ontario. Ron Turcotte, famous ten years later as the rider of Secretariat in his memorable US Triple Crown victories, said he immediately knew the horse was something special. "When I called on him for extra, he moved to the lead immediately but was satisfied to stay head to head with the other horse. As I was instructed not to touch him with the whip, I refrained until we were past the 16th pole, then I decided to disregard orders and turned my stick up. In order not to be seen by the trainer, I switched the stick to my left hand and tapped him one time. To my surprise he exploded, and within 70 yards he opened up an eight length lead, which is what he won by. Had I done that at the quarter pole he surely would have won by 15 to 20 lengths."

Turcotte was again in the saddle when Northern Dancer won the Coronation Futurity at Woodbine, the richest two year old race in Canada, by six lengths. "This was the last time I rode the Dancer," said Turcotte, "I just couldn't slow him down to win by less than six or seven lengths, which is why I got taken off him. God knows how good he really was, for he was never a completely sound horse most of the time I rode him, and I still could not slow him down more than that."

Despite now having to contend with the beginnings of a quarter crack, a vertical split at the top of the wall of the hoof, Northern Dancer went out and won the Sir Gaylord at Aqueduct by eight lengths with a bar shoe to help stabilise and support the troublesome foot. Nine days later he won the Remsen by two lengths at the same New York track, but the quarter crack had worsened. This same problem had twice interrupted his sire Nearco's racing career and had forced him to miss the Kentucky Derby. Lightening had struck twice. Northern Dancer's participation in America's most iconic of races, run every year since 1875, was over.

Desperate times sometimes require desperate measures. Just as they were about to ship Northern Dancer back to Canada, trainer Luro read a story about the success a California blacksmith had when applying a vulcanised patch to a star trotter on the West Coast, who won several big races with the patch over the quarter crack on his injured hoof. Bill Bane warned it was still at the experimental stage. Taylor said let's go with it.

Bane travelled all the way to Belmont Park in New York and spent six hours working on the material with an acetylene torch to properly vulcanise it to increase its strength and elasticity before attempting to apply it to Northern Dancer's hoof. For once the head strong colt stood quietly throughout the whole process. Early in January 1964, Northern Dancer was able to resume training; the patch had worked, he was no longer in pain from the quarter crack. The Kentucky Derby dream was back in play.

Northern Dancer disappointed on his seasonal reappearance at Hialeah Park, Miami, though he didn't get a clear run. So when the Flamingo Stakes came along at the same Florida track on 3 March the pressure was on. Legendary jockey Bill Shoemaker was on board and the Canadian colt beat a decent field decisively by two lengths. Next up was the Florida Derby at Gulfstream Park and, despite running away with his work rider on the track the day before when he covered five furlongs in a blistering 58.6 seconds, Northern Dancer coasted to a one length victory with Shoemaker sitting motionless. The story was building.

Northern Dancer being ridden by his trainer, Horatio Luro.

However, the Taylor camp were knocked back yet again when Shoemaker deserted Northern Dancer for the Kentucky Derby and chose instead to ride Hill Rise, the outstanding 3 year old colt on the West Coast. He believed Hill Rise was the better horse. Horatio Luro decided on Bill Hartack, a particularly outspoken and opinionated jockey, as his replacement. Arrogant and volatile, he was well known to lash into trainers and spit insults at the media. An interesting choice, which did not appear to meet with the approval of the owners, but he had other form. He had already won the Kentucky Derby on three occasions.

Northern Dancer next took in the Blue Grass Stakes at Keeneland, nine days before the Derby.

Hartack kept a firm hold on the little colt as he eased to a half length victory. He was now ready to run for his life in "The Run For The Roses" at Churchill Downs. In the final days before the big day Northern Dancer was in peak condition, bouncing out for his sunrise canters around the historic track.

The key now was to keep him calm and relaxed but there was a complicating factor - the dawn patrol of the media army. In 1994 there were 1,200 accredited print, radio and television representatives, who arrived early at the track stables in search of a story. Unlike Europe, where training yards are privately owned and therefore off limits to outsiders, nearly all American horses are trained at the racetracks themselves and therefore open to public scrutiny 24/7.

For many of the media present in Kentucky it would be the only horse race they would attend all year. Knowing very little about racing, they followed the obvious leads, and the little horse from Canada was a stand out story. An endless procession of photographers converged on Barn 24 asking for Northern Dancer be taken out of his box for a photo shoot. The trainer had a cunning little plan to help deal with the stress for the horse and himself. He knew that few of the photographers would recognise any of the Derby runners, let alone Northern Dancer.

All they did know was that he was small. So Luro used his own lead pony as a photo double for Northern Dancer. The pony didn't resemble the great racehorse in anyway other than size, but no one seemed to notice. The Kentucky Derby Festival had been in full swing for more than a week, bedlam on the streets, in the parks and on the beautifully manicured lawns of Louisville.

On 2 May 1994, Derby day finally arrived. Muriel Lennox couldn't attend in person, but watching on television back home in Canada she was there in heart and soul. Muriel lived on E P Taylor's private estate in North Toronto for 12 years, keeping his riding horses schooled and fit. She accompanied Taylor whenever he chose to ride, which he did frequently until he was almost eighty. Whenever the Taylors flew to the USA to visit their stud farm at Chesapeake Bay in Maryland, where Northern Dancer stood for most of his stallion days, she would work away to get in on the trip if there was a spare seat on the company jet. She never missed any opportunity to see the great stallion. This is how she saw him win the Kentucky Derby.

"In the starting gate, Northern Dancer stood patiently as the remainder of the field were secured in their stalls. Seconds after the last horse, Roman Brother, was led in, the bell clanged, the stall doors flew open, and the field was charging down the track. Past the stands, the outside horses moved toward the rail in anticipation of the first turn. Northern Dancer was on the rail, sitting seventh, with ample running room in front of him. Hartack continued to restrain him, and kept him on the rail as they ran around the bend and into the back stretch. As the field charged into the final turn Northern Dancer was still on the rail, trapped by a solid wall of horses. Hartack's strategy had backfired.

"Northern Dancer had easily caught the front runners and now had no place to run. Any hope of cutting around them was dashed by Hill Rise, thundering alongside, like a predator keeping his quarry hemmed in.

"Suddenly Northern Dancer shot sideways, right under Hill Rise's chin, and blazed around the front runners. His neck stretched full out and his short, choppy stride was so fast his legs were a blur. When Shoemaker realised what had happened, he quickly rode Hill Rise in pursuit, but it took several seconds for the lanky horse to get into gear. Once he got rolling, Hill Rise chased Northern Dancer with a vengeance, gaining ground with each long, powerful stride. It seemed impossible that little Northern Dancer, straining with every short, choppy stride, could stave off the mighty Hill Rise.

"His head was at Northern Dancer's hind quarters, then at his flanks. Mere yards from the finish Northern Dancer must have felt Hill Rise's hot breath on his shoulder, and stretched his neck even further. As the horses flew across the line it was Northern Dancer by a neck. And a new track record of two minutes flat! In that instant Northern Dancer became 'our' horse. Canadians poured into the streets to celebrate. Car horns honked, total strangers patted one another on the back.

"His victory was our victory and we basked in the triumph he had given us. Northern Dancer had not only waltzed off with America's greatest horse race title, but had sprinted around Churchill Downs track faster than any other horse in the Derby's illustrious 90 year history."

Canadian journalist Trent Frayne was there. He was in a car load of sports writers who had driven to Louisville in the hope of witnessing history being made. His account shows exactly how much Northern Dancer had captured the hearts and minds of the Canadian people.

"But now from the roof of the ancient grandstand where I was standing (and, I realised, screaming) it became apparent that

36

Hill Rise's advance had stopped, that Northern Dancer was fighting him off. There were still many strides to the wire, but Hill Rise was stopped there, his snout at Northern Dancer's neck. The little horse had his head thrust out in that driving style of his, and nothing was going to stop him. I found myself pounding my fists repeatedly on to a restraining railing there on the roof, and shouting over and over, 'He's going to make it! He's going to make it! He's going to make it! He's going to make it!'

And, of course, he did."

Northern Dancer defeats Hill Rise in the Kentucky Derby

Only two other horses in the 140 year history of the Kentucky Derby have run faster times than Northern Dancer and the great Secretariat is still the record holder. He ran 1.59.40 in 1973, just .6 of a second faster than Northern Dancer. Both horses went on to win the next race in the American Triple Crown, the Preakness at Pimlico, Maryland. Whereas Secretariat then won the third race in the history making series, the Belmont, Northern Dancer's blazing trademark run wasn't there and he finished third to horses he had left standing on other occasions. His last race was to be in his homeland. His left foreleg, strained in the Belmont, was now bothering him, but he won Canada's top race, the Queen's Plate, on three legs and sheer heart.

He had run four classic races in six weeks, but Northern Dancer was much more than facts and figures to Canadians, they had taken him to their hearts like no other. Sacks of fan mail arrived at Windfields from across Canada, the United States and the Bahamas and the Taylors ensured all letters and requests for a photograph of the horse were answered.

Then there were stories to tell, like the one about a letter sent from a young student at the Brantford School for the Blind, who had written to ask if he could meet Northern Dancer. Winifred Taylor immediately wrote back to say she would be pleased to introduce them. Mrs Taylor's fondness for the horse, from the time he was a foal, was reciprocated by Northern Dancer. They were kindred spirits, small of stature but big of heart.

When Mrs Taylor and the 13 year old blind boy arrived at Woodbine, Northern Dancer recognised an approaching voice. He went to take a look. It was Mrs Taylor. Luro was extremely apprehensive about her promise to the blind boy. He had fled Northern Dancer's stable not long before when the volatile colt had turned on him. Yet as Mrs Taylor approached him he lowered his head to her. He was uncharacteristically relaxed as she patted him and spoke about her young guest and his letter. Slowly and gently she guided the blind boy's hand to the horse's nose, and for as long as the young lad wanted to stroke him, Northern Dancer stood there as quiet as an old carthorse.

He sired 635 foals over 23 seasons at stud, a fraction of what stallions produce today, with 80% of them getting to the racetrack and 80% of them winning. He sired 26 champions in Ireland, England, France, Italy, the US and Canada. He began his stud career in 1984 at a fee of $10,000 and by the time he came to the last three years he stood at up to $1 million per mating. In Europe, his champion sons like Nijinsky, The Minstrel, Nureyev, Storm Bird, Secreto, El Gran Senor and Sadler's Wells are still regarded as some of the greatest racehorses ever seen.

In the autumn of 1981, Windfields Farm received a firm bid from a French bloodstock agency to buy Northern Dancer. It was believed it probably came from shipping magnate Stavros Niarchos, but it was never officially confirmed. They were prepared to pay $40 million outright for him. Over half the shareholders wanted to sell. It was an unheard of amount of money for any horse, let alone a stallion who was 20 years old.

The man who sank the proposal was one of the richest in the world; art collector, philanthropist and racehorse breeder, Paul Mellon of Virginia, who said it was an outrageous idea to take the stallion who had been so good to everyone for so long, put him on a plane and send him away from his home. He threatened to take out an injunction on the horse and go to the highest court in the land to prevent it happening.

Mellon was the breeder and owner of Mill Reef, trained by Ian Balding to win the Epsom Derby, Eclipse, King George and Arc in 1971. In addition to being a shareholder in Northern Dancer, he had also been a member of the syndicate financing Sangster's foray into the US yearling sales. He was heir to one of America's greatest business fortunes, the Mellon Bank, but gave away millions to the arts and culture, in England as well as America. He was an enthusiastic supporter of the Grayson-Jockey Club Research Foundation, his country's leading source of equine research funding which helps all breeds. He ensured Northern Dancer saw out the rest of his life where he had lived for so long.

No one was more relieved or happier than Windfields' Joe Thomas, who was an integral part of the Northern Dancer story right from the start, when Nearco and Natalma first met in the covering shed in 1960 and the future hero of Canada came into the world 11 months later. It was Thomas, a genial, gentle giant of 6'3" and liked by everyone, who watched him develop as a foal and yearling and who stood at E P Taylor's shoulder during the racing career which culminated in glory in the Kentucky Derby. It was Thomas who masterminded Northern Dancer's breed-changing stud career.

Having secured the horse's future, with Paul Mellon's help, Thomas was cruelly cut down by cancer in June 1994 at the age of 60. It was the year of El Gran Senor, yet another brilliant son of Northern Dancer trained by Vincent O'Brien in Co Tipperary. Thomas had done a deal for The Senor to go back to Windfields, where he had been born, as a stallion after his racing days were over. When the day came for the Epsom Derby, Thomas was desperately ill but knew what was going on in the build-up to the big race. Secreto, also an outstanding son of Northern Dancer but trained by Vincent's son David, beat El Gran Senor in a pulsating, driving finish. Joe's daughter Lesley didn't want to tell her father El Gran Senor had been beaten. She just said: "You came first and

Joe Thomas and Northern Dancer

second, Dad.""That's great," he said, "that's just great." Joe passed away that night.

Northern Dancer died six years later, on the morning of 16 November 1990, at the grand age of 29. He had colic the night before but appeared to have recovered. It struck again early the next morning and the horse was in severe pain. Surgery might have saved him, but at his age that was a huge ask and it was decided the most humane action was to euthanise him. An oak casket had been built in readiness for this day and Northern Dancer was placed in it and taken from Windfields Farm in Maryland in the US back to the Taylor farm outside Toronto, where his journey began.

It was past midnight, cold and wet, when Northern Dancer arrived back in Oshawa. The entire farm staff had turned out to welcome him home. He was buried in the heart of Windfields Farm, just over from the barn where he was born. He was in good company. Buried alongside was South Ocean, one of his harem. Together they had produced Storm Bird.

The day Northern Dancer won the Kentucky Derby for Bill Hartack, E P Taylor and Joe Thomas.

Northern Dancer as a stallion.

Chapter 3

THE BRETHREN

THE BRETHREN

*"Twenty years from now you
will be more disappointed by
the things that you didn't do
than by the ones you did do.
Explore. Dream. Discover."*

Mark Twain

American civil rights campaigner Martin Luther King also had a dream, in1963, that all men are equal. John Magnier's dream, ten years later, was the polar opposite of equality, though his interest was in the business world rather than civil rights. With Vincent O'Brien and Robert Sangster, he was going to rule the thoroughbred breeding and racing world. For Magnier, it became more than a dream, it was an obsession and he pursued it relentlessly.

In the early 1970s, he correctly predicted that bloodstock values were going to explode and he was desperate to get in early. For years American breeders had been raiding Europe for their best horses. Top stallions went to Kentucky because that's where the big dollars lived. When a Champion racehorse retired to stud owners were delighted to sell to the Americans, who could put a syndicate together for the kind of money the Irish would have no hope of matching.

Magnier laid it on the line to Sangster in one of their long chats about the state of the industry this side of the pond. US bred horses were regularly winning Europe's top races and most were then returning to America to stand as stallions. Sir Ivor, Nijinsky, Mill Reef and Roberto all won the Epsom Derby between 1968 and 1972 and all were born and raised in America. Only Mill Reef, at the English National Stud, stayed in the Europe for a stallion career.

Magnier painted a gloomy picture. He said the sheer weight of US dollars would come to dominate the industry. Europe, and particularly Ireland, would be standing second rate stallions who would get second rate racehorses which in turn would make third rate stallions. "In this business you have to get the best and breed to the best. There is no other way and I'm afraid the Americans could cause us to become a strictly third line power in the bloodstock business," he told Sangster.

When they first met at Haydock races in 1971, Magnier was just 23 and Sangster 12 years older. Magnier had an old head on young shoulders and had done a deal to buy the top sprinter Green God and Sangster was fascinated to learn of the business intricacies of standing stallions at stud. Green God then went out and won the Vernon's Sprint Cup, sponsored by Sangster's business, Vernons Pools, which his father started with £400 and five staff in 1926. The Sangster empire was the lottery of its day, giving working people the chance to gamble a few pence with the dream of winning a hundred thousand pounds by predicting the outcome of football matches each week.

Author Patrick Robinson, brother of Nick Robinson, one of Sangster's early friends, had an inside handle on this first meeting. He said there was a quick and early bond between Sangster and Magnier.

"That bond was money. Robert, having inherited his first one third of the Vernons empire, had a considerable amount of it. John had long had far reaching plans to make a considerable amount of it, but in broad terms, it occured to him that he could go further, faster, with some serious Sangster money behind him. In turn, Robert did not care how far John went in the stallion business, nor how rich he became in the riveting business of syndicating expensive stallions, just as long as he took him along with him. This partnership was destined to go every step of the way."

Sangster was old money, his family wealthy since Edwardian times. His grandfather Edmund founded the fortune with a large warehouse and wholesale business in Manchester. Sangster country became the historic golf links of Hoylake, home of the Royal Liverpool Golf Club and the venue of 12 British Opens, the latest version in 2014 when won by Rory McIlroy. It was known as the course which beat the legendary Jack Nicklaus. Robert was a useful golfer and rugby player, but boxing was his forte.

His godfather was Dr Joe Graham, a British Boxing Board of Control official fight doctor, who took him to the big boxing shows in Liverpool and London involving fighters like Randolph Turpin, Sugar Ray Robinson, George Walker, Freddie Mills and Terry Downes, all great boxers of their time. Mills, World Cruiserweight Champion, taught Sangster to spar and he was undefeated at school and remained unbeaten in Germany during his two years' National Service, becoming Berlin Brigade Light Heavyweight Champion.

His interest in racehorses was sparked by Nick Robinson, who recommended a bet on Chalk Stream, owned by his grandfather, to win the 1960 Lincoln. Robinson gave Sangster a crash course in racing in the weeks before the Lincoln and when Chalk Stream won Sangster was so hooked he went out and bought the horse as a wedding present for his soon-to-be wife, Christine, a beautiful, well educated, impeccably mannered and surprisingly shy model. Chalk Stream cost a grand to buy. In no time Sangster would be paying millions for yearlings in America and revolutionising the thoroughbred world.

Sangster's father, Vernon, was an avid sports fan and encouraged his son to put his interest in racing on a business footing. In 1964, when 28 years old, Robert bought a 200 acre run down farm in Cheshire which he re-developed into Swettenham Stud, breeding horses to race in his famous blue and green colours. When he met Magnier his own racing interests were growing rapidly, but he was hungry to go faster and higher.

In July 1972 Sangster agreed to accompany Magnier to the Keeneland yearling sales in Kentucky, where he was first introduced to his new hero, Vincent O'Brien. He was captivated by the American scene and took a share in a yearling with another wealthy Englishman, Charles St George. Named Cellini and trained by O'Brien in Co Tipperary, he won his first two races comfortably before taking the 1973 Dewhurst, a championship race for two year olds in England. He was now worth a million dollars as a stallion back in America, whether he won another race or not. O'Brien had selected him, supported by Magnier, and Sangster had quadrupled his investment. When they went back to the Keeneland sales a year later it was to a backdrop of excitement flooding both the racing and breeding industries by Secretariat's Triple Crown wins in the Kentucky Derby, the Preakness and the Belmont, the first horse to achieve this feat for 25 years. An imposing chestnut colt, he was nicknamed Big Red for the striking colour of his coat and became a huge celebrity in 1973, appearing on the covers of national magazines like Time,

Newsweek and Sports Illustrated. His times for running the three Triple Crown races were the fastest ever seen and still stand as the record today, 42 years later. He won the third, the Belmont, by 31 lengths, also a record.

He won $1.3 million in prize money and was syndicated to stand as a stallion in Kentucky. When his first yearlings appeared at the sales, one subsequently named Canadian Bound made $1.5 million (nearer $10 million in today's value), the first time a yearling anywhere had broken the $1 million barrier. Yearling sales and stallion values were being set on fire, exactly as Magnier had predicted. Secretariat went on to sire some good horses but, unsuprisingly, nothing as exceptional as he was. Canadian Bound never won a race and Secretariat's legacy was more as a sire of top class fillies for the breeding industry.

In the autumn of 1989, Secretariat was afflicted by laminitis. When his condition failed to respond to treatment over the next month he was euthanised on 4 October at the age of 19. He was buried at Claiborne Farm in Kentucky and given the rare honour of being buried whole. In America, it was the tradition for only the head, heart and hooves of a horse to be buried and the rest of the body cremated. Dr Thomas Swerczek, head pathologist at the University of Kentucky, carried out a post mortem on Secretariat.

"We just stood there in stunned silence. We couldn't believe it. The heart was perfect. There were no problems with it. It was just this huge engine. We estimated his heart weighed 22lbs, about two and threequarters bigger than the average horse."

In the summer of 1973 Sangster and his Irish friends went back to the States for the yearling sales at Keeneland. He was determined to get involved in something big, but when the big one came along he got cold feet. Vincent O'Brien chose a striking son of Bold Ruler. Magnier said he thought it would take $500,000 to buy him. When he came into the sales ring, Sangster stunned everyone by pitching straight in at that price, but the Yoshida family from Japan trumped him with a bid of $600,000. O'Brien wanted to go higher, but Sangster had become very nervous, kept his head down and didn't look at the auctioneer again. The colt went to Japan, was named Wajima, won nine races and nearly $600,000 in prize money and at the end of his racing career was syndicated as a stallion for $7.2 million.

O'Brien was disappointed not to have secured the colt, but as a shrewd businessman Sangster was careful with his money, he just wasn't ready to dive in as he felt out of his depth as far as O'Brien and Magnier were concerned. In his own words, he felt "bloody ignorant" compared to the two Irishmen when it came to horses. Later that night Magnier told Sangster he thought the Bold Ruler colt was cheap at $600,000. He said they had two of the best judges of a racehorse in the world, O'Brien and Tom Cooper of the British Bloodstock Agency, who had also been advising, telling them to buy.

He told Sangster, firmly but quietly: "When we come here again, we have to be much more serious, much more organised. We have to come with several million raised from a syndicate so that nothing frightens us off. We must be in a position to back our judgement." And that's what happened. When they returned in 1975 they had everything in place. O'Brien and Magnier had pored over the catalogue of yearlings for sale, listing the ones they were interested in as potential stallions; Tom Cooper had already scrutinised them on the farms where they had been reared and Phonsie O'Brien had also cast his eye over them at the sales; and Sangster had put a syndicate together of wealthy speculators, from Europe and America, with funds of over $3 million to spend.

The most important person in this alliance was Vincent as he had the final say on which yearlings they were going to buy and then had to turn them into champion racehorses. His record on both counts is second to none. The facts and figures behind his legendary career are well documented: the Cheltenham winners, three consecutive Grand Nationals and six winners of the Epsom Derby. In 2000 the Racing Post compiled a list of the greatest flat trainers of the 20th century. Vincent O'Brien came top. They did the same for jump trainers and Vincent O'Brien came top of that too. In 2003, he was voted the greatest influence in horse racing history in the Post's worldwide poll.

His background with the stories and anecdotes from his early life help explain the why and how he became who he was, the greatest of the greatest trainers. He was born in 1917 and eventually was one of seven brothers and one sister. His father Dan had four boys with his first wife, Helena, who died in child birth aged 36. When Dan remarried it was to Kathleen Toomey, a cousin of first wife Helena. Vincent was their first born and he was followed by Dermot, Pauline and Phonsie, christened Alphonsus Septimus no less.

Kathleen had eight children to care for in her family and one day a further three suddenly arrived. When Mrs O'Sullivan, a widow and neighbour, lay dying in her cottage, she sent one of her three boys up to Dan and Kathleen with a message asking if they would look after her sons when she was gone. And that's what the kind and compassionate O'Briens did, taking the three little orphans into their home. One of those boys was Danny O'Sullivan who worked for many years for Vincent at Ballydoyle.

Dermot later became Vincent's right hand man as assistant trainer at Ballydoyle and Phonsie, nearly 14 years younger than Vincent, looked up to him as a father figure when Dan died suddenly of pneumonia in 1943. The family were in some difficulty when Dan died; farming in Ireland had been in dire straits for years thanks largely to the punitive taxes of up to 20% imposed on Irish produce by the government away in London. Dan had made a living by buying and selling horses and training point-to-pointers, though it was a very young Vincent who did most of the training as his father had little patience for that side of it, wanting to find out too quickly how good they were.

Patience and a natural feel and understanding of horses became central to the way Vincent faced up to his responsibilities in those early days after his father's death. Getting a horse fit and ready to run and knowing when to have a good bet was how Vincent helped keep the family together.

His special abilities were apparent from an early age. His schoolmaster, Tom Tierney, said of him: "This lad is something different." A few special horses in those early days in Churchtown were able to demonstrate how different he was. In 1936, at the opening of Killarney Racecourse, one of the most beautiful venues anywhere in the world, the O'Briens had three runners. The horses had to be walked four and a half miles down the road from their farm to catch the train at Buttevant Station for Killarney, with Vincent leading one of them.

During the trip Solford, who Dan had bought as an unbroken three year old, developed colic and was unable to run, though thankfully he recovered as he was about to become an important horse for the family. Vincent felt Solford was the first horse he had trained properly. "The day my father did the deal for him he jumped a wall into a graveyard. Fortunately he didn't hurt himself, but later on his legs gave trouble. I blistered him myself and knew he had to be rested. When he was ready to be ridden I rode him every day to a particular area of the farm down by the river where the ground was spongy - every day for weeks and months. I brought him back really slowly. His legs never gave trouble afterwards, even on the hard ground," Vincent said.

This patience and innate horsemanship were the hallmarks of O'Brien throughout his life as a trainer. Solford went on to win six flat races and one over hurdles for the O'Briens. In 1938, he showed his toughness by winning the Irish Cambridgeshire under top weight on desperate ground. Vincent was 21 years old. Solford was afterwards sold to the wildly eccentric British racehorse owner, Dorothy Paget, and won the Champion Hurdle for her at Cheltenham two years later.

Paget, the daughter of an English aristocrat and American heiress, was worth well over £100 million. She would regularly bet £10,000 (worth over £300,000 today), all on her own horses. She owned Golden Miller, famous for winning five Cheltenham Gold Cups and still the only horse to win the Gold Cup and the Grand National in the same season, 1934.

She hated men. She said the mere sight of them made her want to vomit, and apart from a gardener, unfortunately nicknamed "The Eunach", she only employed women. She said the worst experience of her life was being kissed by a drunken Frenchman. What happened to the Frenchman afterwards remains a mystery. She assigned her staff different colours, with the exception of green which she believed was unlucky, and would use their allotted colour when speaking to them or about them.

She was expelled from six schools by the time she reached 15 and her main accomplishment during this time was singing in front 400 inmates at Wormwood Scrubs Prison at a Christmas concert in 1924. She won a total of 1532 races as an owner, including the 1943 Epsom Derby with Straight Deal, but she was far from straight to deal with herself, often telephoning her trainers in the middle of the night wanting a lengthy chat about her horses.

On one occasion, when Fulke Walwyn trained five winners for her on a six race card, she wasn't pleased at all. She threw a screaming fit because he didn't land the sixth race and told an assistant to go and "kick him in the balls." Dorothy Paget died of heart failure at the age of just 54 on 9 February 1960. Smoking a hundred cigarettes a day and weighing over 20 stone wouldn't have helped.

Although she had a connection to Ireland as the owner of Ballymacoll Stud in Co Meath, where Arkle was born, Vincent O'Brien's name never featured on her list of trainers, many of whom didn't last long with her. Which was a shame, because Vincent would have sorted her out. And if he was struggling he could have called for a dose of Irish charm from Phonsie, who had a glowing reputation for his story telling and wit.

Through Irish connections in America, Phonsie became a good friend of President George Bush Snr. They shared a love of fishing and from the late

Quare Times gets a rousing reception after winning the Grand National in 1955, the third consecutive year Vincent had won the race, each with a different horse. "Those three National winners were the greatest piece of training I've ever known," said Kildare vet Bob Griffin.

1950s Phonsie and the President would fish together most years in the Florida Keys. Relaxing over a drink in the evening, Bush loved to hear Phonsie's stories of life back in Ireland.

Phonsie knew Vincent better than anyone and they were as close as brothers could be. Reflecting on the early years, he said: "I remember when he ran away from Mungret College, and him coming home and my father having a big row with him and saying he was going again, and I remember him running down a field and the crying coming out of him. He wasn't going back there. He got a job with Fred Clarke, who trained horses in Leopardstown at the time, and he went to night school there at the same time. That's where he educated himself."

"He was a perfectionist. He didn't have much but what he had was perfect. His clothes were always immaculate. And he had an amazing brain for pedigrees. His knowledge of the stud book was second to none. That's why he was totally responsible for getting those good horses in America. He had a bit of experience with Fred Clarke, he saw a bit of training methodology there, but that was the only experience that he had before he started training himself. He learned as he went."

He had a plan to train two horses, one called Good Days belonging to English owner Sidney McGregor and the other a horse he bought at Newmarket Sales for a few hundred pounds, Drybob, to win the autumn double on the flat in Ireland, the Cambridge and the Cesarewitch. "Vincent had a £2 double the pair of them, both at 20/1. Drybob dead heated for the Cambridgeshire and Good Days won the Cesarewitch. It was incredible, and it won him the first few quid he ever had. The betting end of it was the most important thing in the early days." Phonsie recalled.

Phonsie also had a part to play in another horse from the early days which demonstrated his brother's inevitable climb to the top. "I remember being sent with another chap, Andy Daly from Cork City, and we went about 16 miles on a pony and trap to collect a horse. The horse was "broken" all right, we led him along behind the trap on the way home for about nine miles, until he couldn't go any further. So we tied the rope around his neck and drove him along the road for the last four or five miles. That was Cottage Rake. Two years later he won the first of his three Gold Cups.

O'Brien's early success as a gambling stable, training out in the sticks and not being part of the inner racing circles at the Curragh and in Dublin, caused jealousy and resentment within the sport's ruling classes. He was banned from training for three months in 1954 because the stewards found four of his horses were guilty of inconsistency without the trainer being able to explain, other than by saying they were horses and not machines.

Vincent O'Brien and Lester Piggott

Worse was to follow in 1960 when one of his horses was allegedly found to have a minute trace of a stimulant "resembling" an amphetamine and he was banned from training for 18 months. He had never heard of the stimulant and he vehemently protested his innocence. The testing procedures, which used samples of sweat and saliva combined with highly questionable laboratory techniques, saw Vincent sue the Irish Turf Club for libel. After fighting them for 12 months he was belatedly given his licence back. The whole drug testing programme for racing was soon overhauled. The slate was officially wiped clean when Vincent was invited to become an honorary member of the Turf Club in 1999 and then he and Lester Piggott became the first inductees to the Club's Hall of Fame in 2003.

O'Brien's eye for a good horse is legendary. His eye for a good wife was just as important. He met Jacqueline Wittenoom, the daughter of an Australian MP, in Dublin in May 1951. Twenty two years old, she had completed a scholarship studying industrial relations after university and then worked as an economist. She was soon to return to her home town of Perth in Western Australia and Vincent had to make up his mind pretty quickly, which he did. They announced their engagement that August and were married in Dublin the following December. In her fascinating 2005 biography of her husband, Jacqueline recalled arriving back in Perth to tell her father she was getting married.

"And breaking the news to my father was a little daunting as he wasn't too pleased with horse trainers. As an MP, several years earlier he had decided he should have a racehorse because it

would win him more votes. The horse was called St Paddy, and the first time out he streaked thirty lengths in front and dropped dead of dope. My father was furious. So I told him I was going to marry an Irish farmer!"

The statistics which show how good O'Brien was are endless. None more so than the astonishing treble he had in 1953 when winning the Cheltenham Gold Cup with Knock Hard, the English Grand National with Early Mist and the Irish Derby with Chamier. In 1955, switching over steadily from jumps training to the flat, he went to Tattersalls Sales at Doncaster and bought seven yearlings for millionaire builder John McShain, whose father had emigrated from Northern Ireland to Philadelphia. McShain's construction company became one of the biggest in the US and built the Pentagon, with its 18 miles of corridors, in 14 months. He restored the White House and built Washington and Philadelphia airports. One of those yearlings he bought for McShain was Ballymoss, who was second in the Epsom Derby but won the Irish version and the English St Leger, O'Brien's first English Classic, in 1957.

As a four year old he won the Coronation Cup, the Eclipse, the King George and finally the Arc. In that same year, O'Brien also won the Gold Cup at Royal Ascot with Gladness, a tough as teak filly he had also secured for McShain. Despite all this, the American was eventually to take his horses away from O'Brien because he could get them trained cheaper elsewhere

While many remembered the brilliance of O'Brien when winning the biggest races on the flat and over jumps, Sangster would also tell the story of Boone's Cabin to explain the genius of the little maestro from Co Cork. One of the lesser lights, Boone's Cabin knocked around Ballydoyle for four years, a strong and sturdy sprinter but not top class. He won a few races now and then and every time Sangster expected the trainer to say he had gone as far as he could with him he would say he needed a bit more time.

At five he won the Ballyogan Stakes at Leopardstown and Sangster thought they would now be able to move him on as a prospective stallion to one of the smaller racing countries, to recoup some of the costs of keeping him in training so long. O'Brien had a different plan. He told Sangster the horse had just about come right and suggested a run in the highly competitive Wokingham Stakes at Royal Ascot. "He might just surprise you. I've always thought a lot of him, but he's just taken a little bit of time to come to himself," O'Brien said.

Ridden by Lester Piggott against 19 battle-hardened sprinters primed for the day, Boone's Cabin won by three quarters of a length with a blistering display of speed and courage. The trainer said to a delighted but bemused owner: "He's a nice horse. I always thought he had a nice race in him." Boone's Cabin had now stamped himself as a decent stallion prospect, he was sold very well to stand in Australia and Robert Sangster pocketed another pile of cash. He was never slow to tell anyone and everyone his trainer was a genius.

Back at Coolmore, Magnier had been busy bringing the stud up to the standard required for the business he now expected to bring in when the three partners went back to the yearling sales at Keeneland. They now owned all of Coolmore between them, they were going to breed the best to the best and they had to match that with the best facilities. In 1975, Magnier was still only 27 years old but had an air about him of being at least ten years older. His new position as the head of Coolmore gave him the extra confidence which belied his relative lack of experience, certainly as a big player on the world stage. He was now always to be seen smoking a cigar, wearing a tailored tweed jacket, open neck shirt and a cravat, the style beloved of the English landed gentry and aristocracy. He is still fond of his cravat forty years later.

The partners worked hard at refining their game plan. Buying ready made stallions was impossible, their pockets were just not deep enough to compete with the Americans. The plan they all agreed on was to buy the best yearlings, get O'Brien to turn them into champions on the racetrack and then let Magnier weave his magic in the breeding shed. Sangster painstakingly compiled a chart showing how the best, and therefore the most expensive, yearlings sold at auction in America had fared as racehorses and then stallions. They had to try and buy them all from here on. They were about to re-write the rules.

O'Brien had already shown that it could work, that America was where the best yearlings in the world lived and they were the world's best racehorses of that era. Sir Ivor, Nijinsky and Roberto, all American bred and trained by O'Brien, proved the point emphatically. Nijinsky highlighted, yet again, the genius of O'Brien, who had been asked by Charles Engelhard, a billionaire racehorse owner on the grandest of scale from Ohio, to go to E P Taylor's Windfields Farm in Toronto to look at a yearling by Ribot he was interested in buying.

O'Brien didn't much like the Ribot yearling, but he was very taken with one he saw from only the second crop of Northern Dancer, still an unproven stallion with no suggestion that he was about to change the face of thoroughbred breeding the world over. O'Brien strongly urged Engelhard to buy the Northern Dancer colt out of Flaming Page, which he did for $84,000, a Canadian record, when he came up at the sales. That was Nijinsky, the only horse to win the English Triple Crown in the last eighty years.

He was a highly strung horse and needed firm but patient handling throughout his career at Ballydoyle, from both O'Brien and his expert staff. He would always be worked alone before the other horses as he would become impatient and restless if he couldn't get his own way. But for two work riders, in particular, Nijinsky could have easily gone wrong. He was very difficult, but they had the strength to handle him and the patience not to knock him about, O'Brien said. Those riders were Johnny Brabston and Danny O'Sullivan, the same Danny O'Sullivan who Dan and Kathleen O'Brien took into their home when he was orphaned over thirty years earlier.

Nijinsky even had a touch of colic the day before the Epsom Derby in June 1970 but, luckily, recovered in time to take his place in the great race and deliver an appropriately great performance to add to the Two Thousand Guineas a month earlier. He went on to win the Irish Derby, the King George and then completed the Triple Crown with victory in the English St Leger. He was retired to stud at Claiborne Farm in Kentucky, syndicated for $5.5 million.

He was a champion racehorse who then became a champion sire. John Magnier wanted to stand him at Coolmore but couldn't get anywhere near the valuation the Americans put on him, but he did stand two of his finest sons, Caerleon and Royal Academy, who both contributed significantly to Coolmore's spectacular rise in the thoroughbred breeding industry.

Now, in July 1975, Magnier, O'Brien and Sangster were ready for their assault on the American yearling sales and the offspring of Nijinsky and Northern Dancer were at the top of their must buy list. O'Brien had absolutely no doubts. "We must buy the Northern Dancers. We must buy them at all costs. And the same goes for yearlings by Nijinsky. I am telling you. We must have them. I am very certain of that," he told Magnier and Sangster.

While beset by personal difficulties - he had been forced into exile against his wishes by Britain's extortionate tax regime and had recklessly fallen for the charms of the glamorous and vivacious wife of an Australian politician which was to end his marriage - Sangster had succeeded in putting together a syndicate with cash of over $3 million to invest in yearlings. It was just the start of a crazy upward spiral, before long they would be lucky to get one top yearling for $3 million.

Rudolph Nureyev (pic) and Vaslav Nijinsky were Russians who changed the face of classical dancing in the same v Northern Dancer and his sons Nijinsky (opp.) and Nureyev (below) revolutionised racing. It is uncanny how Nijinsky d Nureyev, the horses, mirrored the lives of their human namesakes in many ways. Nijinsky was a highly-strung, vola stallion who could have easily gone the wrong way, which is exactly where Nijinsky the dancer did go, spending his l thirty years of his life in and out of mental asylums. Rudolph Nureyev's free spirit inspired and enthralled a generat before he lost a brave battle against AIDS in 1983. The fighting spirit of Nureyev, the horse, was no less inspirational wl he faced life-threatening inury.

Epsom Derby winner Australia, a great grandson of Northern Dancer, walks in the shadow of the statue of the legendary Nijinsky at the Curragh

Top: Nijinsky at the Curragh where he won the Irish Derby
Bottom: He cruises into the lead in the Epsom Derby

There was an impressive list of wealthy men joining up with Sangster and his two Irish partners. Charles St George was an immensely rich Lloyds insurance broker; Alan Clore, a son of one of England's wealthiest financiers, Sir Charles Clore; and Simon Fraser, from a long line of Scottish aristocrats whose ancestral home was Beaufort Castle in the Highlands of Inverness.

Also recruited was steel tycoon Jack Mulcahy, who had left Ireland as a 20 year old to make his fortune in America, and Walter Haefner, the Swiss businessman who became a billionaire through car dealerships and computers in Europe, the UK and America. He turned the 400 acre Moyglare Stud into a leading farm in Ireland and enjoyed considerable success as a racehorse owner in his own right, thanks to the brilliance of another Irish trainer, Dermot Weld.

Magnier, O'Brien and Sangster, together with their back up team, became known to the Americans as The Brethren. O'Brien included bloodstock agent Tom Cooper, who did all the leg work before they got to the sale in Kentucky, his brother Phonsie, who had a good eye for a horse, and he never bought anything in America until vet Bob Griffin had checked a likely yearling over.

Sangster liked to take his own bloodstock adviser, P P Hogan, along as an aide. He had bought some good yearlings and broodmares for Sangster's personal racing and bloodstock operation and as much as anything was there to make sure Robert didn't get too carried away when the bids were flying around at the sales. John Magnier just put his total trust in Vincent O'Brien. They left for America on the morning of Wednesday 16 July 1975. Can you hear the soundtrack to the Magnificent Seven?

A week later, a DC8 cargo plane was crossing the Atlantic with 12 highly prized and expensive yearlings on board, heading for Shannon Airport. The Brethren had bought every one of the yearling colts they decided would fit into their master plan, plus a couple of well bred fillies Sangster wanted as eventual broodmares, for a total cost of £2.4 million. At Keeneland that year they had been the biggest buyers in the history of thoroughbred breeding. Nine of the 12 yearlings on that flight traced their origins to Ireland; four of them were direct descendants of the Tipperary born stallion Princequillo, three descended from the former Kildare horse Turn-To, one was a grandson of Kildare's Nasrullah and one a son of Vaguely Noble, who started out from County Meath.

These yearlings were, effectively, coming home. The symbolism was striking, because Ireland's sometimes sad history has all too often been defined by the emigration of its people during times of famine and poverty. Many went to

America, just like their best stallions had done in the recent past, but there was a chance the balance was about to be redressed, atleast as far as the thoroughbred horse was concerned. Now Magnier just needed O'Brien to deliver one champion out of these 12 yearlings. The horse that did it for them was The Minstrel.

They were somewhat surprised when they first saw The Minstrel on the sales grounds. As a three quarters brother to Nijinsky, he did not look as they expected. Nijinsky was big, dark bay, impressive looking. The expression that the Irish love for this kind of animal is that he filled the eye when you looked at him. By contrast, The Minstrel was small, only just big enough according to Vincent O'Brien, and chestnut with a white face and four white socks. O'Brien went back to look at him several times, looking him in the eye, just staring at him. He could accept his lack of size if he had inherited Northern Dancer's character; the courage, the determination to battle in a race when the fight was at its fiercest, inside the last furlong.

Someone said he had a labrador at home not much bigger. Phonsie said if it was only about size a cow would outrun a rabbit. Sangster asked him if he liked him. "I bloody love him," said Phonsie. Vincent did, too, and told Tom Cooper to buy him when he came into the sales ring. No limit, he said, buy him, which he did for $200,000. Afterwards, they all thought he was a bargain, there was something about him, particularly for Vincent. For Magnier, if this horse could run, as a three quarters brother to the great Nijinsky he would start to fulfill his dream for Coolmore Stud.

And run he could. He won his first race as a two year old at the Curragh by five lengths in a new course record for six furlongs. He again won easily next time out and in October 1976, travelled over to England to contest the Dewhurst, which Nijinsky and Mill Reef had both won in recent seasons. He won again, impressively by four lengths.

The Brethren had much to look forward to and their smiles grew ever bigger in the last days of the 1976 season when Alleged flew home by eight lengths in a Curragh maiden in the manner of a really good horse in the making. The syndicate Sangster had put together not only had the chance of recouping all of their investment in 1977, but moving into serious profit.

So it proved. The Minstrel won the Epsom Derby with as brave a fight as any horse could give in an epic duel with Hot Grove. The Minstrel ran for his life in pursuit of Hot Grove, who had looked in control having got first run three furlongs out. Responding to every crack of Lester Piggott's whip, the little horse dug deep from within and at the line was a heart-stopping neck in front. He had shown he possessed every bit of the mystical fight and courage displayed by his father, Northern Dancer, in the Kentucky Derby 13 years earlier.

Vincent O'Brien, generally an understated and pragmatic sort of fellow, admitted he was trembling with emotion as he watched The Minstrel flash across the finishing line. When he was looking at yearlings at the sales he always tried to peer inside a horse's mind and character to try and work out if he had the necessary courage to win at the highest level. He had been proven right about The Minstrel.

Whether a horse wins the Epsom Derby by sheer athletic brilliance, like Nijinsky, or by sheer gut-busting bravery, like The Minstrel, it is the race that has defined the thoroughbred breed for over 200 years. Muriel Lennox summed up perfectly what the race stands for in her superb book on Northern Dancer.

"The Epsom Derby not only bestows tremendous prestige, but also assures the owners a place in history. The winning horse will be standing on the same ground as its celebrated ancestors. If you listen closely, you can almost hear the hoof beats of the great legends galloping across the turf on their way to Epsom's winner's circle: Hyperion, Sir Ivor, Mill Reef, Sea Bird, Shergar, Nijinsky. Their sweat is in the soil, their breath in the air."

The Minstrel (left) wins the Epsom Derby

Nijinsky was a phenomenon. The Minstrel showed that Northern Dancer horses could also win ugly, by having more heart than the others. It would lead to Northern Dancer's offspring becoming more valuable than gold as yearling prices went through the roof. In the first four years of following their plan at the yearling sales, Sangster and his team had spent close to $11 million, but they had doubled the return on their investment from the sale or re-syndication of the good horses within the first two years.

They had sold a 50% stake, worth $4.5 million, in The Minstrel to go to stud alongside Northern Dancer at Windfields in Canada and after his victory in the Prix de l'Arc de Triomphe Alleged was valued at $7 million. Other good horses like Transworld, Artaius and Solinus would bring in another $6 million and Try My Best and Godswalk were retired to stand as stallions at Coolmore in Co Tipperary and they would eventually be joined by Thatching, soon to become a champion sprinter for Ballydoyle. Lady Capulet and Fairy Bridge were top class fillies now added to the broodmare band and after Alleged won his second Arc in 1978, his valuation jumped to $16 million. They were rolling in cash.

Not quite everything had gone to plan. Try My Best had failed to build on a brilliant two year old season so his value was a fraction of what he would have been if he had won a classic or two a year later. He was, nevertheless, a very good looking horse and had been a very fast two year old, so Magnier was delighted to keep him at Coolmore. Simon Fraser and Alan Clore had found investing in the unknown too much of a risk after only one year and pulled out, but Billy McDonald brought in two even better partners, Bob Fluor, chairman of one of the six biggest corporations in the US, and Danny Schwartz, a very rich Californian builder.

Sangster's team went to Keeneland and Saratoga in 1978 and spent even more, over $7 million on nineteen colts and three fillies. The real drama concerned the yearling they didn't buy, the first time they failed to secure one of the horses on Vincent O'Brien's must buy list. Greek shipping billionaire Stavros Niarchos outbid everyone at $1.3 million to secure the yearling who became known as Nureyev, a brilliant racehorse horse and stallion who one day would be valued at $40 million.

While the Sangster consortium was making plenty of money, they still had yet to achieve what they set out to do - make a racehorse and stallion like

Nijinsky to stand at Coolmore. Part of the problem was that American racing and breeding were on an incredible high. After only one Triple Crown winner in 25 years, they now had three in five years. Secretariat was followed by Seattle Slew in 1977 and Affirmed a year later. The Kentucky breeding industry was awash with money thanks to Northern Dancer and the men from Coolmore.

They spent nearly $9 million on 16 colts in 1979 and that didn't include the two they were really after. O'Brien told Tom Cooper: "No limit, buy them both." Cooper paid $1 million for a colt by Northern Dancer and $1.4 million for a son of Nijinsky. Just two years later they were to sell the Northern Dancer for a staggering $28 million in the most bizarre of circumstances. That was Storm Bird.

He was a brilliant two year old, the complete package, showing great speed and the all-important courage to go with it. He won yet another Dewhurst for Vincent O'Brien and was then put away for the winter with the following year's Classics firmly on the agenda. This could be the one they had been waiting for. One night during that winter a disgruntled employee who had been sacked from Ballydoyle crept into Storm Bird's stable and hacked off his mane and tail.

While a mane and tail can grow out again, Storm Bird as a racehorse was never the same. He contracted a virus and between the physical strains of the illness and mental stress of that winter night at the hands of his assailant, he became a shadow of the horse he was at two years old. He missed all the Classics but did eventually race once, finishing well beaten. It was a disaster. Magnier still wanted to stand him as a stallion, but the figures didn't add up to anywhere near what he would have been worth as a champion three year old.

In the July of that year, 1981, Sangster's Gangsters, as they were now known by some of the more irreverent inhabitants of Kentucky, returned to the sales and spent another $9 million on yearlings. The previous three years had not gone badly, they were still making money, but they had failed to find the supreme champion by Northern Dancer they wanted to stand at Coolmore. Their grand plan had, so far, not worked out and it was about to get a lot more difficult. Already faced with increasing competition for the best horses from America's domestic owners and breeders as bloodstock values rocketed beyond anyone's understanding, something happened in the summer of 1980 which would change racing and bloodstock forever. The United Arab Emirates struck oil, lots of it, in the desert south of Dubai.

One year later the ruling Maktoum family of Dubai joined the mad throng at Keeneland, intent on building up their interest in the best thoroughbred racehorses. Prince Khalid Abdullah of Saudi Arabia was on a similar mission. Not forgetting Greek shipper Niarchos, who had even more funds available for re-investment thanks to Nureyev.

They were all particularly interested in three impeccably-bred sons of Northern Dancer and Sangster had to go to $3.5 million for a full brother to Storm Bird, more than double the price ever paid for any yearling in history. Sheikh Mohammed bought another Dancer for $3.3 million and Niarchos went to $2.95 million to secure the third.

The whole world now wanted to get into the bloodstock game, which Magnier, O'Brien and Sangster had set on fire. Explaining how his team had captured the imagination of not only the horse industry, but big business too, Sangster said: "A top racehorse, or a top stallion, is an international commodity. He has a major value anywhere. He can be moved instantly to where he is most valued. Better still, he never answers back."

Out of the blue, the Sangster team did a deal to sell Storm Bird to another oil man, this one from Oklahoma, Robert Hefner, who had developed Ashford Stud in Versailles, Kentucky, into a stunning showpiece which Coolmore were eventually to own. Magnier led the negotiations with Hefner and his bloodstock adviser, George Harris, who had been born on Christmas Day 1942 in the Golden Vale of Tipperary.

While the plan had been to make champion racehorses into champion stallions to stand in Ireland, when the Americans came calling with an open cheque book the dream had to be parked up for a while longer. They couldn't turn $28 million down. They were all smiles when the deal was finalised in the Hyatt Hotel in Lexington. Vincent O'Brien was even seen to do a little Irish jig. Storm Bird was worth more than three times his own weight in gold.

Instead of standing Storm Bird at Coolmore, Magnier stood the Irish Two Thousand Guineas winner Kings Lake, syndicating him for £22 million. Everything continued to go the way of Sangster's mob in 1982. Golden Fleece, yet another strapping son of Nijinsky who O'Brien had bought at Keeneland for $775.000, won the Epsom Derby in breathtaking fashion, coming from last to first with a devastating run in the fastest time for 50 years. He had his problems in training, both physical and mental, and he became another prime example of the skills and commitment of O'Brien and his staff at Ballydoyle.

Golden Fleece

He only ran four times before he was syndicated to stand as a stallion with a huge future. This was the horse Magnier had been looking for at Coolmore. His stud fee was £100,000 and breeders queued up to send their mares to him.

He only stood for one full season, then the desperate curse of cancer which had struck down Windfield's Joe Thomas a year earlier also descended on Golden Fleece. Top surgeons from America were brought in to operate and the horse initially recovered, but the cancer came back and he was eventually euthanised in February 1984. Magnier had to fight long and hard to get the insurance pay-out on the massively talented but ill-fated son of Nijinsky.

In addition to Golden Fleece winning the Epsom Derby, Northern Dancer's grandson Assert won the French and Irish versions when trained by O'Brien's son David from a separate yard at Ballydoyle and Sangster became the first owner to win all three derbies in the same year.

At the end of his three year old season, Sangster and Magnier sold Assert for stallion duties in North America, syndicated for $25 million. But that was only half the story, because Assert was by Coolmore stallion Be My Guest, who also had a Classic winning filly, On The House, representing him on the racecourse that year. They helped Be My Guest become Coolmore's first ever Champion Sire in only the seventh year since Sangster, O'Brien and Magnier had formed their partnership.

Be My Guest, Coolmore's first Champion Sire.

It was ironic that Be My Guest should turn out to be such an outstanding success as a stallion, because it flew in the face of The Brethren's master plan. He was by Northern Dancer but not a top flight racehorse and was bred in America by a member of Sangster's syndicate, Walter Haefner, and then sold at Goffs Sales in Ireland. He was bought by Diana Guest Manning for £127,000, then a European record for a yearling but way behind what they were making in America. Her son, Raymond Guest, became US Ambassador to Ireland and had horses with Vincent O'Brien, including Epsom Derby winners Larkspur and Sir Ivor. It wasn't supposed to happen like this, but with O'Brien as the trainer anything could happen.

There was, however, a revelation regarding Be My Guest's success which rocked the bloodstock world. In 1978, the first year he started out as a stallion, Magnier had allowed him to cover 97 mares, breaking the guidelines followed by thoroughbred breeders for centuries, that no stallion should cover more than 55 mares in one season. This was an unwritten rule which had been strictly followed by all breeders, both large and small, in the long history of the thoroughbred and was intended to make sure the breed was not abused but allowed to flourish into the future. Magnier was severely criticised in the press for over breeding the stallion. He apologised, saying he had not meant it and that he wouldn't do it again.

With 97 mares at a stud fee of £7,000, Be My Guest had virtually paid off his syndication costs in one year. Now that he was Champion Sire, which brought a big increase in his stud fee, Magnier and his partners were going to make a fortune out of the busy stallion. Patrick Robinson wrote a fascinating book about Sangster, with his full co-operation and called Horsetrader, in which he tells of a conversation between Magnier and Sangster in the Turf Club bar at the Curragh in 1982.

" ...he (Magnier) confided in Robert, with a terrible Irish chortle: 'I'll let you into a shocking secret, with which you must go to your grave. If I could live 1978 all over again I'd still breed Be My Guest to 97 mares!' And they both fell about laughing..."

Magnier didn't get his stallions to cover 97 mares again, that became a low figure, they would soon be regularly covering twice that number. Some of his National Hunt stallions cover three times that number – Leading Light served 320 mares in his first season in 2015. The two Coolmore men had driven a bulldozer through one of breeding's great traditions which gave the stud an edge over everyone else. In the Coolmore stallion book for 1985, Magnier said: "We are forever looking for ways to improve ourselves and our facilities, as for example keeping our breeding sheds open 24 hours a day."

But it didn't stop there. The two businessmen next turned their attention to sending their stallions to Australia and New Zealand, so called shuttling, for the southern hemisphere mating season, which occupies the opposite time of the year to the northern hemisphere breeding season. This now meant stallions could be breeding throughout the year and, therefore, doubling their earning capacity for the partners. Some of these stallions were soon covering 150 mares in each hemisphere, a staggering increase on the maximum of 55 per year which had been the standard for the previous 200 years.

Shuttling stallions from the northern hemisphere to the south first took place in the 1970s but it was sporadic and not particularly successful. In the 1980s Sangster went into partnership with Australian horseman Colin Hayes at Nagambie Stud in Victoria and they set about perfecting the art of shuttling. The first really serious shuttler of the modern era was the Coolmore stallion Godswalk and from there a whole new industry was spawned, led by the phenomenal success of Danehill.

Coolmore built their own stud in the Hunter Valley in the mid 1990s and many of their stallions now shuttle regularly to Australasia and South America. When Sangster and Magnier revolutionised the practice, not only were the Coolmore owners able to double their income through breeding throughout the year, but all their earnings, even those earned in Australia, were tax free because of Haughey's infamous concession to stallion owners, of which he was one.

For a savvy and professionally run operation like Coolmore, the roads leading to Fethard became paved with gold and Magnier became rich beyond those wildest dreams of 1975 when he first joined forces with O'Brien and Sangster. Only time will tell if this huge explosion in breeding to the most commercially popular stallions, and in particular Coolmore's now routine policy of saturation inbreeding to the Northern Dancer stallion line, will have a detrimental effect on the breed as some experts predict. By then it might be too late.

In their acclaimed book, Thoroughbred Breeding, Dr Matthew Binns, a former Professor of Genetics at the Royal Veterinary College in London, and Tony Morris, an expert writer about horse racing and breeding for nearly fifty years, cautioned that the dramatic changes that have taken place in the thoroughbred breeding industry require careful monitoring and statistical modeling to look out for signs of genetic health problems. It is already thought that breeders' relentless quest to make racehorses faster has resulted in a considerable increase in stress fractures in the breed. They said one consequence of intensive inbreeding can be a decrease in reproductive fitness and advances in veterinary intervention could be masking inbreeding problems.

This new anything goes order in the thoroughbred breeding world traces directly to Magnier and Sangster treating bloodstock on a strictly commercial footing, just like battery hens in the intensive farming of the modern age. In particular, to when they took the number of mares covered by their stallions to unprecedented levels and then pioneered shuttling between hemispheres. It was all about money and it started in 1978 with Be My Guest covering 97 mares.

The feeding frenzy reached fever pitch at the American yearling sales in 1982. Sangster's syndicate thought they might need $15 million cash to spend. Sheikh Mohammed and his brother Hamdan were increasing their interest all the time and the upward spiral in the cost of these stunning yearlings showed no signs of slowing down.

Danny Schwartz was one of the biggest builders in California when he sold out to a major national construction company in the States for a gigantic sum of money. He was a typical all American hero. At the age of 19, in June 1944, he was with General George Patton's Third Armoured Division in the Second World War.

He had been involved with some of Vincent O'Brien's horses for a couple of years when Sangster asked him to take up a bigger stake in their syndicate and he agreed. Concorde was packed with horsemen when it flew from London Heathrow on 15 July and when the iconic jet landed in New York there were three privately chartered Learjets waiting to take them on to Kentucky - one each for Sangster's Gangsters, Prince Khalid Abdullah and Sheikh Maktoum. When they landed at Lexington there was a Boeing 727 belonging to Sheikh Mohammed parked up and a few hours later Niarchos' personal Boeing 737 touched down. Welcome to the real world.

Unsurprisingly, Kentucky's horsemen were in a high state of anticipation. They were not disappointed. Sangster and his team, which also now included Niarchos, parted with $14 million for 12 yearlings, Prince Khalid took six home for $3.3 million and Sheikh Mohammed and his brothers trumped them both with a $20 million haul. The gross take for the sale hit $100 million, more than $56 million of which was for yearlings destined to race in Europe.

When Magnier and Sangster completed the syndication of Assert for $24 million to stand as a stallion in the US, the Coolmore team were sitting on cumulative deals of around $96 million in the stallion business. Storm Bird had realised $28 million, Kings Lake $16 million, and Golden Fleece $28 million. With Be My Guest being crowned Champion Sire, Magnier, O'Brien and

Sangster had reached the top of the mountain. With the exception of Vincent O'Brien, who was working away creating the next champions at Ballydoyle, the lads went off to Barbados on vacation.

In 1983, Lomond won the English Guineas for O'Brien and then Caerleon followed up with victory in the French Derby, but in the Irish Derby he was beaten by Sheikh Mohammed's Shareef Dancer, a portent of things to come on the racetrack and at the yearling sales. The Dubai bandwagon was beginning to pick up speed and after Shareef Dancer gave Sheikh Mohammed his first win in a Derby, the Arabs were ready to show the scale of their ambitions - in the sales ring with their oil dollars. Shareef Dancer's win had added insult to injury to the Coolmore team, they had been beaten in a bidding duel with Sheikh Mohammed when the colt was sold at Keeneland for $3.3 million.

It wasn't just about ambition now, it was more about raw, ruthless pride. One powerful man beating another, no matter what the cost. One of Sheikh Mohammed's advisers said he was surprised, when he first came to England, to find out that Sangster was regarded as a rich man. There's rich and then there is Arab rich. As Phonsie O'Brien remarked on the night of 18 July 1983, the craziest ever seen in the history of bloodstock sales: "We're bidding against an entire bloody nation!"

All of the major players in world bloodstock's premier league were in place when a stunning colt by Northern Dancer out of the mare My Bupers, a half brother to the brilliant filly My Juliet, an Eclipse Award winner as the best racehorse of 1976, came into a packed sales ring as lot 308, with hundreds of onlookers outside and unable to get in. Vincent O'Brien had said he was the most beautiful of movers. California trainer D.Wayne Lukas was in for him until the $5 million dollar mark was passed and from there on it was a straight fight between the Sangster and Sheikh Mohammed camps.

The bidding went on up in millions at the start, then in five hundred thousands and sometimes on by a mere hundred thousand. The auditorium sat in hushed disbelief as the bids went over $7 million. When the Sangster team took it to $10 million the crowd inside stood up and cheered and outside a massive roar burst into the night air. But Colonel Dick Warden, bidding for Sheikh Mohammed, came back once more and the colt was his for $10.2 million.

When the sale ended the gross take was a staggering $147 million. Foreign buyers accounted for $96 million of that with 129 yearlings bought. Sheikh Mohammed and his brothers spent $43 million on 26 yearlings, Sangster had

14 for nearly $18 million and Prince Khalid bought nine for just short of $6 million. The sale ring which had belonged to Sangster, O'Brien and Magnier since 1975 was now under the control of the men from the Middle East. And the stunning yearling who cost $10.2 million? Author Patrick Robinson summed it up beautifully.

> **"The horse was taken home to England and trained by John Dunlop. Named Snaafi Dancer, he could not beat a fat man going downhill. Sheikh Mohammed's dreams of Derby glory with this highly bred son of Northern Dancer withered on the vine. A mile and a half at Epsom? Snaafi Dancer could not have got the trip in a horsebox. And as a stallion? He was infertile - $10.2 million catastrophe, which will live forever in the folklore of thoroughbred racing."**

Sangster was lucky to get away with that one. The yearling cost $5 million more than he was really worth, even in a bull market, because misplaced personal pride wouldn't allow either of the two protagonists to back down. The difference was that $5 million was a drop in the ocean of Dubai oil for Sheikh Mohammed. It was Sangster who would have picked up the largest part of the tab if he had won the fight for the Northern Dancer colt.

While it was the Sheikh who became infamous for paying $10.2 million for the yearling who was incapable of being a racehorse or a stallion, his personal sales ground feud with John Magnier eventually saw the head of Coolmore score an own goal of epic proportions nearly 23 years later. The Coolmore boss led his new partners, Michael Tabor and Derek Smith, into the purchase of a two year old colt for $16 million at the Calder Select Sale in Florida. Named The Green Monkey after a golf course in Barbados, he couldn't win a minor race in three attempts and went to stud in America for a no-hope fee of $5,000. It was slightly better than Snaafi Dancer, but it was Magnier's turn to be the chimp.

Lady Luck was still with Sangster as 1983 came to an end. Ballydoyle had two very exciting two year olds, both by Northern Dancer, heading into the winter with the following year's Classics well within their grasp. One was El Gran Senor, a champion at two and three whose only defeat in eight races was when he was touched off by Secreto, trained by Vincent O'Brien's son David, in the Epsom Derby of 1984. He was named after Northern Dancer's trainer, Horatio Luro. The other was Sadler's Wells, home bred by Sangster out of Fairy Bridge and the stallion who made Coolmore.

It is said every cloud has a silver lining, and it was Robert Hefner who was that cloud for Coolmore in 1984. He went spectacularly bust, even taking a bank, the Penn Square in Oklahoma City, down with him. At one time he had assets in excess of $2 billion from the oil and gas he owned deep underground the plains of Oklahoma. That was when the price of natural gas was $9.50 per one thousand cubic feet.

When the price torpedoed to $1.50 in 1984, Hefner's colossal borrowings of $770 million sank him when he still owed the Coolmore partners $14 million for his purchase of Storm Bird. Hefner had pledged his stunning Ashford Stud farm against the deal Magnier had negotiated. To settle the debt, Hefner had to give Ashford and Storm Bird to the Coolmore partners. Thanks to Magnier's tough negotiations, the cloud ended up with a mighty impressive silver lining.

Storm Bird

The Maktoum family continued to expand their bloodstock interests. Sheikh Mohammed had bought Dalham Hall Stud in Newmarket, Sheikh Hamdan had Derrinstown Stud in Ireland and Sheikh Maktoum was developing Gainsborough Stud near Newbury in England. Out of the blue, Sheikh Mohammed invited Sangster, O'Brien and Magnier to fly out to Dubai for a chat; he wanted to be rivals on the racecourse but friends off it. In particular, he didn't believe it was wise to fight each other in the sales ring. O'Brien couldn't go as he was too busy training his horses at Ballydoyle, but Sangster and Magnier were collected in Sheikh Mohammed's private Boeing 727 and flown for formal talks at the ruling family's royal palace.

Sheikh Mohammed then asked Sangster and Magnier to return when Vincent O'Brien was available and to bring their wives, which was a bit of a problem for Robert because he was about to change his again. They all went back in March 1985. Robert did take a wife, but she wasn't yet his wife. Susan Lilley was at the time married to Peter Lilley, of the Lilley and Skinner shoe empire, but she did eventually become Sangster's third wife. How he must have envied Sheikh Mohammed, who not only had far more money than he did, but under Muslim law the Bedouin prince could legally have up to four wives without lawyers divesting him of his wealth in divorce actions.

The summit in the desert was held behind closed doors. The only public announcement was that Sheikh Mohammed had taken a share in two horses which Sangster had bought at the last yearling sale in America. The implications were massive; the two rival camps were now aligned together and would not be bidding against each other at future sales.

Within two years the American bloodstock industry would be in total meltdown, unable to service unparalleled amounts of debt built up by stud farms caught up in the gigantic inflationary bubble caused at the yearling sales, which Sangster, O'Brien and Magnier had started ten years earlier when they went in pursuit of Northern Dancer's best colts at any price.

There was one more moment of total madness at the Kentucky sales in 1985 before everything came crashing down in 1986. Sangster got into a dogfight over a colt by Nijinsky out of My Charmer, the dam of both the brilliant US racehorse and sire, Seattle Slew, and Lomond, a Classic winner for Ballydoyle and promising stallion at Coolmore.

His opponents weren't his new friends from Dubai, but a very rich syndicate of Americans put together by leading trainer D Wayne Lukas. On they went,

Lukas against The Brethren, until bidding reached $13.1 million, when the Californians decided to walk away. That was Seattle Dancer, who did win a Group 3 race for O'Brien and became a stallion, but was worth nowhere near $13.1 million.

This was the end of it all for Danny Schwartz, who now questioned the wisdom of what they were doing. He said there was no clear strategy or budgets, he could not agree to be in for an open ended ten or fifteen per cent. He admitted later his involvement with Sangster, O'Brien and Magnier cost him $10 million, but he particularly cherished the friendship he had built up with Vincent, Jacqueline and their family. He liked nothing better than to take his private jet to New York once a month, pick up the Aer Lingus flight to Shannon and be in time for breakfast with Vincent at Ballydoyle. He said:

"Vincent O'Brien was basically interested only in being the best trainer in the world. John Magnier was interested in the yearlings as future stallions, from which he would make money for the next twenty years. Robert was a partner in Coolmore and this applied to him too. They were magical years for me. I loved Ireland and the people, and I loved my involvement in the racing in England. I look back on wonderful times. And when I do, I understand that some things are beyond price."

Schwartz exiting was a big blow to the Sangster team and their financial muscle all but evaporated. Niarchos also left to go his own way and the racing landscape in the UK and Ireland continued to change dramatically. Apart from Law Society winning the Irish Derby, 1985 had ended up a poor year by Vincent O'Brien's standards and the Arabs were now growing ever stronger. Sangster had been leading owner in England since 1977, but top place now went to Sheikh Mohammed, thanks to his home bred filly Oh So Sharp, who won three Classics. He also owned another brilliant filly, Pebbles, who won the Breeder's Cup Turf Championship in New York.

Prince Khalid Abdullah was runner-up in the leading owners list and fourth and sixth were Sheikhs Hamdan and Maktoum who, with their younger brother Mohammed, had spent over $200 million on yearlings during the 1980s. Sangster dropped to seventh in the list, with prize money of less than £250,000.

John Magnier was also having his difficulties the following year. Lloyds of London were still refusing to pay out on the death of Golden Fleece, saying they weren't liable for what happened to him, and El Gran Senor had major fertility problems at stud in America, getting only 22 mares in foal, which resulted in a significant loss of revenue. O'Brien didn't have a winner at Royal Ascot that year and Ballydoyle was beset by a virus.

The Kentucky yearling sales were another bloodbath, with only the Maktoums keeping it afloat. They spent $40 million on fifty seven yearlings and they followed the trend pioneered by the men from Coolmore, buying stock by Northern Dancer and his sons like Nijinsky, Danzig, Nureyev and Lyphard. Sangster's name was way down among the minor purchasers, just three yearlings booked to his account for a total of $3 million.

The next year at Keeneland, he was listed as buying just one yearling, a filly by Northern Dancer out of his own mare, Detroit. He was just buying out a partner in the filly. Ballydoyle had not had a truly top notch horse for the last three years. Bluebird was a good sprinter, but in Alydar Sheikh Mohammed had a better one, which was the way everything seemed to be going. The grand plan to corner the best of Northern Dancer's yearlings was over. The Brethren were history.

Sheikh Mohammed

Chapter 4

TOUGH BRAVE SPIRITED

Three Galileo weanlings enjoy the soft going at Barretstown Farm

TOUGH BRAVE SPIRITED

*"A horse runs with its lungs,
perseveres with its heart,
and wins with is character."*

Federico Tesio

Until his untimely death from a paddock accident at the age of 17 in 2003, it had looked as if Danehill would be the stallion who would have a greater influence than even Sadler's Wells at Coolmore and leave the biggest legacy through his sons and grandsons. Magnier doesn't acquire too many stallion prospects off the racetrack; his business model is mostly about buying and breeding yearlings to turn into champion racehorses before retiring them to Coolmore as stallions.

He bought Danehill at the end of his racing career, in which he was crowned champion sprinter in 1989, from his owner Prince Khalid Abdullah, whose seriously successful Juddmonte Farms has substantial breeding operations in America, England and Ireland. It was a brilliant piece of business, because right from the start Danehill's offspring fired in winner after winner, particularly in Australia. This was Magnier mining more gold from a source he knew so well, as Danehill was by Northern Dancer's son Danzig and from Northern Dancer's own family.

He initially stood in partnership with John Messara's Arrowfield Stud in New South Wales for the southern hemisphere breeding season and shuttled to Coolmore in Co Tipperary for the northern hemisphere. He was an outstanding success in Australia, becoming champion sire nine times. When

Coolmore decided to set up their own stud operation in Jerrys Plains, New South Wales, in the mid-1990s, they bought out Arrowfield Stud to own Danehill outright in a $24 million deal which made him the most expensive thoroughbred in Australian breeding history. He had cost Magnier just £4 million when he bought him from Prince Khalid.

Siring brilliant racehorses like Dylan Thomas, George Washington and Rock of Gibraltar, his reputation in Europe was growing all the time. He became champion stallion in the UK and Ireland three times and twice in France. His loss to Coolmore on 13 May 2003, when he broke a hip while rearing up in his paddock, was huge. According to newspaper reports, Coolmore received a £36 million insurance pay out on his death, but the way he was going as a stallion at the time they would have made much more from his future sons and grandsons if he had lived on.

As with so many of the Northern Dancer clan, Danehill's offspring were noted for their mix of toughness, courage and dash of brilliance. He was the sire of 2008 runners of which nearly an incredible 77% (1545) were winners. He sired 89 Group 1 winners, more even than Sadler's Wells, including Duke of Marmalade. He came from Danehill's final crop in 2003 and won five Group 1 races, so Danehill's prepotency was showing no sign of waning at the age of 17. It is safe to say there were many more top flight winners to come if he had not died so suddenly.

At the last count he had left 114 stallion sons and 56 grandsons at stud in Australia. In Ireland, Danehill Dancer and his sons have continued to fly the Danehill flag for Coolmore. Many of his daughters have since become outstanding broodmares and, among a glut of top class racehorses in both hemispheres, is the broodmare sire of the superstar Frankel, Arc winner Danedream, dual Classic winner Golden Lilac, two year old champion Teofilo and Melbourne Cup winner Shocking. He is the paternal

Danehill

80

grandsire of superstar mare Makybe Diva, who won the Melbourne Cup three times and had winning prize money of over A$14 million. Some record for a horse the experts crabbed for having less than perfect knees.

As Danehill was siring his final crop in 2003, the heir apparent to Sadler's Wells was just starting out on a stud career which would see him scale even greater heights. Galileo was to become the best stallion in the world following a brilliant break through year in 2006 with his first three year olds. Just eight years later he reached the astonishing landmark of a century of group winners when Marvellous, a home bred from Ballintemple Farm, landed the Irish One Thousand Guineas. In 2008, the first year Galileo became Champion Stallion in Europe, Sadler's Wells was retired from his own breeding career at the age of 27.

Just as fate played such a big hand in the creation of Northern Dancer, a chance conversation and a $100 note were the forerunners to Robert Sangster breeding Sadler's Wells. Billy McDonald was a colourful and charismatic Irish bloodstock agent who relocated to California in the 1970s, where he also ran a Rolls Royce dealership. Paying tribute to McDonald when he died on 19 November 2009 at his home in Belfast, trainer John Gosden said he was in the Guinness Book of World Records for selling the most Rolls Royces in a day.

"He could sell ice to an Eskimo. Billy was one of the great characters of the game. He was a man who lived life to the full and had a great eye for a horse. He was an immensely popular and loveable man who was totally at ease in all the great watering holes, restaurants and racecourses of the world. There will never be another Billy."

McDonald was an adviser and friend of Robert Sangster. He found an unraced two year old by American stallion Hoist The Flag for him. The racing experts at the Keeneland July Yearling Sale in 1975 had turned the colt down because of some minor imperfections. He had been unsold at $34,000, but six months later he was owned by Monty Roberts, of 'Horse Whisperer' fame, who was preparing him for a breeze up sale. McDonald persuaded Sangster to buy him privately for $120,000. Sangster named him Alleged and Vincent O'Brien trained him to win consecutive Prix de l'Arc de Triomphes in 1977 and 1978 in a glittering career on the racetrack.

McDonald had been prepared to back his judgement when buying Alleged, and later in the same year he backed it again though in slightly more unorthodox circumstances. Magnier and the Coolmore team had gone to Claiborne Farm in Kentucky on a scouting mission ahead of the sales to look at yearlings which might make future champions. Taking yearling manager Gus Koch aside, McDonald put a $100 bill in his hand and asked him: "Which one do you like best?"

Koch replied that he would go for the little Bold Reason filly every time. "They always race over to this gate from across the far side of the paddock

and that little filly is always yards in front when they arrive. She's the racehorse." Using the salesman's pitch which Gosden said could sell ice to an Eskimo, McDonald persuaded Sangster to buy the diminutive filly for $40,000 when she came into the sales ring. Sangster named her Fairy Bridge. John Gosden said McDonald lived life to the full. He did that

Robert Sangster (right) and Billy McDonald viewing a yearling in America

alright. He was engaged seven times but only married once, for two years. He was friends with racing heroes in the US like jockey Bill Shoemaker and trainer Charlie Whittingham and great mates with film stars like Roger Moore and Pierce Brosnan. He was close friends with movie producer David Giler, who gave him a small role in the Richard Dreyfuss film Let It Ride in1989.

Then there was Frank Sinatra and a restaurant in Los Angeles called Le Dome, where all the racing people would go in the 80s. Billy was friends with Sinatra and one night he took a date to the restaurant and quietly asked Sinatra to drop by his table on his way out to say hello, to impress his new girlfriend. Which Sinatra did, and Billy said: "Frank, not now, can't you see I'm busy."

Restauranteur Eddie Kerkhofs owned Le Dome and McDonald decided to give himself a party there when he turned 40. "He rented out the whole place,"

Kerkhofs recalled. "He was inviting 130 people and wanted pasta, caviar and Roederer Cristal Champagne. So 130 people came, and it was a lot of noise, and this and that. All of a sudden I got a phone call from Palm Springs. It was the Chairman of the Board, Mr Sinatra himself."

Sinatra couldn't get to the party, but he told Kerkhofs to send him the tab. "And that's what I did, he picked up the check for Billy's party. I didn't tell Billy until the day after, because he would have done even more damage. He was the one who introduced me to the horse racing world, to Bill Shoemaker and those guys. Le Dome became their hangout. We would have a fantastic week during the Breeders' Cup. All of that, from John Magnier to Michael Tabor, was because Billy introduced us," Kerkhofs said.

McDonald, perhaps unsurprisingly given his lifestyle, suffered a stroke in his mid fifties and eventually returned to Belfast, where he helped care for his mother and brother Calvin, who had been paralysed when thrown from a horse, until he passed away in his sleep one night at the age of 65. Gosden said there would never be another Billy. If the people and horses he was associated with were world class, then so too was McDonald himself. As Johnny Jones Jr, who stood Alleged at his major American farm, Walmac International, said: "The best story I have about Billy is this. I bought his share of Alleged the night before he won the Arc. When Alleged won the value of the share obviously increased tremendously. But Billy didn't back out of the deal. He stayed with it, and did what he said he'd do."

In 1975, Sangster went into tax exile on the Isle of Man, buying The Nunnery, a dilapidated house set in 90 acres, which he renovated and developed into his own stud farm. He named the filly McDonald had recommended to him at Keeneland after a mythical place nearby. Superstition said that before anyone crossed Fairy Bridge they should say "Good Morning Fairies!" The locals followed the ritual without fail, it was believed bad luck would descend on anyone who did not speak to the fairies at the bridge. It was even said taxi drivers wouldn't drive over it until their passengers greeted the fairies. To think the world believes the Irish are crazy.

Fairy Bridge won two races for Vincent O'Brien in 1977 on the way to becoming champion two year old filly in Ireland. She was aptly named and created her own place in folklore when she returned to America at the end of her racing career to be bred to Northern Dancer. Her first foal, born in 1981, was Sadler's Wells.

Fairy Bridge

Further matings with Northern Dancer also produced a Champion two year old colt, Tate Gallery, and Fairy King, a successful stallion for Coolmore in Europe and Australia until he was euthanised because of laminitis at the age of 17 in 1999.

Two years after Sangster bought Fairy Bridge for just $40,000, and before Sadler's Wells came along, the deal began to look more inspired almost every day. Stavros Niarchos paid $1.3 million for her yearling half brother by Northern Dancer, whom he named Nureyev after the famous Russian ballet dancer, and he went into training with Francois Boutin in France. Nureyev only raced three times, winning his first two starts comfortably. He then also won the first Classic of the 1980 European racing season, the English Two Thousand Guineas, but was disqualified and placed last for interference by his jockey, Frenchman Philippe Paquet, who impeded several horses as he barged his way to the front.

Despite the disqualification, Nureyev was clearly a top class racehorse. He was due to run in the Epsom Derby next, but a virus laid him low and he never raced again. Renowned French horseman, Alec Head, put a syndicate together for him to go to stud at Walmac International in Kentucky, which valued him at $14 million. With this backdrop, expectations were huge when Sadler's Wells went into training at Ballydoyle as a two year old of 1983.

History shows that he didn't disappoint, though he wasn't the best three year old at Ballydoyle in 1984; that was El Gran Senor, another son of Northern Dancer. Just like his sire, Sadler's Wells stood out for his toughness, courage and will to win, attributes which he also passed on to his foals when he went to stud.

These are the same qualities which are often the only difference between gold and silver medals at the Olympic Games or champions and runners-up in just about any other human sport. Humans, though, have the benefit of sophisticated training schedules and sports psychologists to help show them the way forward.

Racehorse trainers have to look at it from a different angle, not to screw up what selective breeding has been trying to achieve for centuries, to make horses faster, stronger and tougher than the previous generation. Sadler's Wells had the supreme equine sports psychologist as his trainer. This is how journalist Tony Morris, a pedigree and racing expert for over fifty years, saw Sadler's Wells.

Sadler's Wells

"It was his good fortune to go into training with a master in Vincent O'Brien, but it was the colt's own merits as an athlete that were crucial in enabling him to earn the opportunities to start at stud with the prospect of success more expectation than hope. Unbeaten as a two year old and a triple Group 1 winner at three, his results were first class. But other horses have compiled similar records without achieving much at stud. Sadler's Wells, in addition to his class, impressed for his physique, his toughness, his honesty, his temperament and his soundness. He had everything breeders wanted in their stock."

When he went to stud at Coolmore, Sadler's Wells also had the good fortune to be looked after by stallion men who shared his qualities, people like Noel Stapleton and Paul Gleeson. Paul was working in the stallion yard thirty years ago and led Sadler's Wells off the horse box to start his new life as a stallion. Both Noel and Paul emphasise the horse's superb temperament, that he was a gentleman to deal with. Noel and Paul are out of a similar mould.

The best photograph I saw in my time at Coolmore was the one of Paul walking beside Sadler's Wells as he reared up high above him. The stallion was just showing his joy of life and there was Paul calm beside him as if he was out walking a puppy. To me, this is an iconic image of Sadler's Wells which also sums up life in the stallion yard; the power and beauty of the horses and the underplayed skills of their handlers.

John Magnier had only returned from his winter's tax exile in Barbados a couple of days when Sadler's Wells passed away on 26 April 2011. The legendary horse was 30 years old and died peacefully of old age. Noel said it was like as if he waited for everyone to get there before he took his leave. His heart was buried in the stallion yard as a gesture of what this wonderful horse had done for the Magniers and Coolmore.

Mrs Magnier organised her chef to knock up some sandwiches for those who stayed behind. There were jobs to be done, getting him ready to go to a taxidermist in Germany for one. When I was first told what was involved I felt sick. Why not just let him go quietly and with dignity were my first thoughts. Having now seen him returned in all his glory as the focal point of the stud's museum, built specially at a cost of over €4 million, it was a good decision. The Magniers were right to want to preserve him for the benefit of future generations to view, apart from it being an extremely clever marketing initiative for the Coolmore brand.

The Coolmore boss is in exalted company, because German king Frederick The Great had his favourite horse stuffed in 1754. His hide caught fire during a bombing raid in the Second World War, but his skeleton was saved and is still on display in Berlin today. Taxidermy has been around for centuries but very few horses are remembered in this way. The most famous of Napolean's many horses was Le Vizin, who died in 1829, eight years after Napolean. Le Vizin was stuffed and is also still on display in a Paris museum. So the chances are Sadler's Wells is going to be around for a few hundred years at least.

He sired 2,259 foals in the 23 years he stood as a stallion. He was champion sire a record 14 times and 18 of his sons and daughters became champions. His runners earned prize money just short of £100 million. "He was a truly amazing sire," Ben Sangster said of the horse who ran in his late father's colours. "He's been lucky for anyone who had anything to do with him, especially us. He was the bedrock of our Swettenham Stud and the bedrock of Coolmore."

John Ferguson, bloodstock advisor to Sheikh Mohammed, so often the bitterest of rivals with Magnier, also paid tribute. Ten of the stallion's Group 1 winners were campaigned by either Sheikh Mohammed or Godolphin in their early days of involvement in European racing. It's a fair argument their success at the highest level has declined markedly since Sheikh Mohammed decided to boycott Coolmore stallions in a very public stand-off in recent years. "Sadler's Wells has been one of the greatest influences on the thoroughbred breed ever. Phenomenal, that is the only word to describe Sadler's Wells," Ferguson said on learning of the stallion's death.

Magnier fully expected Sadler's Wells to succeed as a stallion. He told Sangster when the horse arrived at Coolmore: "This fellow will sire Classic winners for years to come. That's not said in hope, that's a promise." Coolmore didn't show the same confidence about dual Derby winner Galileo. He stood his first season at stud for €50,000, half of what Giant's Causeway started out for the previous year and €75,000 less than Sadler's Wells's initial stud fee.

Coolmore rarely support their first season stallions with the best of their own mares, they prefer to let outside mare owners have first strike and discover if a new stallion is any good. They will send a few of their older mares to a new stallion, those getting close to the end of their breeding days. If a new stallion turns out a failure, like so many do, they haven't then wasted a year or two of the breeding life of their best broodmares. If they are a success they will then quickly row in behind their latest sire sensation, as they did with Galileo.

It was Irish trainer and breeder Jim Bolger who did most to make Galileo the champion he is today. He believed strongly in the son of Sadler's Wells, supporting him with a number of mares from his own relatively small broodmare band during Galileo's first seasons as a stallion. The horse had few two year old runners and no big winners in his debut crop of 2005, Bolger's Heliostatic being his first winner, but one year later the picture started to change dramatically. His three year old daughter Nightime became his first Classic winner in the Irish One Thousand Guineas, for Dermot Weld and bred by his mother, and his colts filled the first three places in the English St Leger. Red Rocks, third that day, then went out and won the Breeders' Cup Turf in America.

Teofilo became Champion two year old when winning a quality Dewhurst for Bolger, who did the same double with New Appproach the following year. In 2008, New Approach won the Epsom Derby and Lush Lashes, another bred and trained by Bolger, won three Group 1s. Galileo has been Champion Sire ever since.

Only one of his early successes, Irish Derby winner Soldier of Fortune, was trained at Ballydoyle and he was bred by Bolger. The majority of Magnier's mares were soon being put in foal to Galileo each breeding season and Aidan O'Brien was training around 60 of his two year olds every year. The transformation has been such that Ballydoyle had six Group 1 winners by Galileo out of Coolmore's own mares in 2014, their best ever home bred results, and that trend has continued into 2015.

Phonsie O'Brien reckons that Bolger is the nearest in comparison as a trainer to his famous brother. "Vincent never believed in working over long distances. Even the jumpers never worked beyond 10 furlongs. It was all about speed. A number of trainers employ his training methods now. Aidan O'Brien does, and I'm sure Jim Bolger does too. I have never been in his place, but what I read about Jim Bolger, he would remind me most of Vincent," he said.

Bolger would also bear comparison with the great Federico Tesio, the outstanding breeder and trainer of the first half of the 20th Century. Bolger's success with small numbers of horses compared to the big battalions in the thoroughbred racehorse world is hugely impressive. Whether it's Dermot Weld, as a pioneer of training horses to travel all over the world to win the biggest of races, or John Oxx, with his faultless campaigning of World Champion Sea The Stars, Ireland consistently produces trainers to match, and beat, anyone anywhere.

Galileo's lowest advertised stud fee was E37,500 in the year before he had his first runners. It has since risen to E350,000, potentially earning Coolmore E70 million a year if he covered 200 mares, which he has been doing. With his home bred foals going on to win Group 1 races and the colts then joining the stallion roster and his fillies selling for up to $5 million, as Better Better Better did, there is really no ceiling to what this fantastic stallion can make for Magnier and his partners.

In September 2008, the year he first became Champion Sire, the wheels very nearly came off the gravy train as it was only just leaving the station. Galileo went down with colic and had to be rushed to John Halley's equine hospital in Fethard to undergo surgery, not once but twice. Vets had to remove a significant section of his intestines.

Colic is a term used to describe all types of abdominal pain in horses, with the most common problems being a build up of gas or fluid, a blockage from impacted food, an intestinal infection, a twisted gut or plain stress. Horses can't vomit, so digestive problems can quickly build up and cause colic, which is why it is a leading cause of death. Compared to humans, horses have a relatively small stomach but very long intestines to facilitate a steady flow of nutrients. The large colon is usually 10-12 feet long and the small intestine is up to 65 feet long. Most cases are successfully cured medically but up to 10% will require emergency surgery and performing it as early as possible is critical to its success and dramatically improves the prognosis for the horse's survival.

Studs and racing yards are well aware today of the latest horse management procedures to follow to reduce the chances of a horse getting colic as much as they can. The problem is the design of the horse's digestive system, which has evolved over 50 million years from when they first roamed the planet in the wild.

By about five million years ago the modern horse had completed its evolvement. The world has changed a bit since then; horses were not intended to be stabled for long periods as they are now for the many sporting disciplines and recreational pursuits enjoyed by mankind everywhere. Their digestive system is best suited by around 18 hours of grazing time each day, as was intended in the wild, but the modern thoroughbred has no hope of getting that once they go into training. That's why they get colic and why it can easily lead to their death.

Galileo had a considerable length of his intestine removed and a resection carried out, which is not an insurmountable problem as horses can have as much as 80% removed and still function normally, even without needing a special diet. The key elements are the speed with which a potential case of colic is picked up, how early a definitive diagnosis is made, how quickly surgery can be performed if that is what is required and the expertise of the veterinary surgeons. Coolmore and the Fethard Equine Hospital are at the top of their game on all counts, but that doesn't mean every horse can be saved. Thankfully, Galileo was, but sadly, St Nicholas Abbey wasn't.

Galileo came through his surgery well and was soon back in the stallion yard. I happened to be covering for one of the regular night men patrolling the stallion yard following his life saving operation. CCTV had been installed in his box, so with monitors in a tack room at the yard and in the nearby security office, his every movement is scrutinised 24/7. Someone said even Magnier can watch him on a screen in his mansion whenever he wants to.

Galileo

Since his colic in 2008, Galileo has never been allowed to run free in his paddock, he is always grazed in hand during the day and regularly exercised the same way. That will be the case for the rest of his working life, no chance can be taken that he might get down and roll out in his paddock or do anything extravagant that might kick off the colic again. He is just too valuable to take any chances with.

I hardly took my eyes off him during the couple of weeks I was monitoring him at night, dreading a disaster to such an important horse on my watch. One night he became uneasy, pawing the ground, shaking his head, he'd got up and down a couple of times, all classic signs associated with colic. Something was bothering him but it wasn't desperate, yet. I went to his box, felt under his rug to see if he was sweating up, he wasn't, but he kept pawing the ground, so I called head stallion man Gerry St John in for a second opinion.

His temperature was fine, he still wasn't sweating up, so we just watched him and eventually he settled down again and the night passed, thankfully, without incident. What was so noticeable about Galileo is his temperament, you could do anything with him, and that would have been an important plus when dealing with the major colic surgery he underwent. Since then he has gone on to become the best thoroughbred stallion in the world, but those early days after surgery were a worry for everyone.

Another reason for his success, apart from the obvious one that he was the best Epsom Derby winner for ten years when he won in the second fastest time ever in 2001, is the physical quality of his foals. They just look so well formed and correct from the moment they are born. Foals by all stallions come with defects from time to time, it's what nature can throw up and some are recurring faults, but the Galileos we had in the foaling barn where I worked at Ballintemple Farm usually seemed to be as near perfect as you could realistically hope to expect. Some would be bigger, or smaller, than others, but the stallion has a well deserved reputation for getting so many foals with strong, correct limbs.

Much has been said and written about the character of Northern Dancer horses; their spirit, their attitude. They certainly haven't all had the same temperament as Galileo, but most have inherited Northern Dancer's toughness, his heart for a battle, his will to win. St Nicholas Abbey had all that courage, and then some more, as he faced a monumental battle over six months to survive from a fractured leg, colic, laminitis and then colic again, which eventually claimed his life.

90

Yet another top class middle distance runner by the great Montjeu, St Nicholas Abbey was Champion two year old in 2009 and only ever finished unplaced in three of his 21 lifetime starts over four seasons of racing, earning a few quid short of £5 million in prize money. His record would have been even better but for Aidan O'Brien over training him in readiness for the first Classic of the 2010 season, the English Two Thousand Guineas, and jockey son Joseph overdoing the waiting tactics until owner Derrick Smith suggested a change of plan.

St Nicholas Abbey finished sixth in the English Guineas and didn't race again that year. When he won his first of three record breaking Coronation Cups at Epsom the following year, O'Brien admitted he had "messed him up last year." In 2013, he also admitted that he had always felt that the horse needed holding up and a change to the more suitable tactics of riding him closer to the pace of a race was initiated by Smith. St Nicholas Abbey was top class and was hugely popular on the racecourse for his toughness and bravery in winning top races in England, America and Dubai.

He needed every ounce of that bravery when he fractured his right pastern during routine exercise at Ballydoyle on the morning of 23 July 2013 and underwent surgery at Fethard Equine Hospital the next day in the hope of saving him for a career as a stallion. Over the next six months the stud's regular updates, which included a superb short film shot at the hospital, detailed how the horse's improvements and setbacks ebbed and flowed, from heartbreak to joy and back again. Through it all, St Nicholas Abbey's fighting spirit shone like a beacon.

Two days after the first successful surgery, which required 20 screws and two bone plates being used to reconstruct his leg and a bone graft taken from his hip to replace segments which had lost their blood supply, he underwent emergency surgery for a serious colic. The prognosis was "very guarded."

The next two bulletins gave hope. On 21 August, almost one month on from the initial fracture, he was reported to be in his best shape so far. He then had a setback on 28 August. He had become uncomfortable and x-rays showed a steel weight bearing pin in his canon bone had broken. It was decided to take it out and let him support his own weight.

September went well, his appetite was excellent and he was starting to thrive, his surgeons were upbeat although they emphasised there were still many weeks before he would be out of danger. On 30 September, his recovery was reported to be on track, the vets couldn't be happier with his progress.

Top Left: Nureyev defied all the odds to recover from his catastrophic injury.
Bottom Left: Montjeu first, the rest nowhere in the Irish Derby.
Main Photo: Lady Luck ran out on the tough and brave St. Nicholas Abbey

A new problem came to light on 23 October. St Nicholas Abbey had laminitis in his left fore, the opposite leg to the one with the fracture and which had borne much of the horse's weight while the right leg was in a cast. Coolmore said: "Although laminitis could be a life-threatening complication, we are hoping the condition will stabilise. Obviously the next weeks are crucial in his recovery, but St Nicholas Abbey remains comfortable, with a good appetite and incredible attitude."

Late in November it was said he had reached a "critical" stage in the fight to overcome the laminitis - it was now the most serious complication he had faced since surgery on 26 July. It was revealed on 10 December that part of the intensive veterinary treatment he was receiving included maggot therapy for a discharge at the toe of the laminitic foot. Vets were hoping to see progress over the following few weeks.

St Nicholas Abbey died on the morning of 14 January 2014, due to complications from a second bout of colic. He had a severely twisted gut that was found to be unviable when he underwent surgery yet again. He was euthanised on humane grounds. The vets reported that the laminitis had been steadily improving and the fracture had healed better than expected, but his six month fight for survival was over. Nothing more could have been done and the horse himself could not have fought harder, every step of the way.

He had the best possible care from surgeons Tom O'Brien and Ger Kelly at John Halley's equine hospital and they were advised by two top American specialists, Dr Dean Richardson, head of surgery at the New Boston Centre, Pennsylvania, and Dr Nathan Solvis, a medicine specialist from the Hagyard Equine Medical Centre, Lexington, Kentucky.

Sometimes, with horses, it can all come down to a bit of luck. St Nicholas Abbey's luck ran out, but 27 years earlier another descendant of Northern Dancer survived a similar potentially catastrophic leg injury and went on to become a stallion of some significance. Although the lives of St Nicholas Abbey and Nureyev ultimately took different forks in the road, both displayed the toughness and courage for which Northern Dancer horses have become famous.

Nureyev had cost $1.3 million at the Keeneland Sales in Kentucky in 1978. He was the second best two year old in France and in 1980 was their champion three year old miler. He retired to stud at Walmac Farm in Kentucky without fulfilling his true potential on the racetrack because of a virus, but like so many sons of Northern Dancer he proved to be a sire of champions.

Wayne Reinsmith turned him out into his paddock after an early morning mating in May 1987. Minutes later, Nureyev was standing at the gate, holding up his right hind leg. Reinsmith realised, to his horror, that the leg was shattered. All that held it together was the hide. The stallion had been feeling full of himself when he was turned out and had kicked out with such force that his leg became jammed between the planks of the paddock fence. He managed to free himself and hobbled back to the gate, where he waited for help.

The Walmac staff were mobilised immediately and assistant manager Kenneth Aubrey and resident veterinarian and farm manager John Howard were at Nureyev's side in minutes. Like so many of Northern Dancer's offspring, Nureyev was tough. And in the end it was his fighting spirit and the dedication of Reinsmith, Aubrey, Howard, and a small team who lived with the horse 24 hours a day for the next seven months, that brought about one of the most dramatic recoveries in thoroughbred history.

At the Hagyard-Davidson-McGee Veterinary Hospital, x-rays confirmed the desperate diagnosis. Many horses would have been euthanised in circumstances less critical. Determined to do everything possible to save the horse, John Howard decided to take a chance on surgery. Surgeons inserted screws in the shattered bone of Nureyev's hind leg to form a double X shape and the entire area was encased in a large cast. A special sling was then wrapped under his belly and across his chest so that when he came to after surgery the horse could be hoisted upright to prevent him from putting his full weight on his shattered leg.

It was a situation fraught with danger, for the horse and staff, as there was no way of knowing how a stallion with an aggressive temperament like Nureyev would react. He spent the next five months in the sling with one of Howard's team with him the whole time, day and night.

He had some very bad times in those early days, when the severity of the situation he was in made him depressed, but then his handlers would shout and slap him. They believed if they could get him angry enough to want to fight them he might just stay angry enough to live. And it worked, but the battle had a long way to go. Nureyev began to improve and, supported by the sling, he was soon walking around his box. When the team was changing his cast one day, they discovered that the leg was healing well except for one place. There was a lot of fluid, a sign of infection.

It was cleaned up and his leg put in a new cast. Nureyev then developed a respiratory infection and had to be treated with antibiotics. He was off his feed and became depressed again. A damp spot appeared on the cast, the infection was getting worse, there would be no hope for him if it found its way into the bone of his injured leg.

Then fate stepped in, just as it had done when Nureyev's father, Northern Dancer, was in danger of missing the Kentucky Derby with a foot injury 23 years earlier. While trainer Horatio Luro had at the last minute discovered a blacksmith with a new technique for dealing with the quarter crack on Northern Dancer's foot which secured his participation in the Derby and his place in thoroughbred history, John Howard received the latest copy of the New England Journal of Medicine on the same day the hospital's laboratory gave him details of the infection now starting to ravage Nureyev's leg. There, on the front page of the journal, was an article about exactly the same bacterium, at the time the second leading cause of deaths from infection in US hospitals.

A new drug had been developed to treat this infection in humans. Howard decided to try it on Nureyev. The drug was administered to the sick stallion for the next 21 days at a cost of $400 a day. It worked, the infection began to clear up.

There were still more battles to be won. The physical and mental reserves of this once great racehorse had been drained over his period of confinement. On one occasion his temperature rose to 103 degrees, he stopped eating and began showing signs of colic. If it took hold he would certainly have died as he had such little strength left. He was given electrolytes and nutrients intravenously, and he survived that scare too.

Eventually, after months in the sling, Howard decided they had to run the risk of allowing Nureyev to lie down. They lowered him, inches at a time, with the hoist. Seconds after he was lying safely on his side, Nureyev fell into a deep sleep. For the next few weeks Nureyev was hoisted up and down in the sling, with the usual team ever present to reassure him. Sometimes he would just lay his weary head on the lap of whoever was nearest.

He began to improve again, but there was one more desperate setback. He leapt back and landed on his injured leg. He was in extreme pain. When the vets x-rayed the leg they found that, although the screws were still holding the fractured bone together, two of the inch long screw heads had, incredibly, sheared off in the impact. Surgery removed the screw heads and the horse survived another potential disaster. As autumn arrived, the cast eventually came off and was replaced by a brace. He was now being taken outside for brief walks without the sling and the final test came when they allowed him to lie down unassisted. It was a hugely tense moment for his carers, but he did it.

If the three men had any doubts that Nureyev was now back to his old self, they were soon forgotten when the stallion kicked out exuberantly with his once shattered leg and broke John Howard's arm. In mid-December, Nureyev finally left the hospital which had been his home for the previous eight months and returned to Walmac Farm, where a specially designed complex had been built for him. As the new year arrived his life was no longer in danger, but the question remained as to whether he would be able to resume breeding. On 1 April 1988, nearly a year after he shattered his right hind leg, the French mare Histoire was led into his own personal breeding shed. Three years later he was the leading sire of two year olds in Britain and Ireland and fourth best in the world.

Nureyev died at the age of 24 on 29 October 2001, 14 years after his life threatening injury. Among the brilliant racehorses he went on to produce after his amazing recovery were Peintre Celebre, European Horse of the Year; Spinning World, a Champion in France and Ireland; Reams of Verse, English Champion two year old filly; Stravinsky, European Champion Sprinter; and Fasliyev, unbeaten European Champion two year old colt. Peintre Celebre, Spinning World, Stravinsky and Fasliyev all stood as stallions at Coolmore Stud in Ireland.

Nureyev was also an outstanding sire of fillies, his best being Miesque, who became the first horse to win two consecutive Breeders' Cup races in 1987 and 1988. In 16 lifetime starts, she won 12 races, was second three times and third once. She was a Champion racehorse in Britain and Ireland on seven occasions. When she went to stud, she was just as brilliant as a broodmare, producing Kingmambo, a triple Group 1 winner on the track who also became a hugely influential stallion.

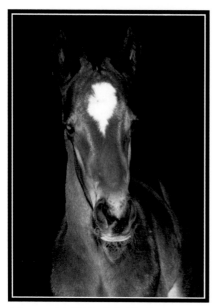

Monevassia's 2013 colt foal by Fastnet Rock

She also foaled Monevassia, whose daughter Rumplestiltskin was a Champion two year old filly for Aidan O'Brien. Rumplestiltskin has produced the Group 1 filly Tapestry and the hugely disappointing John F Kennedy at Ballintemple Farm. While he turned out to have feet of clay in 2015, his beautifully bred dam is more than capable of providing Coolmore with another champion racehorse when everything falls into place.

There is one more stallion story to tell. That's about Montjeu, in my eyes the bravest of all Northern Dancer's descendants. The courage, the will to survive and the will to win displayed by Northern Dancer, Nureyev and St Nicholas Abbey spanned weeks and months. For Montjeu, a brilliant racehorses and a spectacularly successful sire, it all came down to one night of unimaginable agony in March 2012, his last one alive.

He was bred in 1996 by Sir James Goldsmith, a controversial billionaire financier and politician, and named after his 17th century chateau in the Burgundy region of France. Goldsmith had dropped out of Eton School in 1949 at the age of 16 after he had bet £10 on a three horse accumulator, winning £8000, nearer £100,000 in today's equivalent value. He told his headmaster: "A man of my means should not remain a schoolboy." Magnier and McManus would have been impressed with that.

In 1953, he ran away with Isabel Patino, the daughter of a Bolivian tin mining magnate. She tragically died of a brain haemorrhage in the seventh month of pregnancy when just 17 years old. The child, also Isabel, was delivered by caesarean section and survived. Goldsmith's family helped raise her as he turned his attention to business, running a small enterprise selling a quack arthritis remedy in France. After a publicity stunt involving an arthritic racehorse, sales took off and the company grew from two employees to over a hundred.

He never looked back, expanding into slimming remedies and manufacturing own brand prescription drugs. He remained a controversial and divisive figure throughout his life, whether in business as a ruthless corporate raider accused of taking over companies and cynically stripping out their assets or privately as the father of eight children from three marriages and numerous affairs. British media claimed he was the father of Diana, Princess of Wales, because of his close friendship with Diana's mother and, later, Diana herself.

Goldsmith owned Montjeu's dam, Floripedes, who was Champion 3 year old filly in France in 1988, but who become blind as a broodmare. During the time she was boarded at Coolmore she had a constant companion mare with a cow bell around her neck. When out in their paddock, Floripedes would follow the sound of the cow bell and in that way her companion guided her and kept her safe.

Jimmy Goldsmith fought a four year battle with pancreatic cancer and died aged 64 before Montjeu reached the racetrack. Coolmore vet Demi O'Byrne saw him impressively win his first race as a two year old and advised Michael Tabor to buy him. He was trained in Chantilly by John Hammond to win 11 of his 16 starts, including two of the most prestigious flat races in Europe, Ascot's King George VI Stakes and the Prix de l'Arc de Triomphe at Longchamp. He was also a dual Derby winner, taking the French and Irish versions easily in 1999. He was some racehorse.

While his sire, Sadler's Wells, was known for his cool and calm temperament, Montjeu became more famous for his quirky and feisty ways. Mick Kinane, one of Ireland's greatest jockeys, rode him to win the Arc and King George. "He had an aura about him and a few issues, and the great horses he's sired have all had that as well," he said. Another top jockey, American Cash Asmussen, was on board when he won the Grand Prix de Saint-Cloud in 2000. "The last time I went so fast, I was landing in a Concorde at New York!" was his view of Montjeu.

Left: Montjeu's son, Leading Light, won the English St. Ledger and Ascot Gold Cup

Montjeu is the sire of Chicquita, who inherited some of his brilliance and most of his quirks. Here she is seen after winning the Irish Oaks at the Curragh, after which Coolmore paid €6 million for her to join their broodmare band.

100

There was an interesting sideshow to the 2000 racing season. Montjeu and Sheikh Mohammed's Dubai Millennium were the two outstanding older horses that year and there had been great rivalry between the Coolmore and Sheikh's camps as to which was the best horse, though they would never usually race against each other because Dubai Millenium was a star miler and Montjeu excelled over a mile and a half. To settle the issue, Sheikh Mohammed challenged Coolmore's Michael Tabor to a $12 million winner takes all contest, but then Dubai Millennium fractured a hind leg on the gallops and had to be retired to stud. After only one season as a stallion, the Sheikh's pride and joy was dead, cut down by the mysterious and vicious disease known as grass sickness.

Montjeu made his own rules up in the breeding shed when he also switched to stallion duties at Coolmore, always taking his time and not consenting to cover a mare until he was good and ready, no matter how long he kept everyone waiting. He passed on some of these traits to his brilliant son, Hurricane Run, who won the 2005 Prix de l'Arc de Triomphe with a stunning burst of acceleration just as his father had done in 1999. After a few years of the mating game, Hurricane Run had had enough of it after covering 90 mares one season and downed tools, as it were, much to the frustration of Coolmore management. There was money slipping away here. They just couldn't get him going again; maybe he just fancied a bit of a break with some sailing and golf in Barbados.

They moved him away from the main stallion yard to a smaller more peaceful unit with just a couple of really pretty mares hanging out with him, but he wasn't impressed. One evening I was checking on him there and came across general manager Christy Grassick feeding him a few carrots. He wasn't fooled by the charm offensive - "I'm a son of the great Montjeu, you know where you can stick your carrots" he would have said if he was Mr Ed the talking horse. A stallion who has lost his libido doesn't stay long at Coolmore. Hurricane Run is at stud in Germany now.

Stallion man Gerry St John said Montjeu was a real character alright. "He was always very impatient to get out into his paddock in the mornings. He would be in a bad mood in his box until we put him out and he never wanted to come back in no matter how bad the weather was." His record at stud as a sire of classic winners was seriously impressive. In his first eight seasons he supplied four winners of the Epsom Derby, the yardstick by which the greatest racehorses have been judged for over two hundred years.

Montjeu had already supplied three winners, Motivator, Authorised and Pour Moi, by the time he died. The last horse to do that was Northern Dancer, which shows how good he was. Camelot then became the fourth in 2012. Hurricane Run, St Nicholas Abbey, Scorpion, Fame And Glory and Leading Light were other multiple winners at the highest level.

His loss was a serious blow to Coolmore, who might have reasonably expected at least another five productive years from him. He was still relatively young, but very well insured. Reports from good sources around the farm indicated the pay out was in excess of €100 million. With stallion insurance there is one vital condition - the horse must die naturally, he can't be euthanised. It's a safeguard against skullduggery for insurance syndicates like Lloyds of London, who would typically be the insurers at this kind of level, but it does absolutely nothing for a horse in Montjeu's situation, who burned to death from the inside out as septicaemia ravaged his body.

Everyone, from MV Magnier down, had to wait and watch as Montjeu gave his all to survive over one very long and horrific night. He had to die naturally to meet the conditions of his massive insurance claim, but they didn't anticipate he would put up such a fight. They didn't expect him to last through the evening let alone the night; maybe a couple of hours at the most, but that's the Northern Dancer heritage for you, fighters to the last breath.

He had first become sick from a blood clot about ten days before he died. He had had this problem before but managed to pull through. This time he became steadily worse and there was no turning back. Septicaemia set in and despite expert veterinary treatment he died in slow motion. Any other horse would have been put down, but to collect the insurance Coolmore had to let him die naturally. This was Montjeu, with unbelievable spirit and courage. He didn't want to die.

Septicaemia is blood poisoning, where bacteria or toxins spill over from a local infection and are carried throughout the horse's body in its blood. Treatment is with intravenous fluids and antibiotics, but if they fail the horse's immune system becomes compromised and eventually it leads to multiple organ failure. If this cycle isn't broken death is inevitable. Please let it be swift.

Rumours had circlulated for a couple of days that Montjeu was in a serious condition. I was working in the foaling team at Ballintemple Farm when, just after midnight 29 March 2012, I had to go over to the main farm to collect some paperwork from the security office. I saw on the cctv screen there what everyone believed were the death throes of the great stallion. He was thrashing around his box and sweating up so badly you could see steam rising from him like he was on fire. He was rolling, pawing the ground furiously, shaking his head, in obvious distress.

The security lads said he had been like that for a couple of hours. Every time he lay down they thought that was it, he's gone, but he would get up again. They had to keep an eye on this all night in security, but thankfully I was able to get out of there and get on with my work. It was a desperate, heartbreaking sight. Adam Perrin was working the night shift checking horses on the main farm that night and he texted me updates.

1.12am: "When I was passing the yard Christy, Halley, Gerry and MV were all there, so the horse is still alive."

4.24am: "Just came out of security, he is pawing the ground, shaking his head, sweating up like fuck, walking the box and rolling. Bobby is outside his stable at the moment. Shane in security reckons they are just waiting for him to drop."

4.31am: "It would be nicer if they put the horse out of his misery."

Montjeu

But they couldn't put him out of his misery because of the insurance claim. There would be a post mortem, the terms of the insurance said he had to die of natural causes. It's possible that, when Montjeu's fate became clear, the drugs he was on were withdrawn to hasten his end. He was clearly in severe distress that last night; maybe the pain killers weren't enough any more, maybe he wasn't on pain killers any more. You would never know the full story because no one would ever tell you the full story.

Coolmore vets would have had to be careful what they gave him because a post mortem would reveal what drugs were in his system when he finally died. Insurers would be delighted to find something that might invalidate a claim and so wriggle out of it.

He did finally die, but it wasn't until much later, around 10am that morning. Someone said he died naturally, another said Coolmore managers were able to get consent from the insurers to euthanise him. Either way, his death was not peaceful. I fully understand the insurance situation and that Magnier had previously had a huge fight to get paid out on the death of Golden Fleece thirty years earlier. But that doesn't change the fact that Montjeu, a brilliant racehorse who captivated the public on the racetrack and a brilliant stallion who made a lot of people a lot of money, died in horrific and barbaric circumstances. He fought every step of the way in true Northern Dancer style. He really was too brave for his own good.

Montjeu with Gerry St. John

Galileo

Thoroughbred royalty in the Coolmore stallion yard.
Clockwise from bottom right:
Montjeu, Galileo and Sadler's Wells

PART TWO

Chapter 5

LIFE ON THE INSIDE

LIFE ON THE INSIDE

"If one tells the truth one is sure,
sooner or later, to be found out."

Oscar Wilde

The need for secrecy in Coolmore is astonishing and comes all the way from the top. There's a code of silence even the Italian mafia would be proud of. Magnier is treated as God, the Pope, Queen Elizabeth and the President of the USA all rolled into one. There might be a bit of Putin in there too, though I haven't seen The Boss riding a horse around bare chested like the Russian. He has built up a deserved reputation as being hard and ruthless and that's the feeling that seeps through every strand of Coolmore and even beyond.

He demands total loyalty from his lieutenants and that's what he gets, no matter what the situation is. They do what he wants, no questions asked. In the couple of weeks before he returns to Ireland every year after his winter exile in Barbados, nerves start to jangle as the main farm is spruced up even more than usual. The main gates are painted; it's important he can see them glinting as his entourage sweeps through on the way in from the airport.

He prowls around those first few weeks, looking for anything to shout about just to let everyone know The Boss is back. He will find something, even if it's not there. As one wag said: "One day he is going to come out the house and complain the daffodils are facing the wrong way."

Magnier is known to detest the press and only gives interviews under sufferance. Any media interest is tightly controlled. When that great mare Goldikova finished her racing career, in which she won 14 Group 1 races, she came to Coolmore to be covered by Galileo. A Frenchman was understandably excited having the pride of his country in Tipperary, so he posted a photograph of her on his Facebook page happily settled into her new surroundings. Coolmore management were not impressed with him sharing this news.

The workforce received a memo which said that it is against the terms of their employment to post photographs of any horse at Coolmore Stud on social media. It was only a picture to say the brilliant mare had arrived at Coolmore, something you would think anyone and everyone in the bloodstock world would be interested in just for the joy of it. There you go, that's their miserable, mean spiritedness for you.

I only ever met Magnier a couple of times at Coolmore, though met would be a very loose description of the occasions. After the foaling season had finished at Fairy King in May 2006, I was sent to help out for one weekend at Danehill Farm, which has an American style barn, a 30 box yard and an isolation unit. Mares with their newborn foals are usually kept here and when they come back into season they are taken over to the covering yard a mile or so away to be mated with their chosen stallion. We had a mare to be covered by Montjeu, so the barn foreman and I loaded her up in a trailer pulled by a jeep, leaving the foal in the stable, and headed to the covering yard.

I took the mare out of the trailer: she was frantic with worry having been parted from her foal and was on my way towards the covering shed when I passed Magnier going the other way. "Hi there," I called out. I didn't catch his reply as I was gone on my way quickly with the mare, who was acting up and a real handful. Montjeu could be a really fussy stallion. Sometimes he could take hours before he would jump up on a mare. There didn't seem to be any particular reason, it was just one of his quirky little ways.

The handlers just had to be patient and wait for him. It could have been made into a Hamlet cigar advert. Montjeu was there, smoking his Hamlet, and he was going to take his time and do nothing until he was good and ready.

He would look like he was good to go, but would then change his mind. This scenario went on and on and all the time we had to keep very quiet and just wait. Senior manager Harry King was there, like he has been for just about every covering throughout the five month season for the last thirty and more years. Authorised, a colt by Montjeu he bred with Mick Kinane, was running in the Epsom Derby a few days later so I wished him the best of luck. He gave me a look as if he had just scraped dog shit off his shoes. He was like that. I never saw him smile in the nine years I was at Coolmore. Authorised won the Derby. Did Harry smile?

114

When they had given Montjeu a good bit of time, they decided on a change of tack and whisked him and the mare out into a paddock and he did the deed as quick as you like. It was raining quite heavily. There you are, you see all sorts of oddballs with all kinds of fantasies in a day in the life of the Coolmore covering shed, and that's just the horses. The day became a whole lot stranger on the way back to Danehill Farm with the mare.

The barn foreman I was travelling with told me if I saw John Magnier again not to say anything to him unless he spoke to me first. I laughed, I thought he was joking. No, he said, that's the way it is. "But I only said hello," I said, still laughing. "No," he replied, "don't do it. If he stops you and asks about the mare you are with that's ok, otherwise say nothing and keep going." "That's how it is with the Queen of England," I said. "You never speak to her unless she speaks to you first." He just looked at me. I had just met Irish royalty.

Nothing much ever gets written about Magnier in the newspapers. You will get something about him maybe once a year in the Racing Post written by Coolmore's favourite poodle, Julian Muscat. One or two papers have tried to delve deeper but get no encouragement. The Observer sent a couple of their reporters over from England in May 1998 to do a bit of digging around Fethard and what's interesting about the report they filed is they could run it again in 2015 and it would be much the same.

The reporters interviewed Father John Meagher at the Augustinian Abbey in Fethard, who spoke glowingly about The Boss. "Mr Magnier is a very fine gentleman. You should see his place, it's like a city where they speak only in millions." Like Vatican City perhaps.

When investigating the relationship between Magnier and former Taoiseach Charlie Haughey the paper's writers faced a wall of silence from rival stud owners and locals in Fethard. "Others have used words like paranoia regarding Coolmore's security. Haughey appointed the taciturn Magnier to the Irish Senate in 1987, a move which was greeted with some surprise. Magnier shares with Haughey a passion for horse racing and mystery. He spoke only three times in his three years in the Senate and, even now, refuses to talk to the press."

One of the mysteries the Observer was trying to solve concerned Haughey granting 11 Irish passports to Saudi racing and breeding enthusiast Sheikh Mahfouz and his family in return for a promise to invest £20 million in Irish job creation schemes. Haughey personally presented the passports to the sheikh over lunch in the Taioseach's grand mansion in Dublin.

"Only £17 million of the sheikh's promised £20 million can be traced as having been invested as planned. But £4 million of the £17 million which was invested ended up in a chain of tennis clubs in Britain in which the biggest shareholder is John Magnier," the report stated. Dennis Brosnan of the Kerry Group was chairman of the British company concerned and JP McManus was also reportedly an investor.

Another one of Coolmore's great mysteries concerns what caused the split with the Tsui family, owners of one of the world's most celebrated broodmares of all time, Urban Sea. Conor Ryan tried to tease out the story for his meticulously researched book, Stallions & Power, which laid bare the scandals of bullying and attempted suicide at the Irish National Stud. He came up against the predictable wall of silence, as I did when I asked several managers what it was all about. They fell out, that's all they would ever say, and neither side involved have cared to expand on that explanation in public. Urban Sea had cost €55,000 as a yearling and before she reached the racetrack she came into the ownership of the Tsui family from Hong Kong, who had a fortune derived from property, manufacturing and international trading.

She won Europe's greatest race, the Prix de l'Arc de Triomphe, in 1993 and when she retired from racing the Tsui's family were advised to keep her at Coolmore Stud in Tpperary by their bloodstock adviser, Brian Grassick, brother of Coolmore's general manager, Christy. They stood the best stallion in Europe, Sadler'sWells, and the Tsuis entered into a foal sharing deal, where all costs and sale proceeds resulting from the mating were split 50/50, to send their mare to the champion stallion.

Urban Sea proved to be an even better broodmare than racehorse, but for some reason the Tsuis decided to part company with Coolmore and the mare was moved to the Irish National Stud for the rest of her days. Coolmore kept three young horses out of Urban Sea and the Tsuis kept the mare. The one colt Coolmore retained turned out to be Galileo, the outstanding Epsom Derby winner who became the best stallion in the world and a gold mine for his owners, now the Magniers on their own. They retained two fillies: Cherry Hinton has produced Irish Oaks winner Bracelet and All Too Beautiful got Classic placed Wonder of Wonders. The Coolmore owners clearly knew that they were doing when the split came.

Conor Ryan said in his book: "The Tsuis had sold their interest in Galileo for a reputed £400,000. Some close to the deal believed this price at least suggested the Hong Kong family underestimated the colt's ability early on. Until that first excursion in Susan Magnier's name, Galileo was sheltered from public scrutiny. It was October before he raced. Little was known about him. But his pedigree, the son of Urban Sea and the consistently brilliant Sadler's Wells, made him an automatic favourite. He eased home on a rain-soaked Leopardstown with the length of two articulated trucks to spare."

The Tsuis did eventually get their share of glory and cash from Urban Sea, getting World Champion Sea The Stars when they sent her to be mated with Cape Cross. It was fitting that they bred and owned this outstanding colt. Their dream was finally realised with his stunning victory in the 2009 Prix de l'Arc de Triomphe, 16 years after his mother had won the same race. The mystique surrounding Urban Sea and her sojourn at Coolmore is unlikely ever to be fully explained.

In 2004, racing journalist Cornelius Lysaght was again only able to scratch the surface in a story about the secretive Magnier for the BBC. He said during three decades that Magnier had ruthlessly built up the Coolmore racing empire, he had always avoided personal publicity. "Hence the huddle of friends and advisers behind the growth of the business from a stud farm in Tipperary to the biggest force in international racing have been nicknamed the Coolmore Mafia," he reported.

Lysaght said that those who know him well speak of Magnier's charm, his private nature, his shrewdness and of his great  **wealth. "Most of all though, they speak of his reputation for being harder than nails. He is renowned for getting what he wants and for not allowing anyone or anything to get in his way. That is how he has built up Coolmore."**

Magnier (right) with his 'enforcer'
– Paul Shanahan.

When Magnier had a bust-up with Sir Alex Ferguson over the stud earnings of the seven times Group 1 winner Rock of Gibraltar, who he had allowed Ferguson to race in his colours and share in the £1.1 million prize money the horse won on the racecourse, it was a fascinating fight between two men with fearsome reputations. In the end it was all about who had the most money to lose. Ferguson's wealth was a droplet compared to Magnier's and if the Manchester United manager lost the planned court case he would have ended up a pauper. If Magnier lost it would up a bit of a dent in his wealth, that's all. One of them had everything to lose.

Eventually, they did a confidential deal to avoid going to court. Ferguson confined his views on the saga to just one paragraph in his autobiography, so it's obvious now who won the argument. The best comment on it all came in Roy Keane's autobiography, The Second Half, in 2014. Keane told Ferguson he was in a dispute he couldn't win. Mysteriously, and a little menacingly, Keane wrote that somebody in Ireland gave him a message for Ferguson: "You are not going to win this." Sounds like that bit in The Godfather when the guy giving Don Corleone a hard time wakes up to find the severed head of his favourite horse in his bed.

I worked in the stallion yard and with yearlings costing millions, but my main job was in the foaling barn at Ballintemple Farm, a couple of miles outside the historical town of Fethard, from January to June each year. We would foal around 70 of Magnier's best mares each season with the majority carrying Galileo foals in recent times. The value of the mares and foals going through our foaling barn each year would be well in excess of a hundred million euro.

In 2014 Aidan O'Brien had six Group 1 winners which we foaled, all by the champion stallion. We also foaled John F Kennedy and Highland Reel. While JFK turned out a disappointment, Highland Reel was second in the French Derby and then got the coveted Group 1 on his cv by winning the Secretariat Stakes in the US in August 2015. We foaled Diamondsandrubies and she won the Group 1 Pretty Polly Stakes at the Curragh and then as August ended the latest crop of two year olds started to sort themselves out. We foaled the first and second in the Group 2 Debutante Stakes at the Curragh; the winner was by Galileo out of Butterfly Cove and given the prestigious name Ballydoyle. She looked a serious classic prospect for 2016 and is pictured here at an hour old. Then Minding won the Moyglare to ensure the stellar year of 2014 continued into 2015 as our pride and joy strutted their stuff. The quality is extraordinary and it is an exciting place to work.

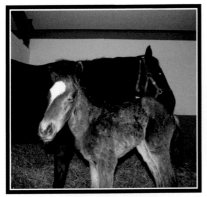 

Two Classic prospects by Galileo for 2016: Butterfly Cove with her filly called Ballydoyle (left) and Lillie Langtry with Minding.

While Magnier and Coolmore won their showdown with Ferguson, Michael Power was a much tougher nut to crack. On 12 February 2015, Power, a former stallion man, commenced personal injury proceedings in the High Court in Dublin against Linley Investments, who traded as Coolmore/ Castlehyde and Associated Stud Farms. He told how his life was devastated when he was kicked by a mare in 2010 after she had been mated with a stallion he was handling. The injuries he received to his left arm had rendered it virtually useless, he was in continuous pain and he had been unable to work since. Michael alleged the injuries he received were the result of negligence because of a lack of a proper safety system in the breeding shed where the incident occurred, exactly the same safety issue I had campaigned about throughout 2014 and which eventually resulted in me leaving Coolmore.

The big difference was Michael had already suffered a life changing injury and I was trying to get Coolmore managers to bring in safety measures for night staff to prevent this kind of disaster happening again. Around the same time Michael was injured, John Magnier's own nephew, Andrew, had been kicked by a stallion and ultimately had to have his leg amputated because of complications arising from his dreadful injury.

There is inherent danger working with horses. Thoroughbreds are unpredicatble, highly strung animals and there are obvious risks which come with the job. Anyone working with them accepts that, but wouldn't you have

Michael Power with Galileo

thought in these circumstances Coolmore managers would want to do all they could to make the working environment as safe as possible, particularly when staff repeatedly flagged their concerns?

I was in the High Court in Dublin on 12 February 2015 for the opening day of Michael's action. I saw him briefly before the start, wished him the best of luck and said we were all rooting for him. He told me he expected the case to last three weeks. Linley Investments denied Michael's claims and said he was "entirely responsible" for his own safety and was guilty of contributory negligence. He had had seven operations on his arm but it was still useless and he was in constant pain. I would see him sometimes when I was driving around checking barns on the main farm in the middle of the night. He would be out walking around with his dog in the small hours unable to sleep because of the pain he was always in.

There was just one day in open court, not even a full day. Only the opening shots were fired before the case was adjourned. On 17 February, Michael's counsel, Turlough O'Donnell SC, announced to the court that after talks between the parties the matter had been settled on undisclosed terms.

It was nearly five years since Michael suffered his catastrophic injury. He had to take Coolmore to the High Court for only a few hours, five full years later, before they would agree to a settlement. Michael was primed and ready to go the full three weeks to prove his case, but Coolmore could not stick the High Court heat for more than a few hours. The farm's rumour mill, as virile as their stallions, suggested Michael's compensation was north of E2 million, with Coolmore also having to pay a similar amount in legal costs. It was no wonder the senior managers present on the opening day, Jerome Casey, Christy Grassick, Harry King and Eddie Fitzpatrick, looked so glum.

In 2013, Coolmore and its partners paid E6 million for the Classic winner and broodmare prospect, Chicquita, and E3 million for just one Montjeu yearling colt. Two weeks after the court case, M V Magnier spent over $3 million buying two year olds at the select horses in training sale in Florida It's all about business and priorities. People can wait.

You don't have to go the Far East to find workers being exploited. Look at stud hands in Ireland in general and Coolmore in particular. Coolmore have a wage system they describe as a "weekly salary." They pay you a fixed amount and you do whatever hours they tell you to do. You fill a time sheet in every week. If you did less your pay could be cut, if you did more it was never increased. The off season, between June and December, is the quieter period but you would never do less than 40 hours between Monday and Friday and then every other weekend.

But during the season, January to June, it's very busy. That's the time Coolmore earns vast sums of money from clients sending their mares to the stud to be put in foal by one of their stallions. Many staff regularly worked 50 to 60 hours per week but were only paid the same basic "weekly salary." Some would never even have one full day off during the season.

I didn't do this job to make money, I did it because I loved the work. You would find that most people who work in the racing and bloodstock industries say the same about their jobs. Many people in these industries are exploited. In recent years, and particularly since the global recession of 2009, Coolmore have relied more on seasonal staff for six months of the year.

121

These are often young people with few, if any, qualifications and in some cases they have been starting every day and work non-stop for the entire season. They have had to make do with two half days in the afternoon as their only weekly rest periods. There is no proper support structure inside Coolmore to help any staff having difficulties and there is no association anywhere in Ireland to represent stud staff. There is the Irish Stable Staff Association, which is controlled by the sport's governing body, Horse Racing Ireland, but that's only for employees working in racing yards – stud staff are excluded.

I worked according to Coolmore's weekly salary system in my first year, regularly clocking up over 60 hours a week and only being paid for 40. I couldn't believe it. I was also called out in the middle of the night to assist with mares foaling. We foaled 130 mares at Fairy King foaling unit that year and I was present for around 75% of them. You would be out for at least an hour a time and you received no extra payment or time off in lieu for being called out. When I took this up with my area manager, Paraic Dolan, he said Coolmore never pay overtime. Like everyone else, I gritted my teeth and got on with the job. The brilliant people I got to know and the fantastic horses I was handling were a measure of compensation for being exploited.

In 2011, the farm took on a young man for the season through FAS, the government's jobs centre at that time. When he found out, on receiving his first pay slip, that he was only being paid for 40 hours work despite doing far more hours than that and he would not be paid any overtime, he went back to the FAS office and told them he wouldn't be returning to work at Coolmore.

The National Employment Rights Authority (NERA), a statutory body appointed to ensure employers compliance with employment legislation in Ireland, launched an investigation into the stud. Employees were randomly selected to answer a questionnaire about their jobs, the hours they worked and the remuneration they received. I received a questionnaire and replied. We were asked on the form to feel free to make any comments and we were assured of confidentiality.

Many people I spoke to didn't reply because they believed their involvement wouldn't remain confidential, that Coolmore would find out what they said and they might lose their job. No one was safe from Coolmore's power, they believed. I replied, saying that young people working there were being exploited by having to work excessive hours and it should be stopped.

A story broke in the Irish Daily Mail on 22 May 2011 under the headline **"Magnier studs charged with not paying their staff properly."** Coolmore and Ballydoyle appeared at Clonmel District Court for alleged breaches of employment law, including failing to provide rest periods and not paying overtime rates. The report stated: "Mr Magnier, who gave Queen Elizabeth a private tour of his stud farm at Coolmore in Co Tipperary this week, has mounted a constitutional challenge to the State agreement which protects the wages of agricultural workers."

The case was adjourned until the following November to allow Linley Investments, under which the studs trade, to lodge papers in support of the constitutional challenge. RTE also reported the case in their news programmes and said the alleged breaches also included that Coolmore had refused to provide records to a NERA inspector. Nothing more was ever heard about it. Mysteriously, the prosecution brought against Coolmore completely disappeared off the radar.

Coolmore denied they were in breach of employment law. A spokesperson said they employ a team of highly skilled, highly trained and highly regarded personnel. She said that NERA had complained about payments to what she called "a small group of employees." If NERA's charge that they had refused to provide one of their inspectors with employment records was true, it would explain why the complaint only referred to a small group of employees. If they had nothing to hide why did they refuse to provide the records NERA had requested to see?

Bullying can be a problem in Coolmore. People have made complaints over the years, even more haven't complained for fear of reprisals. One manager was suspended in 2014 for bullying. One young man made a complaint against a senior manager just before Christmas 2013 and promptly lost his job. Another had to take substantial sick leave because of it and I am aware of another who became ill and was relieved when he was eventually sacked. I was told of another who made a bullying complaint which he subsequently retracted when threatened by a close associate of the manager who did the bullying. There are no hiding places at Coolmore. They don't want you to question anything or stand up for your rights, just do it or you are out on the highway. Their mantra is all about absolute power, but as the famous saying goes – "Power corrupts and absolute power corrupts absolutely."

Yearlings being ridden away at Coolmore.
Centre right: First colt is Ruler of the World, fourth is Magician.

Found beats Golden Horn, Breeders' Cup, October 2015.

Ireland's politicians, from the Taoiseach down, have set the worst possible examples for this over the years, furthering their own situations in whatever way is necessary with every dodgy deal imaginable. Charles Haughey's lecture to the country in 1980, when he told the long suffering Irish people they were living beyond their means and had to change, is a classic which will last forever.

Charlie loved the good life himself, spending thousands on fine dining, £800 handmade French shirts and lavishing gifts on his mistress. Two anti-corruption tribunals found he received €11 million while in office in backhanders of epic proportions from a cartel of the country's wealthiest businessmen. Ben Dunne, the Irish supermarket chief, gave him €1.3 million and the Observer newspaper said: "Since 1985, most of Haughey's mares were serviced by Coolmore stallions, though what if any fees were charged is not known."

There were shocking tales of greed, corruption, embezzlement and tax evasion, all played out in the Moriarty Tribunal which had been set up to investigate improper payments made to Haughey and fellow politician, Tipperary's Michael Lowry. The tribunal ran for nearly 15 years at an estimated cost over €100 million to Irish tax payers. Haughey lived in a grand Georgian mansion on 250 acres and he developed a stud farm and bred racehorses. He had no inherited wealth, having been born into a poor County Mayo family. In 1979, a TD's annual salary was £9,590 and the Taoiseach earned £16,930.

Magnier knew Haughey well. He was an adviser to the charismatic but flawed Taoiseach, who personally appointed him to the Senate, the country's upper parliament. Magnier wrote in Coolmore's 1988 stallion brochure: "The role of today's bloodstock industry is an important one. I see my appointment to the Irish Senate not as a personal honour but as recognition of the contribution all of us in the industry make to the national economy"

In 1968, as Minister of Finance, Haughey made a decision which would begin the revolution that would turn an Irish cottage industry into an international powerhouse envied the world over. He introduced legislation that made stallion owners exempt from tax on stud fees. Incredibly, he removed the requirement to even make returns relating to stallion income.

Stallion masters, in effect, were given a blank cheque. They could include whatever they liked as stud fees with no questions asked, which they did for nearly forty years until the European Commission said it was an illegal, anti-competitive state aid and the Irish government were forced to abolish it in July 2008.

This new non-existent tax regime made it far more advantageous to stand stallions in Ireland than sell them to North America and encouraged an influx of foreign investors. It was Tim Rogers of Airlie Stud who convinced Haughey to go for this scheme and every stallion owner reaped huge benefits as a result, including Haughey himself. When Coolmore Stud hit the financial heights with the phenomenal success of Sadler's Wells, John Magnier kept every single penny the horse made for him.

It is no wonder Magnier told the Racing Post, as Sadler's Wells neared the end of his breeding career and the next generation of top stallions were taking over, that Sadler's Wells would always be the best as far as he was concerned. At the height of his success he was commanding in excess of £250,000 for every mare he got in foal - a licence to print money. Magnier benefited massively from the tax exemption introduced by Haughey and became a tax exile from Ireland, so he had two bites at the same cherry.

"You know, I have a theory about Charlie Haughey. If you give him enough rope, he'll hang you."

BBC Ireland correspondent Leo Enright at the end of Haughey's Premiership.

I had been working in the stallion yard just a few months before Sadler's Wells died in 2011. It was at Christmas and I took some photographs of the legendary stallion in the snow out in his paddock. It was a magical moment. He didn't want to come in to his stable when Gerry St John went to get him, despite the freezing conditions. Gerry had to go into the bottom of the paddock and bring him out. A few days short of his 30th birthday, the equivalent of 90 years old in human terms, he was in top shape physically and mentally right to the end of his great life.

Sadler's Wells at 30 years of age

I always enjoyed my nights with the stallions. My role was mostly only as an observer, to make sure nothing nasty like colic happened to them during the night, but the beauty of it was just to see these fantastic racehorses close up, to look them in the eye, to wonder what made them so special. This was particularly the case with new stallions just arriving to start their stud careers, because their exploits on the track were still so fresh in the memory.

I was in the yard for a few nights towards the end of Mastercraftsman's first season at stud. He is a fine looking horse with size and scope and gave Sea The Stars more trouble than most in his brilliant three year old season. One evening he covered his fifth mare of the day just before 10 pm and then slept like a log until breakfast time the next morning, doing nothing but snoring for hours on end. Perhaps he was dreaming about the fun he had been having all day, though to me he looked as if he was too tired to even dream.

Danehill Dancer

Another time, when I was doing the night shift as part of the quarantine for the stallions before they flew to Australia for the southern hemisphere breeding season, I had to keep a close watch on Danehill Dancer's penis. He had a growth on it which was bothering him so at the end of that season he had surgery to remove it. He was in quarantine and having a short break before heading off to Oz, but vet John Halley wanted him to take it easy for a few weeks and not get himself excited, to give the surgery the best possible chance of healing without any complications.

Stallions, particularly active ones like those at Coolmore who will be covering three or four mares a day, don't need any encouragement to show the world what they've got in their boxer shorts. So Halley gave us the long handle of a lunging whip and told us to go into Danehill Dancer's stable and tap him very gently under his stomach whenever he drew his penis out. It worked a treat. Every time we did this he would put it away very quickly. You had to laugh. It became a game with him, he knew what was coming every time he pulled it out and would just look at you bemused as you tapped under his belly with the whip handle.

Mind you, he was what you would call a real stallion, a bit of a gangster, and you would never want to take him for granted. When he heard you coming around with the feed trolley in the morning he would roar like a wounded lion and stick his head in his feed trough and wait impatiently for you to come along and give him his breakfast, cussing you to hurry on, which he would then attack as if he hadn't eaten for a week. His penis was in perfect shape when he left for Australia with the other stallions.

He went up the stallion ranks the hard way, standing for little money in his first years at stud. Before I went to Coolmore, I negotiated a deal for a friend of mine, trainer Jim Neville, to send one of his jumping mares to Danehill Dancer in an effort to put a bit of speed into a family which was becoming slower and slower when mated with traditional National Hunt stallions, just to try something different. It was the year before Danehill Dancer had his first runners and I was able to get him cheaply - Ir£1500.

He went on to become a great success as a stallion, producing top horses like Mastercraftsman, Choisir, Again, Lillie Langtry, Speciosa and Dancing Rain. He was leading sire of two year olds on three occasions and Champion Sire in 2009. In 2007, his stud fee peaked at E115,000 having started out at a few thousand Irish punts. He did it the hard way, covering lower quality mares to begin with, but his record soon demonstrated he had this rare ability to upgrade those mares and produce tough and talented racehorses who could excel over any distance. He was retired from stallion duties with fertility problems in 2014, aged 21, and has since been euthanised.

And his foal out of Jim's jumping mare? She was stunning, developing into the kind of yearling who would stand out anywhere. Unfortunately, she had been born with only one good eye, the other one had just not developed during gestation. Jim had bred her for jumping and he said it was a tough enough game for a horse with two eyes, so he didn't put her into training. Luck plays such a vital role in the horse game.

When I first arrived at Coolmore I was mad keen to go and see Sadler's Wells in the flesh. He was a true legend and his influence on the thoroughbred breed, in a similar way to his father Northern Dancer, would last for generations

In the beginning, it was touch and go whether I would last long enough in the job to meet the great stallion. I was the victim of appalling bullying right from the start and but for the encouragement and support of one of my early colleagues, Lara Walsh, I would not have stayed. I had been employed as part

130

of the foaling team at Fairy King Farm and the manager would pick on me, and others, relentlessly. According to him we never did anything right and he constantly harassed us.

I found out that over 20 staff had gone to work at Fairy King in the preceding two years but had requested a transfer away within a week or two because of the antics of the manager. After a month I was ready to quit but for Lara urging me to hang in there. She was known for the help and support show would give to all new staff. She told the area manager what was going on but he did nothing to sort the situation out. It was a bizarre time and was nothing like I expected at a major stud farm.

Sometimes, when we were foaling a mare, there would be up to a dozen of the manager's friends gathered around watching, when everyone knows that at that time it is so important to be quiet and unobtrusive. They were always smoking pot and drinking alcohol, it was party time all the time with these guys. This was at the height of the Celtic Tiger and, like it seemed everywhere else in Ireland in those days, there was a serious drugs problem. It was a problem in Coolmore too. There were stories circulating regularly of drunken, drug fuelled escapades. The foaling manager and his mates were the go to guys if you wanted drugs.

He was good at his job when he cut out all the nonsense. One evening, he and I foaled five mares within two hours and got the foals standing and suckling. The rest of the time continued to be a nightmare and I eventually laid it on the line to him that I had had enough and I was going to make a complaint. I did this in front of witnesses so there could be no doubting the seriousness of the situation and my intentions.

He said he didn't care, go ahead and complain, he was too important to Coolmore for them to do anything to him. He then took me off an extra shift I was booked to do watching over the foaling barn on Easter Monday. It paid double rate; the only time you ever got an extra payment was on Bank Holidays, so it was worth doing. He did the shift himself, which he would never usually do.

I made an official complaint, which also included drinking when at work, and told my area manager to back me or sack me. We saw the season out, losing just one foal in the 130 mares we foaled. We came close to losing a second, a filly by none other than Sadler's Wells, but she made the kind of recovery which made up for all the hassle. Owned by an important American client, she had what appeared to be a perfectly normal foaling and there was no cause for concern in the immediate aftermath.

But she was then slow to respond. with no co-ordination, and the vet was called. It transpired somehow her brain had been deprived of oxygen for a few seconds at a crucial stage of the foaling. It had not been a hard foaling, so this was just one of those things that very occasionally happens and cannot be fully explained. We put the foal in an incubator in a specially adapted stable in the foaling barn and, with the mare standing watching, she received constant nursing day and night.

Being a highly strung thoroughbred, the mare was difficult to keep settled in these circumstances other than by sedation, so after a day she was taken away and a foster mare brought in to replace her. With a completely different character, the Clydesdale foster mare was happy to stand quietly and they are ideal in a situation like this. We gave her plenty of hay and she was happy to stay there looking over on the foal for as long as we wanted.

The prognosis was not good and the next week was very long. The foal had someone by her side constantly, turning her over every half an hour to try and keep her internal organs and external limbs moving as she couldn't do anything on her own. Nothing changed for the first few days, but then little by little you could see her get stronger. Eventually, she could hold herself up in the sitting position, she had turned the corner.

The culmination of nearly two weeks of total dedication to the cause day and night by the vets and staff at Fairy King Farm was watching the foster mare with the filly by her side walking out of the barn to a horse box as they were moved to another part of Coolmore to continue her recovery. An amazing sight. I went over to the main farm later in the summer to see how the mare and foal were doing. There they were, in a paddock with other mares and foals, contented and happy. I couldn't believe the progress she had made. Two years later she even made it to the racetrack and is now a broodmare herself. She is a full sister to Champion Turf Horse in Canada, Perfect Soul.

This was the last time the manager was in charge of foaling at Fairy King Farm. The next season he was moved to a barn on the main farm handling mares waiting to be covered by the stallions. Two years later he moved abroad. When he was on good form I enjoyed working with him because he was good at his job.

He was also very good with yearling preparation for the sales. The Queen's racing manager, John Warren, singled him out for praise when going around

Tattersalls Sales at Newmarket with a Racing Post reporter one year giving an insight into what buyers look for when viewing yearlings. Look at the way that guy has that yearling walking, he said of the manager. That doesn't happen by accident, it's a serious skill, Warren said.

But most of the time his behaviour in the foaling barn at Fairy King Farm in my first season was totally unacceptable, as dozens of staff found out before me. His moods fluctuated alarmingly between highs and lows and no one has to put up with this. Other managers knew about it but did nothing until I put my head on the block and spoke up.

The only other time I would come into contact with John Magnier was when he came to Fairy King Farm to look over the yearlings he bought at Book 1 of the Tattersalls Sales in Newmarket every October. Yearlings bought at this sale always go to Fairy King to be let down quietly for a week or so after the stress of the sales grounds. They are then backed and ridden away prior to going to Ballydoyle to begin full time training. This sale has been very productive for Magnier; St Nicholas Abbey, Camelot, Leading Light

Camelot and Jospeh O'Brien win the Group 1 Racing Post Trophy

and Australia all came into this barn from Newmarket in recent times.

Interestingly, when Australia arrived from Newmarket, Coolmore's top vet John Halley left strict instructions that he was not to be ridden and initially only grazed in hand. It was said he had strained his back, which may have contributed to him only making 600,000 guineas in the sale ring when others by his sire, Galileo, made much more. He was given plenty of time to recover. It turned out to be money well spent by The Boss and sound advice from Halley. Australia became a dual Derby winner and grossed over £2 million on the racetrack.

That handy sum will be dwarfed if Australia, who is out of 7 times Group 1 winner Ouija Board and beautifully bred like his sire Galileo, succeeds at stud. He stood at €50,000 in his first season in 2015 and is sure to have had around 200 mares. That's a possible €10 million for just one season, which will be doubled if he shuttles to the southern hemisphere for their breeding season.

Magnier would usually come to view the yearlings with a few people like Aidan O'Brien, Harry King and Demi O'Byrne and would never speak to the staff. His daughter Kate was very nice though. She was there once with husband David Wachman and after the yearling inspection was over popped her head around the barn door to say thanks. It was, after all, a Sunday and we had been called back in on our afternoon off.

As Coolmore has grown to the mammoth size it is today the common touch has been lost as far as stud staff are concerned. I worked a couple of foaling seasons with Patsy O'Rahilly, who was employed for over thirty years by Magnier right from the early days of Coolmore. Patsy is a real character and a legend in his own life time at Coolmore. Sometimes he would sing blood thirsty Irish rebel songs to the mares in the foaling barns. It was always a captive audience. It would frighten me but the mares loved it.

He told me that in those early days at Coolmore, as soon as the evening news on the television was over, Magnier would call up to him at Bawnbrack Yard, where he was foaling manager, and they would walk around looking at the new foals and discussing what had been going on. Every night, regular as clock work. You wouldn't expect Magnier to be doing that today, at 67 years of age and with all the commitments that come with the business empire he heads, but Patsy says those early days were the best of his working life. He was still working the night watch in the foaling season at 70 years of age.

The sights to be seen around the Coolmore farms can be spectacular and I usually had my camera close to hand to be able to quickly catch the unscripted shot. I put them in a photobook a few years ago and a couple of copies did the rounds, with one even sent out to Magnier in Barbados I was told. It's easy to take for granted the stunning sights to be seen around the farms every day. People are often too busy to notice.

Part of the reason for this situation can be traced back to the start of the global recession in 2009, which hit Ireland harder than most countries because it possessed more idiot bankers and greedy property developers than anywhere else. We heard that Magnier told the accountants to slash costs by €2 million a year. One manager told me the accountants received bonuses for meeting the targets Magnier set, which is kind of ironic. Jobs were cut and I have often heard people complain that some barns and yards are under staffed.

Our pay was badly dented by a wage cut and further draconian taxes introduced by the government as they set about repairing the near fatal damage caused to the country's banking system by indiscriminate lending, which fueled the massive property bubble. When I first arrived at Coolmore all you ever heard on the news or read in the newspapers was that Ireland had the fastest growing economy in Europe. Six years later, with world economies picking up, we are starting to hear that Ireland is again the fastest growing economy in Europe. Have the people who run the country learned any lessons?

One of the first things we noticed when the manure hit the fan was the removal of all the spring water dispensers around the farms. Most horse staff don't drink the water out of the taps in the tack rooms and canteens dotted around the stud. The mains water, like in some places in Ireland which are even today subject to boil notices, is not trusted. That is why the spring water was introduced for staff, who were forced to bring their own bottled water in when Coolmore withdrew this concession. The main offices kept their supply, though.

David Gleeson, an accountant who is operations manager, addressed a large meeting of staff at the end of the season in 2009. People were being made redundant in droves. He said everyone was going to have their pay cut between five and seven and a half per cent. It did not go down well. There was nothing given in writing and no vote. The pay cut was forced on the staff. He said with this cut in pay there would be no need for any further redundancies, of which it was rumoured there had been over a hundred.

Many people were unhappy about the cut. They already knew they were working far more hours than they were getting paid for. One stallion man summed up the mood well when he told me later: "What I want to know is where has all the money gone that came in during the good years, when horse boxes were queueing up i n Fethard taking mares to the stallions? Where's all the money gone from those days that they now have to cut our pay?"

According to property developer Bernard McNamara, Magnier put some of the colossal earnings from stallion fees during the good times into one of the most infamous property deals of the Celtic Tiger years, and may have lost it. The developer swore an affidavit for the High Court in Dublin that Coolmore Stud contributed €5 million as part of an investor group put together by Davy Stockbrokers to enable McNamara to buy the Irish Glass Bottle site at Ringsend in Dublin at the height of the boom in 2006.

McNamara and his consortium paid €412 million for the 26 acre site - €17.2 million per acre. The site had been rezoned to permit commercial, residential and retail use, but the property bubble exploded soon after they completed the purchase and those same 26 acres were subsequently re-valued at €30-40million.

The cost for this grotesque transaction to the taxpayer, the ordinary man in the street like most of the Coolmore employees, has not yet been finalised but will be more than several hundred million euro because the State had to bail out the Irish banks involved in the debacle. The stud sued McNamara to get their money back, as he had personally guaranteed their investment. Along with the other elite private investors they were granted judgement, but on 2 November 2012 McNamara was declared bankrupt in London with debts estimated to be over €1 billion.

The general consensus among staff after being told of the pay cut was that at least there would be no more people let go. That's what Mr Gleeson said, but insult was added to injury a few months later when they reneged on their promise and made even more staff redundant. I made a complaint to HR Manager Deirdre Coffey at the time because they also backdated the cut to include any holiday entitlement we had already earned in the previous six months but had not yet taken up. I told Deirdre this was illegal, that it amounted to Coolmore taking money from me and everyone else that belonged to us by law. It was stealing.

She said this decision was made by the accountants and they would not be changing it. I told her I wanted to take this up with those accountants. She advised me not to go any further, she had already raised it and had been told the decision was final. There are no trade unions allowed inside Coolmore, they are not recognised. There is no one to represent employees in any grievance. You are totally on your own against the giant that is Coolmore Stud.

All the while Magnier had been enjoying the sun as a tax exile in Barbados. As Ireland's precarious financial situation unfolded, he gave all the managers on the main farm a group pep talk via video link from Barbados to the board room in the offices. He was very positive at the end of it, Derek Bailey, the manager at Ballintemple, told me. He said it was going to be very tough for the next few years but it will all come good again in time, Bailey said.

So it was from 2009 the power base at Coolmore shifted even more from the managers on the farm to the accountants. The people working on the farms just became numbers, to be carved up whenever it suits, and that's why there have been so many staff problems . The famous Irish writer, George Bernard Shaw, said: "If all accountants were laid end to end, they would not reach a conclusion." Shaw also said: "I learned long ago, never wrestle with a pig. You get dirty, and besides, the pig likes it." Combine the two and you might get: "If I had the choice of a discussion with an accountant or a pig, I would choose the pig. They both have big snouts but the pig can see the bigger picture."

The pay cut was eventually reversed five years later, in December 2014. We heard that management had become concerned about the rock bottom morale in the workforce. At the same time the first of a regular newsletter for staff was published. M V Magnier wrote: "This is the first Coolmore staff newsletter which I hope will be a useful way of keeping everyone in the know on the serious and not-so serious developments in our business." MV had news of a fresh income stream: "We also recently started the 'Coolmore Collection' – selling Coolmore branded clothing online. Early sales have been good."

He also wrote that 2014 was a busy one for Coolmore Australia, where the stallions had covered 1,400 mares in the season just ending. "It was a big year for Coolmore in Kentucky," he said. "Giant's Causeway was America's champion two year old sire for 2014 for the second time. This is the sixth time Coolmore has had the champion juvenile sire. The development of Montague Farm was completed with a 22 stall barn, an 18 stall barn and an eight stall isolation unit. This is a major investment in the American business." There wasn't much interest amongst staff in the newsletter and, ten months later, there hasn't been a second edition.

The recession has been very good for Magnier, which says everything about the strength of his business empire and the shrewdness of the man himself.

Giant's Causeway, "The Iron Horse".

137

In the last couple of years he has been particularly busy buying up the half of County Tipperary he didn't already own. He has been taking full advantage of the massive drop in the price of quality agricultural land, down well over half from the glory days, and has snapped up thousands of acres of mainly tillage farms. Coolmore is the partner the Chinese government has chosen to help them set up a racing and breeding industry and Magnier clearly believes Irish agriculture is in a prime position to exploit fresh opportunities all over the world.

He is a devout Catholic, regularly attending Mass, certainly when he is back home at Coolmore. Derek Bailey told me he often sees him at Church in Fethard, wearing an old coat and blending in with the throng. "You would see him in that old coat and you'd want to give him a few euro to get a new one," Bailey said.

A special Mass is said by the local priest in the Coolmore offices every January, to which all staff are invited. Following the Mass, the priest visits the stallion yard and blesses all the stallions. So there you have it, the real power behind Coolmore's success.

I'm not a Catholic, I find it hard to be a believer at all with all the death and destruction that goes on in the world in the name of religion. So I find it quietly amusing and loudly ironic that the priest is there blessing the stallions and the Coolmore hierarchy are following behind fervently hoping the beasts can keep it up and cover as many mares as possible in the new breeding season about to start.

When Mr and Mrs Magnier had son John Paul, The Boss flew his family to Rome to have JP, as he is known to everyone, baptised by Pope John Paul. When they returned to Coolmore, all the staff were given a special rosary and locket to commemorate the occasion. At that time the staff would have been virtually all Irish, more than likely from in and around Fethard and therefore all Catholic. This would have been a very rare privilege granted to the Magniers by the Catholic Church, though the Vatican bankers would have surely done well out of it.

Many years later, maybe John Paul The Pope was looking out for John Paul The Jockey when he had a very serious fall in Northern Ireland. A talented amateur jockey who won a Grade 1 race at Cheltenham, JP was badly injured when his mount slipped up on a bend and had to be airlifted to hospital.

He had metal rods inserted in his back and there were real fears for days that he might end up paralyzed, but thankfully he made a full recovery. As everyone knows in the horse world, these injuries can often result in life changing situations, so JP was very lucky. He has not race ridden since, concentrating instead on his career in the world of high finance in the City of London.

Katie Magnier married trainer David Wachman in a high profile ceremony in the Augustinian Abbey in Fethard in August 2002. All the good and the great of Ireland attended the reception in a massive marque on Coolmore Stud, an impressive occasion which was noted for three things. The whole extravaganza reportedly cost Magnier €5 million, cabaret in the evening was provided by Westlife, and I was told no ordinary members of staff were invited, just a few senior managers. Magnier has an aviation company as another string to his business bow. When son Tom married in Barbados, The Boss flew many of those attending out to the Caribbean in his own aircraft

When Ballydoyle had a big winner at the Curragh a couple of years ago, Magnier was interviewed by Tracy Piggott on RTE. He told her we were lucky to have Michael Tabor and Derek Smith, his partners in many of the horses trained at Ballydoyle, so involved in racing because they were so passionate about the sport. "I'm interested in the business side" he said.

People interested in business are in it to make money, that's the motivation. It's incredible what Magnier has achieved since Coolmore was started in 1975. You don't become a billionaire, a few times over, if you only have a passing interest in making money. You don't get to that stage either by luck only.

In the Irish Field of Saturday, 23 February, 1991, the Owen Tudor column reviewed the Coolmore stallions for the new season. As Coolmore continued to grow at a furious pace, Owen Tudor said: "There will be misgivings in some quarters that the lion goes from strength to strength as the main body of competitors falter."

Twenty four years on, and 40 years since Coolmore was founded, the lion that is Magnier totally dominates Irish racing and bloodstock and is head and shoulders above the rest of the world. All is not right, as the two suicides among horse staff in recent times show. When I warned David Gleeson this kind of tragedy will happen again because of the bullying culture within Coolmore, he didn't want to discuss it. I told him the employment situation would come full circle, that the stud would be short of staff again soon but they could get all the people they needed from Romania now they are part of the EU. I was told by an insider 79 staff were let go at the end of the 2015 covering season.

With the shocking internal problems Coolmore has faced in the last couple of years, Magnier is said to feel betrayed about what has been going on. He is The Boss. He has made a fortune out of buying into companies and telling them where they were going wrong. The buck stops with him.

Yearling Colts at Godfrey's Farm

Chapter 6

THE FOALING BARN

THE FOALING BARN

"Find a job you love and
you will never work a day
in your life."

Confucius

A foaling barn can make your spirits soar to heights you never imagined, but can also plunge you into the darkest depths of despair. Perhaps it's these polar opposites which combine to make it so unforgettable; the ecstatic highs when you see and help a life being created and the tragic lows when you lose a mare or a foal so young. Fortunately, there are many, many more highs than lows, but I have often wondered how the staff in a children's hospital, particularly those who see many terminal cases, deal with their emotions. I suppose you would call it their professionalism, they just learn to get on with it.

Just like sick children, compromised foals rely totally on help. When you can give them that help and see them walk away later in perfect health, the world can seem a better place after all. When a new colleague, Josie Nolan, joined the night team at Christmas 2011, it didn't take long for her to experience one of the magical highs.

She had previously worked in a training yard so was comfortable around horses, but she had never seen a foaling. She was out checking yearlings in a nearby barn when I called her just after 2am on 12 January 2012 and told her to come on back, a mare we had been keeping a close watch on was starting to sweat up, we were going to have our first foal of the new season. It was a smooth, straightforward foaling and when, a few minutes later, foaling manager Derek Bailey pulled the foal around to the head of the mare, Josie looked at me with a smile on her face brighter than any mid-day sun.

145

You'resothrilling and Gleneagles

Josie and I were left to steer the mare and foal through the rest of the night, making sure the mare suffered no ill effects and getting the foal standing and suckling. The mare was called You'resothrilling, a sister to Coolmore's brilliant champion Giant's Causeway, and the foal was a fine colt by Galileo. He was later named Gleneagles, became a Group 1 winning two year old for Ballydoyle in 2014 and an exciting Classic prospect for the following year.

His year older sister, Marvellous, who we also foaled at Ballintemple, won the Irish One Thousand Guineas in 2014. Gleneagles started to fulfill his huge potential on 2 May 2015 when he impressively took the English Two Thousand Guineas at Newmarket for Aidan O'Brien, training the winner of the race for the seventh time. O'Brien said Gleneagles is very like Giant's Causeway, nicknamed 'The Iron Horse', who won five straight Group 1 races for Ballydoyle in 2000.

"He is by Galileo and out of a full sister to Giant's Causeway. It would be very hard to see any horse anywhere that would have a better pedigree than him. All the traits are very like Giant's Causeway, who was as hard as nails and this fellow is very like that." Jockey Ryan Moore was also impressed: "Throughout the race there was never really any doubt. They weren't fast enough to lead him for long enough. He has a lot of talent and I think there's better to come." Gleneagles went on to gain further top race glory by landing the Irish Two Thousand Guineas and the St James Palace Stakes at Royal Ascot.

He turned out to be an auspicious first foaling for Josie and she became a quick learner. Over the next three years she became a knowledgeable, trusted and well liked member of the night team. She never missed one night's work, loved her job, was passionate about the foaling barn. She could be left on her own with the forty and more Galileo foals we had each season, or be out checking the million dollar yearlings at night, and you knew she could deal with anything that might happen, quickly and calmly.

The quality and value of the mares and foals going through Ballintemple foaling barn is astonishing. Here, on the left, is Classic placed Queen Cleopatra, from a family of champions including Listen and Henrythenavigator, with a colt foal by Fastnet Rock; and in the foreground, a champion filly in California, Golden Ballet, with her Galileo colt. Golden Ballet is the dam of Drosselmeyer, who won the Belmont and the Breeders' Cup Classic.

So it came as a shock that she was let go at the end of the foaling season in May 2014. She had been employed continuously for 18 months in the period before, but now they said she had to go on to seasonal employment, even though one of the most senior managers, Harry King, had come into our barn and said how difficult it was to keep good staff.

This, however, was about pathetic politics and personalities inside Coolmore, who didn't like that I was trying to make night work safer for staff. I had raised a number of safety issues with management in 2013, particularly for the six female staff who worked nights during the foaling season. Josie and two other night staff had also told the safety manager they believed more should be done to improve safety.

147

To be let go like this, which was pure victimisation, broke Josie's heart. It also put her in financial difficulties. It was all done to satisfy inter-managerial conflicts and accountants with inflated egos. The managers were experts with horses and the accountants could add up, but neither cared about treating staff with respect and dignity, the bedrock of health, safety and welfare at work legislation in Ireland and most other civilised countries.

Josie spoke to every relevant manager at Coolmore to try and get this decision reversed. Her line manager Derek Bailey, the top bloodstock man Harry King, the general manager Niall Ryan and the HR manager Deirdre Coffey. I also took it up with Christy Grassick, John Magnier's right hand man since the early days. They couldn't or wouldn't do anything to help her, so I decided to write to Magnier himself and see what he thought of it all. It is notoriously difficult to get through personally to Magnier. Everything goes through the accountants and in particular Jerome Casey, who handles much of his personal business. Mr Casey's affectionate nickname is The Flower Arranger. He deals with virtually everything for Mr Magnier. He even took a wooden seat I had given my colleagues at Drumdeel Farm when I left and put it next to the lake on the main farm for Mr Magnier to sit on in case he got tired on one of his walks around the place. I asked Mr Casey to give him my informal letter. This is the guts of what I wrote.

But I want to tell you a bit more about Josie Nolan the person. She is the bread winner in her family and is totally dedicated to her two children, with son Stephen currently in the Republic of Ireland U 16 soccer team. Three years ago our mare Hveger foaled around lunch time one day but haemorrhaged about 4pm. When Josie and I came in to start our night shift at 9pm the day staff were still there, fighting to keep Hveger alive. She was now sedated and Derek told us to watch over her, to see that she was as comfortable as possible and call him when she became distressed. He did not expect her to last the night and had a foster mare standing-by for her Galileo colt foal.

When everyone had gone Josie asked me if she could sprinkle a few drops of Holy water on the mare. I laughed because I'm

not a believer in that sort of thing, but she meant it. So I said, we've got nothing to lose, they are saying she is a dead mare walking, let's do it. Josie went to her car and collected a small bottle of Holy water her mother had brought back from a pilgrimage to Lourdes.

She sprinkled a few drops on the mare and no doubt said a quiet prayer. Around midnight we suddenly saw Hveger start to nibble a bit of hay. By the morning she had recovered from her ordeal and when Derek came in he could not believe what he saw. She continued her progress and her foal is now a two year old at Ballydoyle, called Highland Reel, and is running for the first time today.

The moral of this story is not whether you believe what happened at Ballintemple that night was a minor miracle, it's about Josie's attitude to her job. She cares passionately about the well-being of the mares and foals and will do everything in her power to see we get the job done to the highest standards. She is always prepared to go the extra mile to get the right result.

The second story is much more recent. Back in this last winter, you will know we had one very bad day and night in Ireland when the worst storm in living memory caused utter chaos, including knocking over massive trees like they were ten pins. On that night Josie had to travel from her home in Templemore to work at Ballintemple. All her close family told her to call in and miss work because conditions were so bad, but Josie didn't want to let anyone down. She started out at 7pm and had to turn back three times and try a different route because she came across roads which were blocked by fallen trees.

Eventually, by going down roads through country she had never been on before, she made it to Ballintemple sometime near 10pm. We went on and did our full night's work despite falling trees and flying debris everywhere. Josie didn't want to let anyone down at Ballintemple, and she didn't, not bothering at all about her personal safety. Now she is being let go. It's unbelievable, because you couldn't get a more genuine and dedicated employee who has all the skills to work in the best foaling barn in the world. And she is Irish. The qualities she possesses are not easily found. If she finds another half decent job outside Coolmore she will not return for the next foaling season. She is heartbroken about what has happened to her and now faces a bleak future without a job and a mortgage to pay. Can you do anything to help her keep her job here? You are her last chance and it should never have come to this.

I have my own issues with Niall Ryan at present over my concerns for the safety of night staff and Josie is paying for this as she is a soft target. I have put all this in writing along the way because no one is listening.

Highland Reel wins the Group 1 Secretariat Stakes in torrential rain at Arlington Park, Chicago in August 2015.

I don't know if Magnier read my letter. I did receive a voice message on my mobile from his son, MV, thanking me for raising these issues and informing me Jerome Casey would carry out an investigation. Josie was still let go and I made a complaint about bullying. The subsequent investigation exonerated Coolmore Stud and said any employer would find my behaviour unacceptable. Highland Reel went on to become a top racehorse for Aidan O'Brien. Thankfully, the outstanding care and attention everyone at Ballintemple gave his dam, Hveger, means she continues to be a valuable producer for Magnier and his associates.

While it's important when working in a foaling barn that you know when a mare is going to foal so you can mobilise the team and get the foal on the ground in perfect shape, the real work starts post foaling. This is when the mare and foal can have various issues which the night staff have to deal with. Mother nature takes care of most things and it's a wonderful sight in the first couple of hours of a newborn's life to see how quickly the foal adapts and develops.

Unlike human babies, who seem to do nothing at all for months on end, the equine variety are usually a tangle of intrigue right from the start and can show incredible awareness, determination and character from the moment they stand up not long after being born. When there is a problem with a new foal, you need him or her to show all the attitude and fight they can muster if it is to survive. They must want to live, as they can go downhill so quickly.

If it's not viewed as a viable foal Coolmore managers will have no hesitation in having it euthanised at the earliest moment. It has been bred to race. If the vets say there is a big doubt about that ever happening a decision will be quickly reached on whether to go on or put it down. A particularly well bred filly might be spared for a future breeding career even if it might not race, but a colt like this is worthless to an operation like Coolmore's, whose modus operandi is to produce top class racehorses who will become top class stallions. It's all about business.

So whenever we had a foal with a serious problem, I would invariably think back to one October morning at Drumdeel Farm, where I lived and worked during the off season of 2011. Senior managers regularly go around all barns and yards and have the horses walked and stood in front of them to be inspected. This is very much the case with foals, weanlings and yearlings,

Looking Back and her son, Rip Van Winkle, winning the Sussex Stakes

where in particular they look to pick up any problems with the youngsters' feet and to see that they are walking correctly. It's a good discipline for everyone, horses and staff.

We had one weanling by Hurricane Run which had a very ungainly walk. She would pick her hind feet up in a pronounced manner, a bit like you might lift your feet up when walking through water and trying not to get wet. It wasn't a pretty sight. The managers that day, M V Magnier, Christy Grassick, Eddie Fitzpatrick and Paraic Dolan, took a long look at this filly as she was walked in front of them. One suddenly said: "I think it should be shot." And that's exactly what happened to her.

That afternoon someone came down from the office and filmed the weanling walking so that her owners, a big German stud, could see for themselves what she was like. They all concurred she was not a viable racing prospect, because the next day a jeep and trailer called to collect her and she was taken to the Tipperary Hunt kennels, shot and fed to the hounds. A summary execution. They didn't believe she would make a racehorse.

When Sumora, the dam of champion two year old filly Maybe, had a big colt foal by Galileo at Ballintemple at 3.40am on 28 April 2013, there was a bit of concern because he was quite badly contracted on his right hind fetlock. He weighed a hefty 146lbs and was unable to stand for nearly three hours, so we bottle fed him on the ground. Contracted tendons are not normally an insurmountable problem. Putting the leg in a splint or in the more severe cases, a cast, will normally sort it out in time. The vets found with this foal there was also significant muscle damage along much of its right hind leg, particularly high up.

He was noticeably lop sided, so vets Tom O'Brien and Denis Crowley put his leg in a full length cast to straighten and support it. The prognosis was guarded. There was a lot of muscle wastage and when Josie and I came in for our shift the next night we were told there was a serious doubt about his future.

He couldn't stand up on his own so our main job with him that night was to get him up when he wanted to suckle the mare. He was big, strong and heavy and it took the two of us to get him up every time. It was hard graft for him and us with this cast on, but this amazing foal had such a positive attitude he thought it was all a game. We were exhausted but smitten by the morning. If Coolmore didn't think he was worth trying to save we were going to throw him in the boot of Josie's car and she was going to take him home with her.

We never usually saw Harry King and M V come into our barn before we finished our shift, but that morning they arrived just as we were packing up to go home at 7am. I made a point of going back into the barn to talk to them as they got to Sumora and her foal. I told them straight that this foal was tough, brave and had such a positive attitude. He's a winner, I said. They didn't say much, Harry just looked at me. He then asked how he was to get up. I said he's heavy but we are getting better at it all the time. It wouldn't make one jot of difference to them what I thought, but I strongly believed I would be letting this foal down if I didn't speak up for him. I said again, he wants to win, we should persevere with him, and went home.

And persevere with him we all did. The vets and the day staff kept working away, changing his cast every three days. He was fostered on to a particularly quiet Clydesdale mare as he was going to be confined to a stable for a good while and his dam, Sumora, wouldn't find that easy and, anyway, was due to be covered by Galileo again in the next few weeks. These foals hardly seem to notice the changeover in mares, as long as there's a plentiful supply of milk it wouldn't bother them if it was a cow standing there.

Josie and I would check the barn diary every night to see what the latest report said about the foal and it was usually positive. Tom O'Brien said keep going as we were, he was improving all the time. His boss John Halley came in to check him out and said he was going the right way. Even John Magnier came in one day when Tom was changing his cast. The lads on the day shift told me Magnier asked Tom straight out, is this foal going to race? Yes, he was told. Then keep going with him, Magnier said.

He was a lively foal and always wanted to play when we went into his stable to give the mare some cut grass or take out droppings. Sometimes he tried to give us a little kick, even with the cast on his leg. He learned that if he lay down on one particular side it was easier to get down and back up again when he wanted to suckle the mare, and nine times out of ten he would lie down on the one side.

The cast came off after a couple of weeks and was replaced by a full length bandage to continue to support the leg. He and the mare were moved into a pen in a barn to give them a bit more room and he was now walked several times a day around the barn. Harry told Derek to push him harder as he was worried he could develop OCD (degenerative joint condition) if he didn't get enough exercise.

Magnier wasn't too pleased when he came back a couple of weeks later, though. It was well into May and the weather was warming up so the large double doors of the barn were left open during the day. The surface of the yard outside was made of stone dust and when vehicles passed the dust was being blown into the barn where the foal was. Magnier instructed Derek to cone each end of the yard off so that no vehicle was able to pass the barn. He was going to be a racehorse, don't let any dust pollute the air this foal is breathing, he said.

Magnier is rightly very sharp on the quality of air around his horses, as is shown by another story which did the rounds of the stud a few years earlier. He was out in the beautifully tended gardens of his palatial mansion one summer's day when he noticed clouds of dust blowing his way. He followed the trail into a nearby yard of the stud, where he found the employee responsible for causing the dust cloud. He was using a hand held air blower on the dusty surface of the yard to clean up the bits of straw, leaves and associated debris which had left it looking untidy.

This is common practice everywhere at Coolmore, in the barns themselves and all areas surrounding them, to keep the farms looking pristine. Magnier could not believe these blowers were used in the barns where there might be horses stabled at the time. He instructed the employee to stop blowing and issued an edict to the top management not to allow the blowers to be used again and have them all removed from the yards and barns on the farms.

Nearly two months after he was born, the Sumora colt was ready to leave Ballintemple and join the other mares and foals a couple of miles away at Godfrey's Farm, where all Magniers best young stock are raised until they are ready to go into training. He continued to develop well and joined Aidan O'Brien at Ballydoyle in November 2014.

We had a similar situation when Absolutelyfabulous, dam of classic winner Magician, foaled a Galileo full brother during the day of 14 May 2014. He was unable to stand because he had badly contracted tendons on three of his four legs, though in this case there was no muscle damage. It was some challenge for all the staff and vets at Ballintemple to care for this fellow with three of his legs in casts and two people were needed to get him up every time he wanted to suckle.

Left: Josie feeds a newborn with colostrum.

Right: Rosie watches over Absolutely Fabulous and Galileo colt.

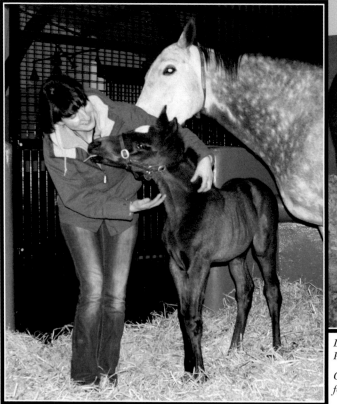

Left: Hanna with Simply Perfect and Galileo colt.

Centre: Josie and Sumora's colt foal by Galileo.

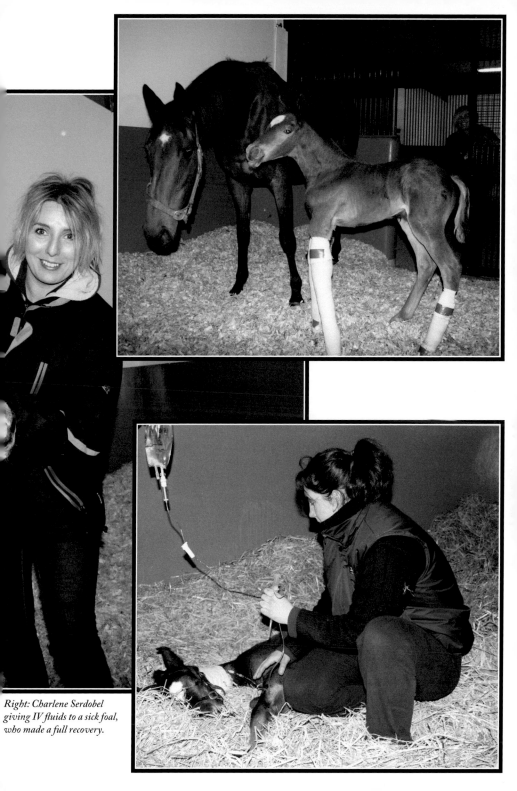

Right: Charlene Serdobel giving IV fluids to a sick foal, who made a full recovery.

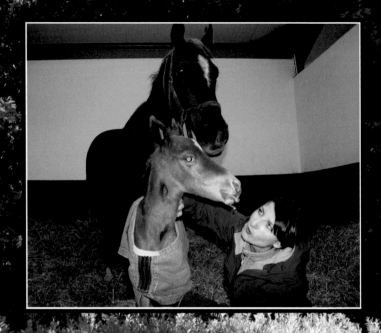

YOGYA
Anabaas - Polar Falls
1997 - 2002
Dam of
SIX PERFECTIONS
Champion 2-Year-Old Filly in Europe in 2002
Prix Marcel Boussac Criterium Production -
Royal Berkshire de Chantilly - Gr. 1
Prix du Moulin de Longchamp - Le Rothold

PETROLEUSE
Habitat - Petroll
1974 - 1996
Dam of
PEINTURE BLEUE Long Island Handicap - Gr. 1
PROVINS William P. Kyne Handicap - Gr. 3
PARME Prix André Baboin - Gr. 3
Dam of
PEINTRE CELEBRE Prix de l'Arc de Triomphe - Gr. 1
Prix du Jockey Club - Gr. 1 - Grand Prix de Paris - Gr. 1

LAGRION
Diesis - Wrap It Up 1989 - 2013 Dam of
DYLAN THOMAS
European Champion 3-Year-Old & Older Horse
Prix de l'Arc de Triomphe - Gr. 1
Budweiser Irish Derby - Gr. 1
King George & Queen Elizabeth II Stakes - Gr. 1
Irish Champion Stakes - Gr. 1 (twice) Prix Ganay - Gr. 1
QUEENS LOGIC
European Champion 2-Year-Old Filly
Cheveley Park Stakes - Gr. 1
HOMECOMING QUEEN
Qipco 1,000 Guineas - Gr. 1

The equine graveyard at Coolmore and (inset) Hanna with Lagrion and Miss Piggy.

A FRANCA
ORPEN
JULES

AUTIFUL
ean Sea

LEO and
E STARS

ONDERS

JUDE

QUARTER MOON

YESTERDAY

ALL MY LOVING

HOLD ME LOVE ME

CC
P
FIN

With the aid of another calm and quiet foster mare he improved steadily, the casts were replaced by bandages and he was eventually able to go out in a small paddock and enjoy the summer sun. To see him integrated with other mares and foals a couple of months after he was born, jumping and messing around, it was hard to believe he was once unable to stand on his own.

I had huge respect for Harry King as a horseman. What he didn't know about thoroughbreds wasn't worth knowing. He had been with Magnier from the early days and now oversaw The Boss' personal bloodstock. He is world class, but could be viewed as the opposite with people. I never saw him smile, let alone laugh. Everything was work and business. He came into the foaling barn one evening at Fairy King when I was on duty in my first season at Coolmore and we walked around looking at all the newborn foals. If the foal was by a Coolmore stallion he stopped and chatted about it. If it was by an outside stallion he just walked on by and said: "Good luck with that." I asked him why he only wanted to look at the foals sired by Coolmore stallions. "They are the only ones which will make me money," he said.

Harry told Josie on a couple of occasions we were caring for sick foals to make sure she didn't make a fuss of them. According to Harry, girls could spoil sick foals with too much caring. They are racehorses not pets, he would say. He said it again about Hanna Boland, another outstanding young woman who spent three years working the night shift at Ballintemple until she left in 2012 to have baby Olivia with husband Tim. It was the time one of Coolmore's greatest broodmares had her final foal and for a while it looked like we might lose the mare and her foal.

Lagrion had just foaled a chesnut filly by Duke of Marmalade when Hanna, who came from Poland to Dublin to teach horse riding before joining Coolmore, and I arrived to start our night shift on 16 March 2012. The foal was small and weak and unable to stand. We were in for a long night, bottle feeding and taking care of her until she was able to stand and suckle the mare for herself. In the early hours of that day we had already helped foal triple Oaks winner Alexandrova and Mariah's Storm, dam of Giant's Causeway. Now Derek went home and Hanna and I were left to guide Lagrion and her little foal through until morning.

An interesting aspect of Lagrion's broodmare career had been that she was usually short of milk post foaling and her foal fostered before the first week was out. Her brilliant son Dylan Thomas, who won six Group 1s including a memorable Arc, was fostered as a foal. So, to start her new foal off, we bottle fed her colostrum and milk taken previously from other mares with plenty and kept frozen until required at times like this.

A short time later we had to call Derek and vet Denis Crowley back out; Lagrion had suddenly slumped distressed to the floor of her box and we initially feared she might be haemorrhaging. Dennis treated her and she was now quiet but exhausted, lying flat out in the middle of the box. Such was Lagrion's reputation, Derek phoned Christy Grassick to tell him of events and say we might have to put her down. Christy said, simply, to do whatever was best for the mare.

For Hanna and me it was now a case of watching and waiting to see which way she would go. One thing was for sure though, she wasn't going to be helping us with her foal for the rest of the night. We decided Hanna would stay with the foal and I would do all the other jobs. We had other mares close to foaling, mares and their newborn foals to watch over and fifty of the farm's best home bred yearlings to check on through the night.

With the mare now in a deep sleep we wanted to keep bottle feeding her foal so that she would gain strength, but also we didn't want her thrashing around and causing distress to herself and her shattered mother. Luckily, the foal was always hungry and Hanna stayed down in the straw with her for the rest of the night, feeding and comforting her.

Around 6am Lagrion suddenly got up, looked at her foal as if to make sure she hadn't been dreaming, and began eating hay. Soon after we decided to get her foal up, too. She had regularly wanted to stand but couldn't; we didn't want her to always be disappointed, so with me holding her back end and Hanna on her front, we helped her up. She stood with us supporting her for a minute or so before we had to lower her gently into the straw again, but in that time she held her head up good and strong, taking everything in around her. Could she see a future?

We went home tired but happy, mare and foal were still in there fighting, but we were also worried about what we might find when we went back in again at 9pm as these situations can be so volatile, particularly for the foal. It was brilliant. Lagrion and her foal were flying along. The mare looked so much stronger and her foal, while still needing help to stand up, was able to suckle on her own. The day staff had done a great job and we went about our work that night with wide smiles and joy in our step. Someone on the day shift had nicknamed the foal Miss Piggy - what she lacked in looks she more than made up with attitude. I took a photograph of Hanna with Lagrion and Miss Piggy that night.

Whenever Hanna went to the box to check on them, Miss Piggy would come up to her, she remembered her from that first night and still expected to be bottle fed. A few days later Derek told Hanna that Harry had been on to him about not making a fuss of Miss Piggy. She's a racehorse, not a pet, he said. We understood where he was coming from but at times like this you wear your heart on your sleeve, proudly. Besides, Harry, we never had bloody time to fuss the foals.

Miss Piggy was fostered on to one of the Clydesdale mares a week later and they were mad about each other. Miss Piggy just loved the endless supply of milk the foster mare had and she thrived. I remember looking in on them one night after they had moved on to another barn and the foster mare was lying down trying to get some rest, but Miss Piggy was having none of it. She was hungry and was biting and pulling the mare's ears to try and get her to stand up. This little foal, who weighed just 74lbs at birth and who was unable to stand for the first 48 hours of her life, was now in full control. She was subsequently named Duchess Diva. She was a diva all right.

I checked on Lagrion over on the main farm the first night she was parted from her foal and she was cool and calm, maybe she knew her broodmare career was over, at 23 years of age she was heading for retirement. Four weeks later her three year old daughter, Homecoming Queen, who we had also foaled at Ballintemple, scorched up the Rowley Mile in Newmarket to win the English One Thousand Guineas, leading from start to finish. Jockey Ryan Moore said he was worried he had gone off too fast but when he asked her for more she kept giving. That sums up Lagrion and her foals perfectly; thoroughly genuine, totally honest, so brave.

I saw Lagrion again in the autumn, she was sharing a paddock with Homecoming Queen who had by then finished her racing career and was preparing to join the broodmare band. There is no such thing as a free lunch at Coolmore, for man or beast, and Lagrion continued to earn her keep during the next covering season, this time acting as nanny to another top class young race mare fresh out of training, Banimpire.

That season at Ballintemple, 2013, we had 72 foals including 44 by Galileo.

It's a place brimming with world class bloodstock and massive expectations. Sometimes we were lucky enough to realise those expectations. We foaled that year's Epsom Derby winner, Ruler Of The World, and as a home bred it doesn't get much better than this as a lot of people at Coolmore and Ballydoyle would have had a hand to play in his progress along the way.

But Lagrion won't be going through the foaling barn again and special mares like her do not come along very often. She produced a Champion 2 year old filly (Queen's Logic); a Champion 3 year old colt (Dylan Thomas); a Classic winning filly (Homecoming Queen); a Classic placed filly (Remember When); and a Group 2 placed filly (Love To Dance). All were by different Coolmore stallions. They couldn't just run like the wind, they would also try their heart out and that was down to Lagrion. A truly great broodmare.

There was another reason why I became attached to this family. One night, on my regular run checking Magnier's best yearling fillies, I came across a very frightened Remember When in her box at Holloways Farm. A night light is left on in the barns but we also carry a torch to take a closer look at any horses we need to without having to switch all the lights on. Remember When was very frightened at the sight of my torch, jumping around trying to run away from it, so I switched it off and turned her light on in her box to see what the trouble was.

Her face was a sorry mess. I later found out she had had an accident in her paddock, probably colliding with the fence, and a large chunk of the skin on her face had been ripped and had to be stapled back together. It wasn't a serious accident as such, though the gash was close enough to her eyes. She had, though, been badly frightened by the whole ordeal. Whenever I went to check on her for the next few weeks, I would switch the torch off, put her light on and go in and talk to her, stroke her neck and help her get her confidence back.

In the end, even when she was lying down, she would get up and come to the door of her box when she heard me coming into the barn and wait for me to open the door and go into her. As anyone who works with horses knows, dog owners too, you can build up a close bond in the smallest of ways and that's one of the things I loved most about working nights – it's just you and the horses.

Remember When with her first foal Wedding Vow

We had foaled Remember When at Ballintemple and she developed into a stunning yearling, so the icing on the cake was to see her go on and do well on the racecourse. She was second in the Epsom Oaks of 2010 and when she finished racing she joined the broodmare band and was covered by Galileo. She came back to Ballintemple to foal and her first was the very useful filly Wedding Vow, a Group 2 winner in 2015. From Lagrion to Remember When and on to Wedding Vow, the wheel keeps turning.

Jude was also a great mare for Coolmore, Ballydoyle and her breeders, Premier Bloodstock, who are a partnership of senior people at Coolmore headed by Richard Henry. He runs Magnier's marketing division, called Primus. She suffered an altogether different end to her brilliant broodmare career, haemorrhaging and dying in agony, aged 17, after foaling a filly by Galileo. All the warning signs of what was going to happen were there two years earlier when she haemorrhaged for the first time after foaling another filly by Galileo, and only survived by the skin of her teeth.

All haemorrhages are bad, but the first one on 15 May 2009 was particularly serious. She had had ten consecutive foals and produced Champion two year old filly Quarter Moon and Irish One Thousand Guineas winner Yesterday, who was also second in a further three Group 1 races and third in the Breeders Cup Fillies and Mares Turf. Her unraced filly, Song, sold for 1.7 million guineas at Tattersalls in 2009. She had been a wonderful mare for breeders Premier Bloodstock and Mrs John Magnier and Mrs Richard Henry, in whose names her offspring raced.

When she haemorrhaged in 2009 she was teetering on the brink of death for two weeks. Tests repeatedly showed she was still bleeding internally. She and her foal were kept in the enclosed indoor lunging ring adjacent to the foaling unit with only infra red heat lamps for lighting. Vet John Halley told us to leave her alone as much as possible, not to go into her unless it was absolutely necessary.

164

She was being treated by the vets but not disturbing her in any way and keeping her calm and quiet was just as important if the haemorrhage was to stop.

Slowly her heart rate eased down, she began to eat again and she looked brighter in herself. It had been touch and go, but after two weeks solitude she was able to go out into a small paddock with her foal and they both enjoyed the early summer weather.

The drama wasn't over. A week later I was checking on her out in her paddock just before midnight as part of my usual night run when in the darkness I could see the outline of the foal but not the mare. I went in to double check all was good and found Jude distressed on the ground. She had colic. I called Derek and we got her and the foal into the indoor lunging ring and kept walking the mare around until vet Ciara Gibney arrived. She was treated and we kept a close watch on her. She would likely have been dead by the morning, from the colic or maybe the haemorrhage could have kicked off again, or both, if we hadn't got her in and treated her so quickly.

Thankfully, she survived yet again, but there was nothing any of us could do to help her on 2 February 2011. I won't ever forget what happened to Jude that day as it was my worst experience at Coolmore. It also happened to be my birthday. When a mare has haemorrhaged and survived the chances of it occuring a second and fatal time are increased significantly, particularly with older mares. A weakness has been found and that weakness is always going to be there, waiting to explode. We had hoped Jude was going to be retired after that first haemorrhage, but when she was put back in foal again in 2010 her owners effectively signed her death warrant.

She foaled a bay filly just after midnight. It was a good, straightforward foaling and all was well. The foal was standing after 35 minutes and started suckling 15 minutes later. The quality of the mare's colostrum was excellent, the reading from the refractometer was 25, with any figure over 20 being viewed as good. Long standing night man Maurice Blake and I were on duty in the foaling barn that night and when we finished our shift we were pleased with the way everything had gone for Jude, though mindful that when she previously haemorrhaged it started two days after she foaled.

When we came back in later that night mare and foal were still doing well. I went off to check other mares and yearlings on nearby farms, but at 9.30pm I had a phone call from Derek Bailey with the news I had dreaded. "Come on back," he said, "Jude is haemorrhaging." When I got back to the foaling barn a few minutes later Jude was on the floor of her box thrashing around uncontrollably. Maurice had taken her foal out as soon as he had spotted the mare rolling and was now holding the little filly by the door, close enough for the mare and foal to see each other but far enough away so that no harm would come to the foal.

Denis the vet arrived but couldn't get near to Jude to do anything for her; she was flailing around in a manic frenzy of fear and pain, bleeding to death in front of our eyes. I couldn't watch it. I went up to the other end of the barn and began preparing a stable for Jude's foal, soon to be orphaned. Jude died at 10.05pm, thirty five minutes after she began to haemorrhage. She died without any veterinary help because it was impossible to get near her. Anyone going into the stable would have been cut in half by her flailing legs and violent contortions.

That is what the life ending heamorrhages are like and we would likely get one, or even two, most seasons, usually with the older mares. They would have had anything between 10 and 20 foals in their lifetime and the continuous pressure on their bodies with carrying a foal inevitably takes its toll and a major artery would burst either during foaling or sometime fairly soon afterwards. You hope, like with Hveger and for Jude the first time she haemorrhaged, the damage wouldn't be too severe and the wound would close and heal, just like it does when you cut your finger. But Jude was beyond redemption that night; if it's a bad haemorrhage there is usually only ever going to be one outcome.

Derek placed a rug over the mare after she died and we put her foal into an empty stable. Paul O'Meara took the jeep and horse trailer to where the foster mares were kept and parted one from her foal and brought the mare back to the foaling barn. Her own foal would be bottle fed until a new owner was found for it, usually the next day. There were no problems fostering Jude's foal on to its substitute mother. The foal was mad hungry and immediately dived under to suckle.

It was a traumatic few hours. I was sick and angry about the whole experience. As Derek was about to leave the barn, I said: "It's a sad day. Jude didn't deserve that." He replied: "These things happen." I shot back at him: "If she hadn't been put back into foal again after what happened the last time, this wouldn't have happened now. After all she's done for them." I was glad to get to the end of the shift and get out of the place.

The next day Jude was collected and taken to the Tipperary Hunt for disposal. In due course a headstone marking her achievements was placed in the equine graveyard on the main farm. It's a beautiful, restful place on a sunny day. It gives the impression the horses are buried there, but that's not the case, the reality is these horses are taken to Tipperary Hunt kennels and fed to the hounds. Such an ignoble end for a brilliant mare who made millions for those connected to her and who literally gave her life for them. It's just business, isn't it?

Her foal did well; she is named Ruby Tuesday and went into training at Ballydoyle. Whether she is sold or retained, she is worth another couple of million to her owners, the Henrys and the Magniers. The Galileo filly from 2009, called Better Better Better, continues to have an interesting history. She was second in the Noblesse Stakes at the Curragh for the same team and was later sold in a private deal to American horseman John G Sikura. He subsequently sold her in foal to

One of Coolmore's greats: Jude with Better Better Better at two days old

leading sire War Front for $5.2 million to Mandy Pope's Whisper Hill Farm at the Fasig Tipton breeding stock sale in Kentucky. That first foal, a filly, was sold for $1.45 million at the Keeneland yearling sales of 2015.

Sikura's father, also John, was a teenage emigrant with his name pinned to his overcoat and a $10 note in his pocket when he arrived in Toronto after fleeing Bratislava in 1950 ahead of the Russian invasion as war tore Europe to shreds. He eventually became a stockbroker, bought land in Ontario and and went on to deal in racehorses for 35 years until his sudden death in 1994. The Sikuras built up Hill N' Dale Farm into one of the leading thoroughbred sales agencies in North America, with one operation in Ontario and another in Kentucky. A self made millionaire, Sikura was a classic rags to riches story.

Michael Tabor and Derek Smith, John Magnier's partners in many horses at Ballydoyle and Coolmore, paid $1.9 million for a filly at the September Keeneland Yearling Sales in 2005 and named her Rags To Riches. Tabor and Smith had also came from relatively humble beginnings to amass considerable wealth. The filly herself, though, cost a small fortune to buy and was regally bred. By AP Indy out of the blue chip mare Better Than Honour, she lived up to her price tag and breeding, becoming the first filly in 100 years to take on the colts in the third leg of the US Triple Crown, the Belmont, and win. This is how Tom Durkin, track announcer at Belmont Park, New York, called the race on 5 June 2007.

"Here comes Hard Spun. And Curlin is coming through in between horses. And Rags to Riches is coming with a four wide sweep. And Tiago is in behind them. And at the top of the stretch, a filly is in front at the Belmont. But Curlin is right there with her. These two, in a battle of the sexes at the Belmont Stakes. It is Curlin on the inside, Rags To Riches on the outside. A desperate finish. Rags to Riches and Curlin. They're coming down to the wire. It's gonna be very close. And it's gonna be... a filly in the Belmont! Rags To Riches has beaten Curlin and a hundred years of Belmont history. The first filly to win it in over a century."

Injury brought Rags To Riches' racing career to a premature end and she has been at Coolmore Ireland since 2009, arriving from Ashford Stud in Kentucky in foal to HenryTheNavigator. She was in an isolation unit to begin with and a notice stuck to her door warned us to beware, she was dangerous. When she came into the foaling barn at Ballintemple, manager Bailey repeatedly warned us not to go into her stable alone and when she was close to foaling not to go into it at all. We heard she had broken a girl stud groom's arm at Coolmore America: they considered she was dangerous and they didn't want her there, hence she found her way to us at Ballintemple Farm. We were also told she had been notoriously difficult to train, regularly dumping her work riders on the ground. They said most of the time she would only allow one particular work rider on her back. She was a brilliant but troubled race filly.

In the build up to the birth of her HenryTheNavigator colt foal on 17 March 2010, she showed us that she was also a troubled broodmare. Hanna and I decided we were going to try and kill her with kindness. Whenever she put her head over her stable door we would very carefully and quietly stroke her head ever so gently. We wanted to win her over. She would just look at us - she has quite a menacing, evil eyed look - and when she thought we had relaxed our concentration she would suddenly snap at us. We persevered for a couple of weeks but eventually gave up and completely ignored her from then on. I think she preferred to be ignored.

When the time came for her to foal, she was a nightmare. She had been building up to it for a couple of days, getting more and more aggressive. We had a lead rope permanently dangling from her head collar and a long brush handle with an improvised hook taped on the end which we used to catch the lead rope and so be able to get a firm hold of her. You wouldn't want to be just walking into her box and expect to catch her like any other mare. In the mood she was in those last couple of days, you might not get back out.

She was running milk, walking her box and starting to sweat up when we called Derek in plenty of time for the foaling. We caught her and held on tightly to her as he put the tail bandage on. She was then let go and for the next 15 minutes or so she was manic in her box, rearing up the walls, pacing around, kicking out with her back legs. I've never seen anything like it.

Eventually, her waters broke and she lay down to foal. Derek, wearing a jockey's back protector under his jacket, left her a couple of minutes until she started to push. Then we went to her head and held on tightly to the lead rope, with strict instructions not to let go under any circumstances, as Derek went to her back end to oversee the birth of the foal.

It all went smoothly and the foal was quickly out on the ground, a colt. When Rags stood up she was held on a tight lead rope as she turned around and went to her foal. We held on to her head for the next hour as all the usual checks were carried out post foaling; tying the afterbirth up until the mare expelled it, giving the foal an enema, spraying its navel several times with iodine and checking the quality of the mare's colostrum. While the mare was licking her foal, Derek milked her and gave it to the foal from a bottle while still on the ground, to get him started, before we were ready to let go of her lead rope. He got the foal up and standing on its own and, when we were satisfied everything had been done, we let her go and quickly exited her box. The foal soon suckled the mare on his own and the night moved on.

When we were feeding all the mares at 6am the following morning, we opened her door and Rags charged at us with bared teeth. Her viciousness told us she would have happily torn us to bits. So we just slid the door open a few inches quickly and shoved a bucket in on the ground for her to eat from in her own time. She still wanted to kill us. The skill, nerve and professionalism of Derek and Paul ensured the next week went by without incident and Rags and her foal were moved to Godfrey's Farm a couple of miles away to join the rest of Magnier's mares and newborn foals.

A couple of weeks later Rags attacked and injured her HenryTheNavigator foal, who was immediately fostered on to a Clydesdale mare. The foal was fine, it wasn't a serious injury, but no chance could be taken on whether she might do it again, perhaps even with a fatal ending. From here on she would never keep another foal, he or she would be fostered soon after birth.

When she had a filly by Galileo in 2014 she was out in her paddock one morning when she started to foal. Derek went to bring her in, she charged and knocked him over, swivelled around and lashed out with her hind legs, missing his head by a whisker.

They got her in to the barn and foaled her using the same tried and tested system. A foster mare had been kept ready in a nearby paddock and shortly after foaling Rags was taken away to another barn further down the farm and the Clydesdale became the new mother of her Galileo filly. No chances were going to be taken with a filly foal by the best stallion in the world out of a brilliant race mare, a World Champion in 2007.

170

With bloodstock prices now rising sharply as the world started to recover from the financial meltdown, her value could be whatever a very rich man or woman wanted to pay to obtain a collector's item, certainly along the lines of the $5.2 million Mandy Pope paid for Better Better Better and the 5 million guineas Qatari Sheikh Joaan al-Thani paid for a Galileo yearling filly in 2013.

This filly, too, was the best foal Rags had so far produced. To date, her offspring have been very disappointing. Her first three foals have run a total of three times and none have even been placed. Her Galileo colt of 2011, Rhett Butler, was exported to Serbia in late 2014. Her latest filly, though, could be the one. Sooner or later you would expect the combination of Galileo and Rags To Riches, with the outstanding families they both come from, to hit the jackpot. Rags is highly likely to see the rest of her days out at Ballintemple Farm. Derek and Paul are the only people who are allowed to handle her, even taking her to be the covering shed. They know her as a broodmare better than anyone.

It is interesting to have seen in the foaling barns at Coolmore that these brilliant race mares are often the most aggressive of individuals, even more so than many colts or stallions. The great Goldikova would happily take a chunk out of you just for the fun of it and Red Evie, dam of Breeders' Cup winner Found in 2015, is the same.

Is it natural aggression which helped make them great race mares or is their aggressiveness the result of the strains and stress of training and racing at the highest level over several years?

It was fascinating being part of the team foaling Rags To Riches, fascinating as long as you lived to tell the tale. While it was scary at times, it was a lot easier being a supporting actor in this psychological thriller than being the stars of the show like Derek and Paul. There is one final twist to the story.

In 2013, a camera crew came to Ballintemple to film Rags as part of a series Blood-Horse magazine was putting together to highlight winners of the Kentucky Oaks. It is on Youtube - Stars of the Oaks - Rags To Riches. Rags won it with nonchalant ease to show how superior she was against her own sex and why her owners, Michael Tabor and Derek Smith, decided to pit here against the colts in the Belmont. The clip shows Rags winning the Kentucky Oaks and now, several years later, in a paddock at Ballintemple and being led up by Derek. It features an interview with David O'Loughlin, Coolmore's Director of Sales, which includes the following description of Rags To Riches.

**"A very good mother,
a very placid mare, very
tough and genuine."**

Moving along, the routine for fostering a foal on to one of the Clydesdales is always the same. It would usually be at least an hour from when the foal last suckled, so that the foal is so hungry it will go ravenously in search of milk without giving the new mare standing in front of it a second thought.

The foster mare will be tied up close to a plentiful supply of hay and have a hood placed over its head so it can't see the foal which is suckling. It will have its hind legs shackled to stop it kicking out at the new foal, which will be sprayed in the same way they do with lambs which are being adopted so the mare is unable to smell the difference in her own foal and her new one. The mare will also be given a strong dose of sedative. The foal will usually take to its new mother immediately, but the mares know something is up and can put up a fight. One day and one night tied up, shackled, hooded and sedated will normally see the mare accept the new foal as its own. If it doesn't, the same routine is followed until it does.

Coolmore keeps a band of fifty or sixty foster mares, mostly Clydesdales or Clydesdale crosses, and a couple of coloured stallions to breed with them. When the mares are needed for a fostering, their foal is moved on to one of Coolmore's regular contacts to be reared by hand.

During the Celtic Tiger years, when the country was awash with money, these foals were in big demand and Coolmore could sell them on for between €250 and €500 each. Since the economic bubble burst it has become increasingly difficult to find homes for them, so much so that Coolmore will now not only give them away for nothing but will add a bag or two of milk powder to sweeten any potential deal.

Until last year these mares were usually left to foal out in the fields on their own, but now they are housed in a huge barn on land bought recently and converted into a tillage farm. The barn was previously used to store cattle during the winter but now holds the foster mares in large pens inside from January to April. When they are close to foaling they are separated into single pens and the night staff will check on them regularly to make sure all is well when they foal. It's now a more orderly system for dealing with the foster mares, who are used to foaling on their own and prefer it that way.

When Derek showed me the new arrangements in 2014 he said the demand for the foals had virtually disappeared. "It's very difficult to find people to take them because of the costs involved in hand rearing them with no guarantee there will be a market for them to sell on in a few years' time. There are managers here who would have no problem putting the foals down. You could imagine what that would look like for The Boss if it got into the papers. It's my job to make sure that doesn't happen, but it's not easy," he told me.

The picture he painted was backed up by government figures. Agriculture Minister Simon Coveney revealed that the number of horses being slaughtered in supervised abattoirs increased six fold in the first three years of the economic downturn, from 2,002 animals in 2008 to 12,575 in 2011, as people could no longer afford to keep their stock and there was no market for selling them on. The figures did not include the smaller abattoirs around the country.

The huge numbers of horses being slaughtered in Ireland contributed to the horse meat scandal which erupted in Ireland and Britain in January 2013, when it was found that frozen beef burgers supplied to several supermarkets, including the Tesco chain, contained horse meat. Meatballs in Ikea stores, sausages in Russia and frozen burgers in Britain were pulled from the shelves by the millions as a result. A Dutch meat wholesaler, suspected of being a key player in the scandal in Europe, sourced much of the meat from Ireland. It was estimated as many as 1 in 20 beef meals across the whole of Europe contained horse meat.

Clydesdale is the old name for Lanarkshire in Scotland, through which the River Clyde runs. A breed of draught horse originally used for agriculture and heavy haulage, the Clydesdales were first developed when Flemish stallions were introduced to Scotland and crossed with local mares. The first breed registry was started in 1877. Throughout the late 19th century and early

20th century thousands of Clydesdales were exported from Scotland and sent throughout the world. They became known as the breed that built Australia.

The Budweiser Clydesdales are some of the most famous examples of the breed. These were first owned by the Budweiser Brewery at the end of prohibition in the United States in 1933 and have become an international symbol of both the breed and the brand. Clydesdales are also used by the British Household Cavalry, leading parades on ceremonial and state occasions. They carry an officer and two silver drums weighing over 120lbs each. To that can be added their contribution as foster mares at world renowned Coolmore Stud, including for the brilliant 7 time Group 1 winner Dylan Thomas. Their bomb proof temperament is the key to their role at Coolmore. They are fabulous horses with the kindest of natures and their contribution cannot be underestimated.

Foster mares were originally intended for the inevitable disasters which happen in every barn, when the natural mother dies, is injured or becomes ill. Then there are the times when a mare might be short of milk or becomes dangerously aggressive towards her foal. Coolmore take this practice one step further.

When they have an in foal mare booked to an outside stallion, such as Frankel in Newmarket or War Front in America, the mare will be foaled at Coolmore, the foal fostered on to one of the Clydesdales and the mare then sent away solo to be covered. They always foal their own mares at home and will never send one of their own foals away to another stud with its mother, preferring to keep them under their watchful eyes at all times. So their band of surrogates are kept busy.

Unsung heroine: a Coolmore foster mare

THE FOALING BARN

Rosie Collins, from Cahir in South Tipperary, was the third and newest member of the night team and, just like Hanna and Josie, an outstanding work colleague. She is also a bit of a character. Half way through last season she decided to have hair extensions, which gave us all a lot of laughs. She looked a mass of blonde curls and I told her, with a bit of foam padding here and there, she would be the image of Dolly Parton. If only she could sing she would have a big future as a tribute artist. For some reason which is totally lost on me, the Irish are mad about Garth Brooks, so anything is possible musically in Ireland.

Rosie lost the sight in her right eye when she was seven years old. It was pierced by a splinter from a bamboo cane which snapped, but to her enormous credit she has never let it dampen her zest for life. She did a bungee jump from Wellington Bridge in New Zealand a few years ago.

Sometimes you need a bit of luck when working the night shift, to be in the right place at the right time. Even then, with horses, it is often not straightforward. In 2013, I was doing my rounds of the barns when I came to Shouk, another great mare over many years for the Coolmore men. She's the dam of triple Oaks winner Alexandrova, Magical Romance, Masterofthehorse and Washington Irivine. She was lying flat out and didn't respond when I kicked the door to get her attention. I went in to check her and she had a small patch of cold sweat on her neck. I got her up but she went straight back down. I got her up again, she pawed the ground, went down again and started rolling. It was colic, but I had got her early, it was only just kicking off and I was hopeful all could be right.

I called the barn manager and told him we needed a vet immediately. Before long Shouk was on her way to Fethard Equine Hospital where she successfully underwent colic surgery. When the vets were getting her up after the operation, she broke her neck and died. Vets always do say the key to a horse surviving colic surgery is about how it comes out of the anaesthetic afterwards, but this was a cruel twist of desperate luck for Shouk. She was 19 years old and a grand mare.

Another mare I remembered well was the Queen Mary winner Elletelle. She delivered her first foal on 19 February 2011 and was five weeks overdue when she finally dropped a colt by Galileo, of course. He was a typical first foal, not very big at 106lbs but, nevertheless, very neat and correct. The mare's colostrum was low grade, so we bottle fed her foal some of much higher quality we had stored in our freezer. I remember Elletelle because for the first 48 hours

175

she wouldn't take her eyes off her foal, her head was never further than a couple of inches away, gazing at him like she couldn't believe what she saw. I took a photograph of her resting her head on the foal as he slept.

Elletelle had a second foal, another colt by Galileo, and then she was sent to the December 2012 breeding stock sale at Arqana in France, in foal for a third time to Galileo. She made €825,000 and her new owners sent her back to Coolmore to foal. Horses coming from any sale on to the stud always go into one of the small isolation yards for a few weeks at first because there is a risk that one could bring a disease or infection in with them as a result of mixing with so many horses from so many countries at these sales.

Elletelle can't take her eyes off her first foal.

I was checking on her at Prospect Isolation Yard one night at Christmas. She was a sweet mare and I was glad to see her back with us. I remember seeing her through the night, with her head at times over her stable door and other times eating hay quietly. The last time I saw her an hour or so before I finished my shift, she was lying down, looked comfortable and nothing appeared untoward.

When the day shift came in a couple of hours later to feed her, they couldn't get her to stand up, she had no co-ordination. She was diagnosed with equine herpes virus (EHV), which can cause mares to abort their foals. The likely explanation is that she had picked the virus up somewhere along the way going to and from the sales in France.

It can also attack the central nervous system and this is what happened to Elletelle. She became paralysed and had to be euthanised. The Prospect yard was immediately put into lock down for the next four weeks to ensure this deadly virus did not spread. Thankfully, the mares already there continued to foal without problem. With a bit of luck and because of the good stud management practices in place, the all clear was eventually given and a potential disaster averted.

Elletelle was the only casualty. That first foal she had, which she couldn't take her eyes off, was later named Adelaide. He travelled the world for Aidan O'Brien in 2014 and won The Cox Plate, one of Australia's most prestigious races and its first ever winner trained from Europe. Adelaide is now a stallion at Coolmore Australia.

It is inevitable you will remember the disasters in a foaling barn, when you lose a mare or foal. There are the times, then, when a potential disaster turns into a triumph, a mare or foal recovers from serious illness or injury. Most of the time these blue chip mares foal without hitch and are soon on their way out of the barn. The night team watch over them through most of their pregnancy, the foaling period and then as the foals become weanlings and yearlings before they head off for training.

It's a great feeling to see them go on and claim glory on the racetrack. Homecoming Queen, Ruler Of The World, Marvellous, Bracelet and Gleneagles are our recent Classic winners. Tapestry, Adelaide, Found, Diamondsandrubies and Highland Reel have also all won at Group 1 level. Then Bondi Beach won and lost the final Classic of the 2015 season, the English St Leger, in the stewards' room and Minding and Ballydoyle became Group 1 winning two year olds – some roll call for just one foaling barn.

One horse who has only won a Group 2 race so far but who has given the foaling team a lot of satisfaction is Aloft, as he provided Ryan Moore with his record breaking ninth win at Royal Ascot in 2015. He is by Galileo out of the Storm Cat mare, Dietrich. Most mares follow the same sort of pattern as they get close to foaling so you always have a pretty good idea of what is happening. Dietrich likes to make things as difficult as possible by not showing any of the usual signs you are looking out for. It's like switching a light on; she just gets down and starts to foal as quick as you like without any warning whatsoever, even when outwardly looking to be still a week or two away. She did that with Aloft. We saw him coming at the last moment and he won for Moore in much the same way at Ascot to cap a great week for the jockey and the foaling barn.

Aloft

Chapter 7

GOLDEN ERA

GOLDEN ERA

"If a free society cannot help the
many who are poor, it cannot save
the few who are rich."

John F Kennedy

The death throes of the burst bloodstock bubble in Kentucky in the 80s were long and drawn out and extremely painful for many people, but not for Coolmore Stud and John Magnier, who were going fast in the opposite direction. Just as The Brethren became history, so too did many of the most famous horsemen in Kentucky. Gainesway Farm was the biggest and best-run operation in town, but when John Gaines was forced to sell his beloved art collection, for over $20 million, and then his farm, the bloodstock world finally realised how bad the situation was.

Iconic farms like Calumet, Spendthrift and Bluegrass Farm were either bust or one step away. Bluegrass Farm saw the most complete dismantling of a bloodstock empire built up with total devotion over many years when Nelson Bunker Hunt was forced to auction off every last one of his bloodstock holding - all 580 of them - on 9 January 1988. They made $46 million, a fraction of what they had cost him to assemble.

Hunt, the son of a Texas oil billionaire, was brought to his knees because he greedily tried to corner the market in silver. In 1979 the price of silver jumped from $6 an ounce to $48 and it was revealed he owned a third of the entire world supply, mostly bought with borrowed money. When the price suddenly dropped he was unable to meet his obligations and was forced into bankruptcy facing a potential £1.7 billion loss. The day the horse manure hit the fan became known as Silver Thursday - 27 March 1980.

It was an equine gold rush which Robert Sangster had started when his team from Co Tipperary descended on the yearling sales with their grand plan in 1975. Ten years later there were two main problems for the horsemen and women of Kentucky; they believed it would last forever and they went out and spent all the gold and then some more. It was the bloodstock bubble to end all bloodstock bubbles and was inspired by one five letter word - greed.

Fast forward another twenty years and Ireland, along with much of the rest of the world, experienced the biggest recession in living memory when another bubble came along. This time it was a property bubble, caused by the naked greed of developers and bankers. Nothing much has changed for John Magnier. He came out of the bloodstock meltdown in 1986 in astonishingly good shape, as the rise of Coolmore to be number one in the world since clearly shows. He has also not only survived the financial apocalypse of 2009, but has prospered from it. He has led Coolmore into a golden era of total domination in the bloodstock world. That's some achievement for a boy who had to leave school at 15.

Things were never quite the same for Vincent O'Brien and Robert Sangster, though both tried manfully to recapture past glories. The Brethren re-united for one last desperate roll of the dice. Advised by Dermot Desmond, the Dublin stockbroker friend of Magnier's, O'Brien set up Classic Thoroughbreds with the aim of going back to America to buy yearlings for him to train at Ballydoyle. The same plan as before but now with new money behind it.

O'Brien, Sangster, Magnier, Irish cattle magnate John Horgan and Michael Smurfit of the paper and packaging empire, put £4 million into the venture and invited the general public to buy shares, which they did to the tune of £12 million. While Sangster's and Magnier's names were principally there to give public confidence, it was really all on Vincent's head. He was now the chairman of a public company and he chose and trained the yearlings. There was more pressure than ever as he desperately didn't want to let down all those small investors from his homeland who had bought shares at an opening price of 30p each.

The omens had not improved. The Arabs were still buying all the best American yearlings, Ballydoyle hadn't produced a really top racehorse since 1984 and the dreaded virus was still lingering in that part of Co Tipperary. That didn't deter the people of Ireland, many of whom were mad keen to get involved and have another go. O'Brien bought four yearlings for Classic Thoroughbreds in 1987 and then went back again for more in 1988, when he came across the one he had been dreaming of getting. He had to pay $3.5 million for him, $1 million over his budget, but he managed to persuade Sangster to take a quarter share to get him off the hook.

That was Royal Academy, a son of Nijinsky who reminded O'Brien so much of the great Triple Crown winner the moment he saw him. He won the July Cup for the trainer in 1990 and then, memorably, the Breeders' Cup Mile back in America with Lester Piggott, not long out of retirement, riding a blindingly brilliant race, snatching victory on the line with Royal Academy running for his life down the stretch at Belmont Park. It was an amazing and emotional triumph that, in particular, meant so much to all the small investors back in Ireland, but it wasn't enough to save Classic Thoroughbreds, whose shares had peaked at 41p before plunging to 11p in June 1989 when losses of £8.3 million were posted. The shares continued to drop like a stone and in August

Royal Academy

1991 the company announced that it had ceased trading, with the shares finally at 3p. Remaining funds were returned to shareholders.

Vincent had given his all but the bloodstock world had changed dramatically since he and his two partners set out for Keeneland in 1975. The Arabs had bottomless pockets and were not only dominating racing in Europe but were now breeding their own champions too. It was so ironic - they were pursuing largely the same game plan O'Brien, Sangster and Magnier had set out with 15 years earlier; to buy the best yearlings by Northern Dancer and his sons, and the Arabs were proving to be better at it.

While Vincent was mortified about the losses his family and supporters endured with Classic Thoroughbreds, they knew the risks and took it on the chin in the true Irish way. The only gripes, as you would expect, came from the rich institutional investors who could afford the reckless gamble which failed. When Vincent walked into the company's AGM, with the writing in block capitals on the wall for Classic Thoroughbreds, he was greeted by an astonishing reception, as one newspaper reported with some surprise. "There can hardly be many occasions where the chairman of a company with accumulated losses of over seven million pounds arrives late at his company's Annual General Meeting to be greeted with a spontaneous round of applause. But that was the reception for Vincent O'Brien last Friday evening at the AGM of Classic Thoroughbreds. Many stressed their investment was an enjoyable gamble and the money didn't matter."

O'Brien was a man of the Irish people, who came from nowhere, and nothing would ever change their adoration for him. On reflection, however, Classic Thoroughbreds was a bad mistake which he didn't deserve to have on his record. The training of the racehorse was his forte and it was something he did better than just about anyone, before or since.

Brother Phonsie said Vincent never wanted big numbers of horses in training. "He wanted to keep his string small. Only John Magnier and Robert Sangster wanted to keep on increasing numbers. John Magnier always believed that the more you had, the better chance you had of getting a real one. Vincent wanted 50 at the outside. At the height in Churchtown, we had 42 horses," Phonsie said. At Ballydoyle today the figure would be over 150. In 2008, looking back over the career of one of his racing heroes, Brough Scott, the Racing Post's acclaimed journalist, had this to say.

"There were occasions when you felt that this commercialisation was compromising him, that the younger generation was in danger of prostituting his talent, as in the Classic Thoroughbreds fiasco when the O'Brien-picked yearlings turned out to be a costly embarrassment to all concerned."

Royal Academy was retired to stud at Coolmore for not much more than he cost as a yearling in Kentucky, a sign of those much changed times. But by 2004, shuttling between America and Australia, he had become an elite stallion like his sire Nijinsky and grand sire Northern Dancer. Magnier had done it again, ensuring his partners emerged from the horse manure smelling of roses.

Thirty five years to the day after Lester Piggott had his first ride for O'Brien, when Gladness won the 1958 Ascot Gold Cup, the trainer had his final Royal Ascot winner. College Chapel won the Group 3 Cork and Orrery Stakes in

184

1993 and Vincent led him in to the winner's enclosure. Always preferring to keep out of the limelight, the only other time he had done this before was when Nijinsky won 25 years earlier.

College Chapel, another stallion made for Coolmore, was one of only a few horses now left at Ballydoyle. Even so, the genius that was O'Brien could still hack it at the top table when he had the ammunition. El Prado and Fatherland struck in the National Stakes at the Curragh in 1991 and 1992, but in October 1994 it was all over. O'Brien announced his retirement from training.

Honours, awards and plaudits flowed in for Vincent. Son-in-law Magnier said of him: "At Coolmore, as well as being part owner, he was our most valued adviser. He trained all three Coolmore champion sires to date - Sadler's Wells, Caerleon and Be My Guest. There's another example of his wonderful intuition when he bought The Minstrel at Keeneland. Due to his size we managed to get him for just $200,000. His syndication two years later for $9 million, along with that of MV's dual Prix de l'Arc de Triomphe winner Alleged for $16 million, raised the capital to allow Coolmore to expand and move forward. In anyone else's hands, neither of these colts might have realised their full potential, but MV's unrivalled patience and skill ensured that they did. He was a true master of his profession."

In the summer of 2005, a tribute from the UK's leading breeding expert, Tony Morris, made him so proud. "Proof that Vincent O'Brien's impact has been a global phenomenon came with the recent publication of a list of all-time leading sires worldwide. No fewer than nine of the top 35 - Nijinsky, Sadler's Wells, Southern Halo, Caerleon, Alleged, Sir Ivor, Roberto, Royal Academy and Bluebird, were trained at Ballydoyle and have spread their influence over all five continents. That record indicates that the greatest of racing's greats in the twentieth century is just as surely the most important human contributor to the thoroughbred of the twenty first."

Much to Vincent's relief, Magnier stepped in and bought Ballydoyle from him to ensure the world renowned training establishment not only stayed in racing but stayed in the family. In fifty years Vincent had never found time to visit his wife's homeland, but on his first visit to Perth he fell in love with a house he saw for sale and bought it lock stock and barrel on the spot. He went on to spend half the year in Australia and half back in Ireland until his death on 1 June 2009, at the age of 92.

Vincent O'Brien with his Grand National winner Quare Times

Poignantly, it was the week of the Epsom Derby, which he had won six times. He trained the winners of 44 Classics, 27 of which were in his homeland, and won the Prix de l'Arc de Triomphe three times. Records and statistics are important, but it's what people genuinely believe that counts the most. Mike Dillon, of Ladbrokes, said of him: "Vincent was so modest, warm and generous of spirit. No man in racing, or anywhere else, ever wore true greatness more lightly." Nick Wachman, senior steward of the Irish Turf Club, said Vincent had gone racing to the Curragh the year before he died. "When he came into the parade ring, the whole ring stood up and applauded." Universal and unconditional respect. Vincent O'Brien had helped put Ireland at the top of the world order of racing and bloodstock and no one knew more than his fellow countrymen how much that meant.

Robert Sangster had pre-deceased Vincent by five years and his obituaries were somewhat different. They concentrated more on his playboy image, which probably did him a disservice in the great scheme of things, because he also played a vital role and not just with Coolmore. Ireland benefitted from the involvement of all three partners and, after all, it was Sangster who bred Sadler's Wells.

When O'Brien retired he sold his share in Coolmore to Magnier and Sangster did the same, concentrating instead on his own racing and breeding empire. In his heyday he had around 1000 horses at stud and in training in England, America, Venezuela and particularly Australia, where he was held in the highest regard for raising the country's standing in the racing and bloodstock world.

Despite his image as a rich playboy, which he thoroughly deserved, he was also a clever businessman. He was chairman of his family's Vernons Pools from 1980 to 1988, when he sold it to Ladbrokes for £90 million after becoming aware of early plans to start a National Lottery in Britain. He correctly predicted that could have a disastrous effect on his business, and so it proved. Seven years after selling out, Ladbrokes declared the Vernons business was worthless because of competition from the lottery and reduced its book value in their accounts from £100 million to £1.

In 1985 he had paid £6 million for the 2,300 acre Manton Estate in Wiltshire and spent almost as much again making it the centre of his training operation, with outstanding National Hunt trainer Michael Dickinson in control. In his first season in 1986, Dickinson trained the winners of just four races and Sangster sacked him. He was very good at planting trees though, over 30,000 of them. Despite the efforts of Peter Chapple-Hyam, John Gosden and Barry Hills as trainers, Manton was a debilitating strain on Sangster's wealth. He still had a few great days on the racecourse with the likes of Rodrigo de Triano, but the finances dictated he became a seller rather than a buyer in his stud operation to make the whole show viable.

His problem was that he just had too much going on at the same time around the world, too many balls in the air, which is also an apt if a little crude description of his energetic and complicated love life. He started well, married for 16 years to his first wife Christine Street, but from then on he seemed to be in and out of trouble as often as he was in an out of the winners enclosure, and his shenanigans were usually played out in the newspapers.

He first ran off with the wife of Australian MP Andrew Peacock, who not only lost his wife but also had his promising political career derailed as a result. Susan Peacock, who left her three young daughters in Australia to marry Sangster in 1978, found out four years later he was enjoying a fling with Texan supermodel Jerry Hall, the girlfriend of Mick Jagger. Hall, remembered for her very long legs but little else, told reporters Sangster could buy out Jagger, notoriously careful with his money, ten times over.

Robert Sangster with his third wife, Susan

Hall was just winding Jagger up with the fling with Sangster. She said in an interview she was able to wean the Rolling Stone off drugs but never off girls. Sangster was there just enjoying the ride, as it were, and soon went back to his wife in Australia. But she eventually divorced him in 1984 when she found out in a newspaper he was planning to divorce her and marry Susan Lilley, a former model and wife of British shoe heir, Peter Lilley of the Lilley and Skinner stores. Sangster and Susan Lilley were married for 15 years until divorcing in 2000 and were often in the gossip columns. When she admitted she couldn't cook, Sangster bought her a restaurant.

He spent much of his later years in Barbados and Australia, his famous blue and green racing silks rarely seen on a racecourse in England. He told the Australian newspaper, The Age, in 2002 that he was planning to race his own bloodstock more often in the near future. They reported he was estimated in the Sunday Times Rich List that year to be worth $236 million and he is credited with doing most for selling Australian racing to the wider world after he teamed up with trainer Colin Hayes in the late 70s. He went on to win most of the country's top races, including the greatest of them all, The Melbourne Cup, with Beldale Ball in 1980.

"I am not getting any younger and I probably need a bit of fun," he said. "It's all right getting the bank balance in the black all the time but it's not much fun looking at a bank balance. I will probably race a lot more after this year. I am selling again nearly everything this year but I think my policy is going to change and have the colours race again. I don't mind the bank balance. I would rather have a bit of fun." He didn't get a chance to implement his new plan.

He died aged 67 from pancreatic cancer in London on 7 April 2004. Three services were held for him on the same day, 20 April, in London, Barbados and Australia, a fitting tribute to the standing he enjoyed in the racing and bloodstock worlds. He was an innovator whose influence transcended the globe and he incited blind loyalty from everyone who knew him well. One of his many friends in Kentucky said of him: "Robert was marvellous, square-dealing, honest, unassuming and brilliant."

Racing journalist Julian Wilson said: "His pleasures were boxing, champagne, golf, racing and beautiful women, and often more than one at the same time." In the early days, Sangster and his gang loved their Roederer Crystal champagne, but by the time that became the favourite tipple of some of the world's most famous rappers, referred to as 'Cryssy' in a number of songs, The Brethren had long moved on to a more exclusive and expensive brand. Last word, appropriately, to Vincent O'Brien.

"Robert was a true visionary whose large-scale investment in the best American bred yearlings in the 70s was one of the principal factors in establishing Ireland and Coolmore as major forces in the bloodstock world. We shared some great memories over the years with horses like The Minstrel, Alleged, El Gran Senor, Sadler's Wells and Golden Fleece and I cannot think of anybody with whom I would rather have shared them."

On 16 July 2005, the Racing Post ran a story which said that Sangster, the first man in Britain to turn horseracing into a major international business, left assets worth only £4,500 in the UK according to court papers just released. He's still chuckling about that one somewhere.

While the era of The Brethren ended in major disappointment, they were still responsible for Coolmore's steady rise to the top of the bloodstock mountain. Magnier has been the driving force behind it since its inception, but without O'Brien and Sangster it would be a different beast today. O'Brien selected and trained all those star yearlings and Sangster bred Sadler's Wells, who transformed the bloodstock world in Europe and made Magnier extremely rich. How do you follow all that?

To anyone else that could have been enough for one lifetime, but not Magnier. He wasn't going to be happy until he was the undisputed number one in the thoroughbred world. His wife Sue named one future Epsom Derby winner Ruler Of The World - that says it all.

He bided his time at Ballydoyle, waiting two years before satisfying himself he had found the right man to replace Vincent O'Brien. Like so many important decisions in his life, he got it absolutely right. His choice of Aidan Patrick O'Brien from County Wexford, a one time champion amateur jockey, heralded the dawn of a new golden era for Ballydoyle and Coolmore. Magnier finally began to realise his dream of the 1970s, when he first linked up with Vincent O'Brien and Robert Sangster on the long road to world domination.

Aidan O'Brien

When looking at Aidan O'Brien's career it is impossible to avoid a seemingly never ending list of highly impressive statistics. There are just so many of them, not least that he has been champion trainer in the UK on four occasions and at home in Ireland continuously for the last 19 years. He has won the Irish Derby, Ireland's most valuable race, 11 years out of those 19. At 45 years of age and with nearly twenty years of training at Ballydoyle behind him, 2015 saw him close on fifty winners at Royal Ascot, the most competitive place anywhere in the world to succeed in racing. He has twice matched Vincent O'Brien's record tally of six victories at the Royal meeting. With Ryan Moore in the saddle, he trained five winners there in 2015 to help Moore break the record held by Lester Piggott and Pat Eddery for riding the most winners.

O'Brien's style of training is to bring improvement out of his horses steadily as the season progresses, a method diametrically opposed to the champion Federico Tesio fifty years earlier. Tesio would have his horses fit to fly first time out. He said it was better to lose a race through over training a horse than under training it. Not with O'Brien. He is not afraid to lose a race or two either at the start of its career or at the start of a season if it means that horse will keep improving along the way.

John Magnier once said in a television interview a feature of O'Brien's success is how his horses keep coming back for more through a very long season. He is at his strongest from Royal Ascot on through to October and when it can look like his string is out of form early on in a season when a few favourites can regularly be turned over, they always come good for the second half. It's a meticulously thought out programme as its impossible to keep horses at their peak right through a racing season that lasts eight months.

The 2015 season was a good example of how he makes his plans. Until Royal Ascot, only Gleneagles had shown the champion form Magnier requires to be able to retire elite racehorses from the track to the breeding shed at Coolmore. The horses hadn't really sparkled, but he then had five winners at the Royal meeting and was top trainer there yet again. Diamondsandrubies, who we had foaled at Ballintemple Farm out of champion two year old Quarter Moon, showed great battling qualities to fight to the final stride for an impressive win in the Group 1 Pretty Polly Stakes at the Curragh on the Irish Derby card at the end of June, with the help of a brilliant ride from Seamie Heffernan.

Quarter Moon can be a real worrier in the stable and her penchant for weaving usually means her foals are fostered within a week of being born. There was, however, nothing wrong with Diamondsandrubies temperament in the Pretty Polly and her form sums up perfectly the O'Brien approach, particularly with fillies. She steadily improved on every run up to the Curragh and her all-important Group 1 prize. What's a Group 1 winning filly worth as a breeding prospect with the rapidly escalating values of 2015 and beyond? A few million anywhere in the world thanks to the trainer's patience and skill.

The proof of this approach shows in the results throughout O'Brien's career. Horses he trains regularly put a sequence of winning runs together at the highest level. Rock of Gibraltar, Duke of Marmalade, Dylan Thomas and Giant's Causeway all won five or more Group 1 races in a season. Peeping Fawn, another admirably tough and talented filly, won 4 Group 1s on the bounce. The great George Washington won four as a three year old. High Chaparral and Galileo were multiple winners at the highest level - there are so many outstanding horses you would be afraid you might miss one out. Then there was Istabraq, one of the best hurdlers of all time, who was at the top of his game for three consecutive Champion Hurdle wins at Cheltenham come March. Similarly, the heroic Yeats was brought to a perfect pitch to win the Ascot Gold Cup for four consecutive years, the only horse to ever achieve this feat. Having such superbly bred horses to train is a huge start, but it is seriously competitive at Group 1 level anywhere in the world and those victories don't come along easily.

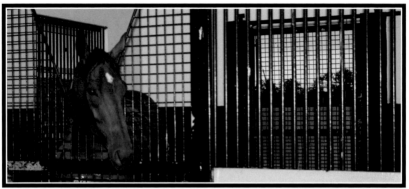

Peeping Fawn prepares for a new career as a broodmare after winning four consecutive Group 1s.

In 2008, O'Brien won 23 Group 1 races around the world, the second time he has hit this figure. That came with the considerable assistance of Johnny Murtagh in the saddle, but if O'Brien does have a fault it concerns his relationships with his jockeys. Mick Kinane, Jamie Spencer and Murtagh all left Ballydoyle in surprising circumstances, the latter clearly feeling he was being pushed out so that O'Brien's son Joseph could take over as No 1 rider. With O'Brien, it's his way or the highway.

Tensions between the Coolmore partners and the O'Briens rose steadily during the 2015 season. Ryan Moore was brought in as No 1 jockey with considerable success, but when he was injured it was believed the owners didn't want Joseph back on the best horses. The breakdown between the Magnier team and their trainer was such that rumours abounded of his imminent departure from Ballydoyle. The troubled waters appeared to become calmer as the autumn approached, but after twenty years in the hot seat it could well be that O'Brien is close to walking away.

While he doesn't have a connection to Coolmore Stud in the same way his namesake Vincent had, the successes he has achieved with the horses running in the ownership of Magnier, Tabor and Smith has seen a steady supply of new stallions heading to Fethard every year of his reign as trainer. For the 2015 breeding season, 20 of the 25 stallions on the roster at Coolmore headquarters had been trained by O'Brien and all had won at the highest level. It's an astonishing record. He has produced a never ending supply of Group 1 winners to keep the bank vaults bulging for Magnier and his associates through stud fees earned. It's a fact that most thoroughbred stallions end up as failures at stud, even at Coolmore, so mare owners are always keen to take a punt on a new stallion in the hope that will become the next big thing. Coolmore need champion stallions standing at the stud, so the pressure is always on O'Brien to come up with champion racehorses at Ballydoyle. The theory for success has been put into practice so well, but O'Brien is sure to feel the pressure involved.

And it is plain to see why the pressure has been building. There have been stories for a while that the close advisers surrounding Magnier, Tabor and Smith have been critical of Joseph's abilities as No 1 jockey. It was Joseph who was on board when Camelot failed to land the elusive English Triple Crown when failing narrowly in the third leg, the St Leger at Doncaster. It was Joseph who was blamed for Australia's defeat by Ryan Moore and The Grey Gatsby in the Irish Champion in 2014. He was also on board Gleneagles when disqualified from first place for interference in France last year. Joseph is a good jockey, but he is no Steve Cauthen at the same age. And look how Kinane, Fallon and Murtagh were at their prime as jockeys in the second half of their careers, with plenty of experience to draw on. There is massive pressure on anyone working as Magnier's trainer or jockey. He doesn't just expect to win everything, he demands it. Aidan has increased that pressure by being so intransigent on riding arrangements. As far as he is concerned, it's Joseph first and the rest nowhere. You can see both sides of the story in this showdown, but unless a

Aidan O'Brien and John Magnier

lasting truce can be forged, there is only going to be one winner – the same one as in the Magnier versus the football manager scrap. But maybe O'Brien isn't that bothered; he's been there, done it and it's time for a change. Maybe Magnier just knows it's time for a change, that the tail seems to be wagging the dog.

It is virtually impossible to come up with a definitive figure for what Coolmore earns from their stallions every year because there are so many imponderables. The most difficult one to evaluate is Galileo. His stud fee is listed as private, for only Coolmore and the mare owner to know, but is at least €300,000 per successful mating. He would cover around 200 mares each season and has excellent fertility so there's a potential €60 million available for just Galileo alone.

However, around half of the mares he covers would be from Magnier's own broodmare band. Bearing in mind the vast majority of these would be regarded as blue chip mares with some of the best pedigrees in the stud book, the value of most of the resulting foals on the open market would be in excess of their €300,000 covering fee. If Galileo produces an outstanding colt like Gleneagles, who will then go off to stud after his racing career is over and earn €40 million each season in fees, his value to Coolmore rises all the time. When you also factor in the current demand for his fillies as potential broodmares, Galileo's worth to Magnier is considerably greater than €60 million a year. Probably nearer €100 million.

When you include the shuttling of so many of the stallions to Australia or South America for the southern hemisphere breeding seasons, Coolmore's stallion income will comfortably exceed €300 million in a typical year.

Then there is the contribution made by the training prowess of O'Brien, who ensures a strong flow of prize money won all around the world to help pay for the costs of running Ballydoyle and enable Coolmore to breed or buy the next generation of star racehorses. On the way to being crowned Champion trainer in Ireland for the last 19 years, O'Brien has plundered the top races day in and day out, consistently underscoring the massive contribution he makes towards the dominant position enjoyed by Magnier and his team.

Taking just the last five years as an example, O'Brien has won over £31 million in prize money in Britain and Ireland for his owners. With those 19 trainer's championships in Ireland, it follows Sue Magnier, Michael Tabor and Derrick Smith have won the most owner's prize money individually or in one combination or another among themselves. In recent times, they have been hoovering up around 20% of the total Irish prize money for flat racing, with O'Brien winning just under €4.9 million in Ireland for "the lads" in 2014. Magnier's son-in-law, David Wachman, is also capable of winning prize money of over €500,000 each season for the Coolmore owners.

While the figures behind the Ballydoyle operation are understandably impressive, this success is proving to be something of a double edged sword.

194

Flat racing has become less competitive at the highest levels, so much so that big foreign owners have steadily reduced the number of horses they have trained in Ireland. The Aga Khan, long regarded as the owner of some of the country's finest racehorses in the past, is one notable example. John Oxx, brilliant trainer of Sea The Stars, has been the main loser for Ireland by the Aga Khan's change of policy i n recent years and France has been the beneficiary.

It seems more and more that if Dermot Weld doesn't have a good one for Moyglare Stud or Jim Bolger can't pull another one out of the hat in which he keeps his small and high-achieving band of broodmares, the O'Brien juggernaut rolls on with little in its way. As a consequence field sizes suffer and the racing becomes less competitive.

In the last few years, the figures show that O'Brien has ended up each season with close to 60 horses in his yard rated 100 plus. It takes the next best five or six trainers as a group to get near to what O'Brien has achieved on his own. And that's including the likes of Dermot Weld and Jim Bolger. Ballydoyle's dominance is frightening but O'Brien can only beat what is put in front of him and that's what he has been doing since he took over at Ballydoyle in 1996. Order of St George became his 242nd Group or Grade 1 winner when he won the Irish St Leger at the Curragh in September 2015.

What of Aidan O'Brien the man? He is naturally shy and reticent in talking about himself. It is a cliche to say that his horses do the talking for him, but that is how he prefers it. He could talk all day about them and their training, but all he really wants is to be left alone at Ballydoyle to work with the best bloodstock in the world. He told the Daily Telegraph in the build-up to Camelot's attempt to complete the Triple Crown in 2012: "If we could never leave this place and hold the races here it would be great."

He is not a natural communicator with the outside world and dislikes being interviewed. When the Telegraph's Paul Hayward asked him if having his jockey son Joseph on board the hot St Leger favourite added to the trepidation, he replied: "I don't know what that means." No pretence with O'Brien, he told it straight. Some might say he needs to get out more, but he would say he has everything he needs in life at Ballydoyle - horses and family. Hayward said that hunched in front of the television in his office, watching a race from England, the sport seems to occupy O'Brien's whole being.

He has a tight-knit family who share his passion, even obsession, with the thoroughbred racehorse. Wife Anne-Marie is a former Champion National

Hunt Trainer herself and apart from assisting Aidan at Ballydoyle, she oversees the couple's own stud farm which operates under the name of Whisperview Trading Ltd with a good deal of success. They bred Epsom Oaks winner Qualify among other good horses.

Apart from a spot of trouble with the tax man in 2011, when their company was listed in the top ten of the latest tax defaulters as a result of an investigation by Irish Revenue's offshore assets team, the O'Briens are generally impeccably behaved. The stewards at the big race meetings in England like to keep him on his toes with a few slaps for not having his horses in the parade ring early enough or not saddling them in time, but so far their fines haven't got too close to the €526,077 settlement the tax authorities hit Whisperview Trading with in 2011.

A senior Coolmore manager has also appeared on the country's list of tax defaulters, as did former jockey and trainer Charlie Swan in 2015. He had to make a settlement of €122,442 for under-declarations of income tax and VAT and for a case linked to an ongoing investigation into offshore assets. It seems to be in the DNA of many horsemen in Ireland – they are either tax exiles or tax defaulters.

One year later, Aidan and Joseph, 19, became the first father and son combination to train and ride an Epsom Derby winner, thanks to Camelot. Joseph became Irish Champion Jockey for the first time and when he retained the title the following year he broke a 20 year record set by Mick Kinane for the most winners in a season, ending 2013 with 126 wins. Joseph has had huge pressure on those young shoulders in a short space of time; if he won a big race it was the horse that did it, if he was beaten it

was his fault and he was only on the horse because his father was the trainer. It can be a lose/lose situation when you are the son of a famous father.

Throughout a difficult 2015, though, he always conducted himself in exemplary fashion, at least in public, which speaks volumes for his old head on those young shoulders. Now that he is doing more and more training of jumpers at his mother's family home at Piltown it is clear the O'Briens are preparing themselves for life after Ballydoyle.

"Yes Mum!" Sarah and Joseph listen while Anne-Marie discusses the tactics.

If Aidan O'Brien turned out to be an inspired choice by Magnier, taking Michael Tabor and later Derrick Smith on as partners in many of the star horses to be trained at Ballydoyle was just as shrewd with Tabor joining the team before O'Brien. Magnier was following the successful blueprint he had forged with Robert Sangster thirty years earlier. By bringing in outside money they could buy more yearlings and thereby spread the risk and increase their chances of finding a champion who would make a stallion. If it turned out a successful venture everyone gained, if it flopped the boss of Coolmore wouldn't take the hit on his own.

But Tabor and Smith were bringing more than just money to the show. They had a lifetime of business experience and success in the racing world, the kind of knowledge money can't buy. Tabor, born in East London in 1941, had become a successful bookmaker, gambler and racehorse owner. His grandparents were Russian-Jewish immigrants, originally called Taborosky, who had moved to London from Vilna in Russia.

He left school at 15 to work in the local Co-op and then enrolled at the Morris School of Hairdressing in Piccadilly, but decided instead to pursue his interest in gambling nurtured at greyhound tracks in London as a teenager, and become a bookmaker. He borrowed £30,000 to buy two bankrupt betting shops in 1968, building the business called Arthur Prince into a chain of 114 shops before selling out to Coral for a reported £27 million in 1995.

It wasn't all plain sailing. In 1970 he was banned for life from all racecourses by the Jockey Club of England, who claimed he had paid two jockeys for information. Tabor had the lifetime ban overturned three years later and said the ban had actually served him well, inspiring him to concentrate on making an even bigger success of his business. From once being thrown out of racing for alleged skulduggery, Tabor is now viewed as a pillar of respectability by the racing establishment. Who said money can't buy love?

His reputation as a gambler was legendary. It was said he would regularly bet in tens and even hundreds of thousand pounds. Derrick Smith worked for Ladbrokes and said they had to stop taking bets from him, such was his success with his monster wagers. The horse which put him into the big time as an owner was Thunder Gulch. He had gone to live in Florida and wanted a horse to race in America. Another fearless gambler, JP McManus, put him in touch with his pal Magnier, whose vet and adviser Demi O'Byrne then found Thunder Gulch for him as a promising two year old. That was 1994, the horse cost him £400,000 and the deal quickly turned to gold. In a brilliant season at three, Thunder Gulch won the Kentucky Derby and the Belmont and narrowly missed out on the Triple Crown when less than a length second in the Preakness. Magnier bought half of the American champion to stand at Coolmore's Ashford Stud in Kentucky and a partnership which was to have far reaching effects was signed, sealed and delivered.

Queen Elizabeth gets a chuckle out of Derrick Smith, John Magnier and Michael Tabor.

It was deja vu - Magnier and Sangster all over again. In 1995, Magnier and Tabor bought three of the top four lots at the Keeneland Yearling Sales and paid 600,000 guineas for the most expensive yearling sold at Tattersalls in Newmarket that year. They named the colt Entrepreneur and he went on to win the English Two Thousand Guineas, their first of many Classics together, and then became another stallion for Coolmore.

He is a good example of the hit or miss nature of the stallion game. As a Classic winner by Sadler's Wells out of a top class race mare, he was given every chance of success by starting out at Coolmore and then shuttling to the major New Zealand stud, Cambridge, for the southern hemisphere breeding season, but had little success. In 2002 he was sold to stand in Japan and three years later was moved on again to the Voskhod Stud in Russia.

Tabor has been involved in all of the major winners trained in the Aidan O'Brien era at Ballydoyle and with French trained horses like Montjeu, Hurricane Run and Pour Moi. While Tabor's financial investment was important, his wealth of racing knowledge and business experience should not be underestimated either. As you would expect from a successful gambler and bookmaker, he knows his racing form inside out. It's a business, but deep down Tabor is a huge racing fan and his interviews are always worth reading or listening to.

He told the Independent: "I get enormous pleasure out of the horses but, it goes without saying, that you're trying to make stallions. You need a stallion, maybe a stallion and a half, every year," he said. With Tabor's help since 1995, Coolmore have comfortably exceeded the quota of stallions they needed to make on the racetrack.

While virtually everything Magnier and Tabor touched in the horse world seemed to be turning to gold, Derrick Smith was in the Caribbean making his own pot of gold in the property game. Born in Manchester but raised in south London, he happily admits he's had a somewhat charmed life, mixing plenty of luck with a sharp brain and sheer hard graft. He went to work for Ladbrokes after finishing at grammar school, only because he met an old school mate one day who told him how well he was doing.

He stayed with Ladbrokes for 24 years, where he became their face around the racecourses, but left in 1988 and became a property consultant. Four years later, having done pretty well for himself, he and his wife Gay decided to move to Barbados. The property market was just about to boom again after the inevitable bust and often in concert with Magnier, Tabor and McManus took his wealth to an altogether different level.

He at first became involved in a few horses with Tabor, including Lion Heart, who became a stallion at Coolmore America, and Sense Of Style, a champion filly in Ireland who later joined the Coolmore broodmare band there. It wasn't until the mid 2000s that he joined the Magnier and Tabor partnership buying yearlings and, as the saying goes, the rest is history.

Over 30 Classic winners and 100 plus Group 1 wins later, Smith has enjoyed every moment living the dream. For a proud Londoner from modest beginnings, the memory of being presented to the Queen in the Royal Box at Epsom two years running when Camelot and Pour Moi won their Derbies will live with him forever.

He loves to see these great horses race, as does Tabor, and in recent years they have been instrumental in quietly pushing to keep some of them in training as four year olds when Coolmore would usually want to pack them off to stud for stallion duty at the earliest possible moment.

While the racehorses at Ballydoyle and the stallions at Coolmore have been more than playing their part in the latest golden era for Magnier, the big picture has been completed by the financial rude health of The Boss and his close associates in their vast business ventures away from horses. Magnier, McManus, Tabor and Smith often combine in property investments, share dealing and currency speculation. They all have palatial homes in Barbados and other significant property holdings all over the world.

Magnier has a villa in Spain in the same neighbourhood as fellow tycoons Alan Sugar, Michael Smurfit and John Fredriksen, a Norwegian-born Cypriot who owns the world's largest oil tanker fleet and has a personal fortune estimated at £14.3 billion. He has homes in London and Switzerland to go with the mansion on Coolmore Stud, which has a secure underground unit built to protect him and his family in the event of any attempted kidnapping by the IRA, who abducted the Epsom Derby winner Shergar and businessman Ben Dunne in the early 1980s and demanded ransoms for their release.

McManus also has luxury gaffs on Lake Geneva and in Ireland and reportedly keeps a permanent luxury suite at a top London hotel. Tabor spends much of his time as a tax exile in Monaco and Smith was originally a tax exile on the Isle of Man. Another member of this incredibly wealthy and powerful clan is Dermot Desmond, or 'The Kaiser' as he is sometimes known after the emperors who once ruled Germany. They also have links to Joe Lewis, the doyen of English-born currency traders, who is a tax exile in the Bahamas.

The Irish Independent and the Sunday Times employ teams of financial journalists to track down the assets and investments which give an indication of the standing of the super wealthy in their Rich Lists published annually. The Independent claimed in 2011 that John Magnier could be worth several billions but that his wealth is difficult to tie down because of the maze of offshore companies and trusts that control his business empire. They have said the true value of his wealth could easily be double, and more, their estimate of €1.02 billion. For example, they tracked down a £35 million stake in Jazz Pharmaceuticals, held through a British Virgin Islands company called Acomita, which reaped him huge profits.

Aside from horse trading at Coolmore, 67 year old Magnier is known as a sharp and shrewd investor, owning a stake in the €600 million Sandy Lane Resort in Barbados, a €245 million share of the Mitchells and Butlers pub chain in the UK as well as an interest in Barchester - one of the largest nursing home chains in the UK - where he was estimated to have netted a £100 million dividend payment when the company refinanced its £1 billion debt pile. He has extensive property interests with McManus, whom he also famously teamed up with to buy a large stake in Manchester United which gave them huge profits and unwelcome publicity when Magnier fell out with manager Ferguson over the breeding rights to Rock Of Gibraltar.

The Independent's report in 2015 said: "Magnier also has a £60 million valued home in Marbella which he developed a decade ago as well as a lakeside home in Geneva. The Coolmore boss and his wife Susan were listed among ARTnews magazine's ten most important art collectors a few years ago. They own a €50 million Modigliani and a €20 million Joshua Reynolds as well as a Giacometti sculpture." He was conservatively listed as the 12th richest person in Ireland. He stays out of the limelight, favouring the discrete company of his equally low profile super rich inner circle.

Three slots ahead of him was his principal ally in that inner circle, 63 year old McManus, who increased his wealth by €50 million since the 2014 list was published and is now estimated to be worth €1.05 billion. Everyone knows JP started out as a gambler and a bookie, but he has made far more money gambling on currency and financial derivatives from his Geneva trading centre. He is a major investor in property, often with fellow Limerick man Aidan Brooks, and is involved in the €250 million Unilever HQ in London as well as a highly valued block of real estate by Place de Vendome in Paris.

He has his well publicised mock Georgian mansion in Martinstown, Limerick, believed to be the biggest private residence in Ireland and valued at over €50 million, and also paid €10 million for Bernard McNamara's home, replete with a dance floor and swimming pool, on Dublin's exclusive Ailesbury Road. He is also into Mitchells & Butlers and Barchester with Magnier. McManus treated himself to a new €55 million Gulfstream G650 jet in 2014.

Desmond, another Irishman now domiciled in Switzerland, is the man acknowledged to have the midas touch, as his spectacularly successful investments have demonstrated over many years. He bought London City Airport for €30 million in 1995 and sold it for €1 billion ten years later, an investment Magnier and McManus were also believed to be involved in.

NCB Stockbrokers, which he started from scratch in the early 1980s and then sold for nearly €50 million, started him on his way. His place in Irish financial history is assured as the mastermind behind the influential Irish Financial Services Centre in Dublin.

He has owned stakes in Manchester United and Eddie Jordan's Formula One racing team and currently is the biggest shareholder in Celtic Football Club. He is in the Sandy Lane complex in Barbados with the rest of the lads and has an €120 million stake in Mountain Province Diamonds, which is developing one of the world's biggest diamond mines in northern Canada. Sixty four year old Desmond paid €147,000 to buy Mel Gibson's sword from the film Braveheart, which complements his beautifully manicured 'Three Muskateers' moustache. He owns a chunk of media group INM, parent company of the Independent Newspaper, who reckon he is currently worth €1.5 billion.

The Sunday Times magazine says Michael Tabor, 73, is worth £600 million, although an American business magazine put him at $2 billion. He has interests in property, brewing and luxury hotels, but gambling is at the core of his success. He owns the BetVictor online gaming operation, which has a £1 billion turnover, and a stake in Ladbrokes. He has a £22 million investment in the Mitchells & Butlers pubs and netted £360 million when he sold his interest in a New York skyscraper and the Next Generation of fitness clubs in the UK. He has also been very successful dealing in currency. His son Ashley founded Global Radio, the UK's largest commercial radio group.

Property and currency are the magical mix for Smith. The Times reported he has substantial property interests in Barbados and Florida "and has done well from currency trading with Joe Lewis and Michael Tabor." He is a part owner in the Sandy Lane hotel complex with Magnier, McManus, Tabor and Desmond and also shared in the fortune made from their involvement in Barchester Healthcare. Smith is valued just shy of Tabor at £590 million.

The phenomenal success of Joe Lewis has been the inspiration for many would-be currency traders and Magnier & Co have teamed up with him in some shape or form over the years. From a Jewish family, he left school at 15 to help run his father's catering business in the West End of London, expanding it by selling luxury goods to American tourists. He sold the business in the late 1970s and moved into currency trading. In September 1992, he and Hungarian born George Soros bet heavily on the pound crashing out of the European Exchange Rate Mechanism.

When it happened on 16 September - Black Wednesday - it made Lewis seriously wealthy. Soros was reported to have made £1 billion and was dubbed the man who broke the Bank of England. Some experts estimated Lewis, who preferred to keep a low profile, made even more, after which he became a tax exile in the Bahamas. Soros is currently rated one of the thirty richest people in the world, with Forbes magazine saying he is worth $23 billion, and the Times made Lewis the 26th richest in the UK with a fortune estimated to be worth £3.25 billion. Both men have given away millions to good causes. Still active in business at the age of 78, Lewis is the main investor in Tavistock Group, which owns more than 200 companies in 15 countries.

The cost of Black Wednesday to the UK, and ultimately the taxpayer, was put as high as £27 billion at the time but was probably a lot less. Lewis and Soros did nothing illegal, they just played the markets and made themselves a bucket full of cash. But when these currency devaluations occur, a few people make unimaginable profits but the loss to the country involved, which means the ordinary man and woman on the street, can be the difference between life and death.

It has been said many times in the press that McManus and Desmond made "an absolute killing" when the Mexican peso was devalued in 1995 in a major currency crisis which had a devastating effect on Latin America. McManus has never admitted or denied it when asked about the story. When he was recently asked what he does in his Swiss office, he replied he does as little as possible himself but tries to get the people who work for him to do as much as possible. Desmond was quoted as saying McManus is 'a wizard' with figures, to which JP replied that was back when he was in school, where he didn't stay too long himself. He puts his success down to common sense; something never taught in schools, he said.

Who knows if the story about the killing McManus and Desmond made in Mexico is true or not, and if true they just played the system, taking full advantage of the flawed policies of the politicians and their expert advisers. There is, though, no ambiguity about what happened to the Mexican people and their economy - it suffered hyperinflation of 52% and several of the country's banks collapsed amidst widespread mortgage defaults. The country experienced severe recession, poverty and unemployment.

Extreme poverty enveloped 37% of the country's people in 1996, undoing the previous ten years of successful poverty reduction initiatives. The nation's poverty levels would not start to return to normal for another five years. Mortality rates among infants and children doubled, more seriously in regions where women had to work as a result of economic need.

This, then, is the world of currency speculation for big boys. A similar scenario will be played out in Greece for the next five years or more. Somebody will have gorged themselves on the Greeks' troubles. The Independent reported as far back as 2012 that Desmond was heavily involved in Greece's precarious position. "Market chatter suggests that he's been extremely active on sovereign bond markets making major bets on whether countries such as Greece or Spain will default," it said.

But not everyone has been happy about the role played by currency speculators. George Soros was accused of triggering the Asian currency plunge of 1997, which brought this damning verdict from Professor Paul Krugman, one of the most influential economists in America and winner of the Nobel Prize in Economics: "Nobody who has read a business magazine in the last few years can be unaware that these days there really are investors who not only move money in anticipation of a currency crisis, but actually do their best to trigger that crisis for fun and profit."

While Mexico lost, Ireland has surely gained, because McManus has given away millions of his wealth supporting good causes with his JP McManus Foundation. He has helped keep a lot of people in racing jobs with the hundreds of horses he has in training with so many different trainers, particularly in the recession post 2009.

McManus and Magnier are joined at the hip in just about everything they do. JP eventually followed the well worn trail of the super rich and became a tax exile in Barbados, where he bought Robert Sangster's old villa and then spent €150 million renovating and expanding it. Labourers were brought in from India, Pakistan and Afghanistan to work night and day with contsruction workers and interior design experts from the UK, German, France and the Caribbean Islands. Middle Eastern expertise was needed to create reception areas in marble and glassblowers were used to create magnificent bespoke chandeliers.

Local workers skilled in the use of coral, which is good for absorbing water and maintaining heat, were used to insulate balconies, walls and balustrades. The project, which includes two wings and 11 huge ensuite bedrooms for JP's family, friends and VIP guests, was finished in 18 months and was ready for Christmas 2013. Some experts have claimed it is the most luxurious and expensive holiday villa anywhere in the world.

McManus was seriously miffed when questioned about being a tax exile at a student awards ceremony in the University of Limerick a year earlier. "I didn't leave this country for tax purposes. I left this country because I wanted to set up a business abroad. I paid my taxes before I left the country, in full. I didn't leave the country in order to avoid paying a tax or to avoid paying a future tax that was coming down the line," he said. "I'm proud to be Irish – and I think I'm doing the country more good by being abroad, trying to earn a few quid. If I decide to bring it back and spend it whatever way I like, at least I'm improving the economy."

Unsurprisingly, the economy needs all the help it can get and both McManus and Magnier have been readily obliging. They had teamed up in 2006 to buy Luttrellstown Castle and its 500 acres on the outskirts of Dublin and spent €20 million on a major upgrade. Dating from the early 15th century, the Castle played host to Queen Victoria when she visited Ireland and then a hundred years later another Queen Victoria became Mrs David Beckham in a glittering wedding ceremony at the 5 star resort, which also comprises a golf course and country club. The notorious Luttrell family owned the Castle for over 500 years and one of them, Henry Lawes Luttrell, was so hated for his role in suppressing the Irish Rebellion of 1798, the Dublin Post prematurely announced his death on 2 May 1811. Still very much alive, he demanded a retraction, which the newspaper printed under the headline *Public Disappointment*.

McManus and Magnier were revealed in December 2013 as the buyers of a multi-million euro land acquisition in the nearby St Edmundsbury in the Liffey Valley. It was sold at auction for €4.3 million, with the buyers wanting to remain anonymous. A local action group had been campaigning to prevent the land being bought for inappropriate development and they forced a spokesman for McManus and Magnier to come out of hiding and say they were going to farm the land.

In 2014, McManus paid €30 million for the 5 star Adare Manor Hotel and Golf Resort, set on 840 acres in County Limerick, where he has held a number of his pro-am charity golf days. He plans to spend another €30 million on a major revamp of the resort next year with the aim of turning it into the best golf course in Europe and ultimately become the venue for the Ryder Cup in 2026.

J.P. McManus is the new owner of the stunning Adare Manor

He has clearly come into a significant pile of cash in recent years. One theory that keeps getting aired is that when Sean Quinn was recklessly betting on the share price of Anglo Irish Bank in 2006 and 2007, losing €3 billion of his personal wealth ahead of the Irish banking system being brought to its knees, McManus was one of those on the other side of the deal, effectively acting as Quinn's bookmaker.

In June 2015, Magnier showed his appetite for quality land was as voracious as ever when it was revealed Coolmore were the purchasers for €4.75 million of Ravensdale House in Co Kildare, which included a period house and 223 acres of land. They said they were going to develop the farm as a stud.

Magnier was spending big in America, too. Bloodstock experts believed he paid around $40 million for the breeding rights to American Pharoah, the first horse to win the American Triple Crown since Affirmed in 1978. Owned by Ahmed Zayat, a controversial Egyptian America entrepreneur, American Pharoah will retire to Coolmore's Ashford Stud in Kentucky to begin stud duties in 2016. Zayat, 52, sold his beverages company in Egypt to Heineken in 2002, after which he moved to America and set up his racing and breeding enterprise. He is known for betting huge sums on horse racing. Huge sums will be happily taken off the world's high rollers in the gambling world if plans come

American Pharoah, the first horse for 37 years to win the American Triple Crown

off to build a mini-Las Vegas in County Tipperary. Richard Quirke, a slot-machine tycoon, has steadily bought up land around Two Mile Borris, near Thurles, as part of his plans to get a proposed €480 million casino and leisure development off the ground. In addition to the casino, a replica of the White House, a National Hunt racecourse, a 7,000 seat greyhound track, a five-star hotel, a heliport and a 15,000 seat concert venue are also planned. And a chapel. No doubt to ask for a bit of divine help before going into the casino or forgiveness on the way out.

The salt of the earth folk of Tipperary have a lot to look forward to if the rise and fall of one of Las Vegas' first hotel-casinos is anything to go by. The Riviera, which opened in 1955, has now been closed, demolished and turned into a convention centre. It had all the star cabaret acts in its early days but went downhill in the 1980s. It was rescued by an Israeli businessman who added three new attractions: a show featuring drag artists, which ran for 23 years; a topless girls show, which ran for 28 years; and one featuring speciality acts, which included an alligator wrestler named Tahar.

They had built a special cage to house the 14 foot alligator, but one day someone left the gate open and the fearsome reptile escaped. It attempted to cross the very busy Riviera Boulevard but was run over by a car. But that didn't kill it. The alligator died when Tahar spray-painted it green in an attempt to cover up the tyre tracks. They buried him in the Vegas desert, so the story goes, next to a murdered mobster.

The casino proposal has, understandably, received enthusiastic support from maverick Tipperary TD, Michael Lowry, in whose constituency the complex will be built. Mr Lowry, a close friend of Magnier's for many years, has said the developers wouldn't be relying on the banking sector to fund the project. That can only mean it will be built with private equity and no one believes in Tipperary that Magnier and his inner circle wouldn't be involved in something like this in his adopted county. The stumbling block at the moment is the government's refusal to grant the Quirke team a licence for a super casino. Few would bet against the gamblers eventually winning that argument.

Magnier, McManus and Desmond invested in the private equity company Lydian Capital Partners, which Denis Brosnan had set up when he left Kerry Group having made his fortune building it into a giant in the food industry with manufacturing plants in 19 countries. In 2006, Lydian bought a company called Castlebeck, who operated 11 independent health hospitals and 12 adult social care centres in the south east of England and over 50 sites in total, for €320 million. In the next five years, two things happened at Castlebeck. Lydian, backed by the Irish tycoons, oversaw an 80% increase in turnover at Castlebeck. Then, in 2011, just five years after they bought the company, one of their hospitals became the focus of a shocking scandal which rocked the UK health sector and the wider world.

An undercover investigation carried out by the BBC's Panorama television programme at Winterbourne View Hospital in Bristol included a secretly recorded film showing horrific scenes of abuse, for which six members of staff were eventually jailed and five others given suspended sentences after pleading guilty to a total of 38 charges of either neglect or ill-treatment. Patients with autism and learning disabilities were seen being restrained, slapped, mocked and doused with cold water, while others were assaulted in showers or encouraged to throw themselves out of the hospital's windows. Frail and confused residents had their hair pulled and eyes poked.

Winterbourne View, the star financial performer of the Castlebeck business, had its licence revoked and was immediately shut down. The Care Quality Commission carried out inspections of the remainder of the facilities operated by the company in the region and found that hundreds of people with learning disabilities and mental health problems had been subjected to inhumane and sub-standard care. Evidence was uncovered which showed residents were routinely locked in their bedrooms, taunted by staff and restrained for no good reason. Several of the Castlebeck units faced immediate closure after inspectors found they were failing to meet legally binding standards to keep vulnerable people safe from abuse and neglect. Only seven of the 23 sites Castlebeck operated met the required standards.

Denis Brosnan owns the successful thoroughbred nursery, Croom House Stud, in County Limerick, was also chairman of Horse Racing Ireland for 22 years and is a close associate of Magnier. After Panorama's revelations about Winterbourne View were shown on prime time television, Brosnan said: "We were shocked and appalled at what happened and determined that this will never happen again." No other investors from Lydian commented.

Mr Brosnan's 35 year old son, Paul, a former banker at AIB in Ireland, resigned as chairman of Castlebeck before any reports were published. The Care Quality Commission's inquiry into the scandal said Castlebeck had not met ten essential standards required by law. The Commission had abjectly failed in its regulation of Castlebeck and its chief executive, Cynthia Bower, also resigned.

Others who presented official reports were more forthright. An independent report produced for South Gloucestershire Safeguarding Adults Board said the private hospital group owned by the wealthy Irish investors had failed to "address corporate responsibility at the highest level" for the ill-treatment of patients. "The abuse resulted from serious and sustained failings in the management procedures of Castlebeck Ltd. Castlebeck appears to have made decisions about profitability, including shareholder returns, over and above decisions about the effective and humane delivery of assessment, treatment and rehabilitation."

Winterbourne View, it pointed out, was planned before Lydian bought Castlebeck but did not become operational until after they owned the company. "Although Castlebeck Ltd claimed high ideals, it has subsequently claimed little knowledge of events at Winterbourne. This plea is not compelling," the report stated. Managers had failed to respond to a whistleblower's allegations made six months before the Panorama investigation or to the 29 occasions police visited the hospital as a result of complaints made about the way patients were being treated.

The report's authors added that an attempt had been made to understand the ownership of Castlebeck but they couldn't make sense of it. All they knew was that one strand of the business, Lydian Capital Advisers, operated from Geneva in Switzerland, and they advised another strand, Lydian Capital Partners, which is based in Jersey. Both countries are tax havens. "Is this a fit organisation to provide health care?" they asked. "Well, the board appeared to melt away when the Panorama programme was broadcast. The regulators would do well to consider complex ownership structures and ask: is this the right way to run a health care business which is entirely reliant on public funding?"

The review of the Winterbourne View scandal by the Care Quality Commission condemned the hospital's owners for putting profits before care. Their report revealed systematic failings across Castlebeck's homes, including widespread use of untrained staff and failure to inform the authorities about incidents of possible abuse or injury. At some homes carers regularly worked 12 hour shifts without a break. Many vulnerable residents were given no say in their lives. The National Health Service watchdog said it was misled by the owners of the private hospital where the safety of its vulnerable adult patients were put at risk by a "culture of abuse." Castlebeck, which had an annual turnover in excess of £80 million, charged £3,500 a week for each resident, which was paid by the NHS and local authorities. Condemnation of the Irish tycoons was equally scathing in the media. The Independent said:

"It is a long way from Ireland's Coolmore Stud to Winterbourne View in Bristol. But the two are linked by a fat trail of cash. JP McManus and John Magnier, the two Irish investors who turn out to own a stake in the Bristol care home at the centre of this week's abuse scandal, are best known for going to war with the Manchester United manager, Alex Ferguson, over the bloodstock rights to the racehorse, Rock Of Gibraltar. It's a safe assumption that the pair, who made their fortunes out of racing, did not invest in the disabled care sector with philanthropy foremost in their minds."

In fairness, the newspaper said, not all privately owned homes are dens of abuse and neglect. "But ownership does matter. There needs to be a fit and proper persons test for those who want to make money out of providing services for the vulnerable and the elderly. When private investors seek to buy into the care home sector we must ask ourselves a simple question before giving the green light: would we entrust our own grandmother with these people?"

A spokesperson for Mr Brosnan and the other investors said extensive changes were quickly implemented, including a new board of directors with a new executive chairman who had extensive experience of the care sector. Managers were now engaging with patients and staff, monitoring of patients had been overhauled and investment had been made in staff training.

The official inquiry heard harrowing stories of how the legacy of suffering lives on for those patients who were ill-treated in Westbourne View. It chronicled the litany of abuses carried out on the patients, whose lives could not have been more different from the wealthy investors who owned the hospital.

Ida had a troubled childhood, she dropped out of school and often harmed herself. As an adult she was raped, had an abortion and was belatedly diagnosed with autism. As if all that wasn't enough, she ended up in Winterbourne View. Another patient, Don, also autistic, longed to go back home. His family were desperate to get him out for a home visit but they were threatened if he didn't return he would be sectioned in a secure mental unit. He talked continually of being restrained.

Simone, an 18 year old who suffered from a generic abnormality, was repeatedly put under cold showers. On one particular day, the film showed she had two cold showers and in between was taken out into the garden, in temperatures just above freezing, and had jugs of cold water poured over her head. She was only taken back inside when she lay on the ground convulsing with cold.

Tom's condition deteriorated badly when he saw the TV images of the abuse when the programme was aired on the 31 May 2012. He told his mother: "I told you, Mum, didn't I? I told you this was happening." His mother had complained to the home's manager but nothing was done. Even after he had been moved away from Winterbourne, Tom burned the clothes from the time he was in the hospital in an effort to get rid of all the memories. The report says that he would urinate into cups. The male member of staff assigned to look after him wouldn't let him go to the toilet, he had to use cups in his room. Tom would have nightmares about his tormentor. The tension in him would build up and he would explode. He became so distressed that he had to be placed in a secure mental unit. His mother said all he ever wanted to know was if his fellow patients at Winterbourne "are all right."

The company said at the time it was shocked and ashamed about what happened. It called in a specialist to try and turn the operation around so it could be sold. They said they spent £8 million on improvements but couldn't find a buyer. When they bought it for £255 million in 2006, it was regarded as the UK's leading provider of specialist services for adults with learning disabilities and complex needs. After it was taken over by Lydian and its millionaires and billionaires, it boasted of its five fold growth in value in just four years. The Panorama exposé demolished the company's reputation and shredded its value.

Castlebeck was put into administration in March 2013 when it could no longer service its debts. Six months later it was bought for a mere £35 million by Danshell, a care operator from Scotland. The Financial Times said the company had effectively been owned by the banks, led by RBS, in the wake of the Winterbourne View scandal. It was £448 million in debt, which included over £220 million owed to its bankers and over £200 million to its investors.

Casterbridge Care, a pre-school nursery operation Paul Brosnan was credited with building up into 26 sites looking after almost 2,500 children, was also in the Lydian Capital Partners'

portfolio of investments. On the morning of 7 November 2007, two year old Rhiya Malin died at Casterbridge's Eton Manor Day Nursery in Chigwell, Essex, after her head became wedged between the roof and the wall of an outdoor playhouse. She was playing in the garden, as she was supposed to be, but no one saw what happened to her. It was 20 minutes after it was noticed she was missing before staff found her hanging in the playhouse.

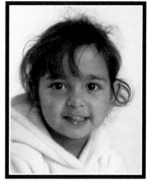

Rhiya

It took her courageous and inspirational parents, Jay and Shatl, over five years to get justice for Rhiya, which concluded at Chelmsford Crown Court when Casterbridge were fined £150,000 plus £70,000 costs and a nursery assistant £2,400 for breaches of health and safety rules. Speaking outside the court, Mr Malin said he was satisfied with the judge's decision. "A fine will never be a reflection of our loss, it's about accountability. No amount of money will ever bring Rhiya back."

It's the long, heartbreaking road the Malin family had to travel to get that accountability, when everything seemed to be against them, including the Crown Prosecution Service, the High Court and even nursery regulators Ofsted, that makes this story so special and even more heartbreaking.

Rhiya had been left without proper supervision during break time. She was eventually found in the playhouse with her head wedged between the roof and a wall. Her feet were off the ground. A toy scooter was nearby. She was taken to hospital where doctors were unable to resuscitate her. The directors of Casterbridge Care and Education Ltd released a statement, which included: "We are obviously co-operating fully with the Essex Police investigation. While we don't want to pre-judge the outcome of the investigation, this appears to have been a freak playground accident. It is a position of great privilege and responsibility to care for children and the safety and security of those children is of the utmost importance to us."

While having to try and come to terms with the loss of his beautiful, mischievous little girl, Jay would not accept what he was being told, that it was just a freak accident. The Crown Prosecution Service decided not to prosecute the owners of the nursery for causing Rhiya's death. Jay and Shatl went to the High Court in March 2010 to try and get that decision overturned. Lawyers for the family strongly criticised the fact that carers had been talking on their mobile phones while they were supposed to be supervising 13 children in the garden of Eton Manor Nursery. Lord Justice Toulson, sitting with Mr Justice Griffith Williams, said: "It reflects badly on the organisation that accepted the care of their child." But they rejected the Malins' challenge and refused permission for them to seek a judicial review. The judges said the CPS had been entitled to conclude against prosecution for negligence or manslaughter, after receiving legal advice.

Rhiya's parents found out the wooden playhouse had been modified by a handyman, with the roof permanently fixed to stop it blowing off in the wind, but it had not been risk assessed to check if it was safe to be used. They also discovered the staff member who gave Rhiya CPR had not been properly trained. They then came across another startling revelation. Casterbridge had changed the name of the company that was operating the nursery when their daughter died, so there was nothing on their record to say a child had died while in their care at Eton Manor. History had been re-written and Ofsted, the regulator, could do nothing about it. Shatl Malin held a demonstration outside Ofsted's offices in London to highlight this deplorable situation. They set up a website, Justice For Rhiya, which further raised the profile of their case and cause.

The inquest into Rhiya's death was finally held in December 2010, three years after she died. The pathologist said she suffered a heart attack due to neck compression. His view was that death would have been instant. Please let it be so. When it looked like there was nowhere else to go, Epping Forest District Council stepped in and made the unusual decision to bring the charges over breached health and safety regulations which eventually led to justice finally being delivered for Rhiya at Chelmsford Crown Court just over a year later. A council spokesman said they had listened very carefully to all the evidence at the inquest and had decided it was in the public interest to prosecute the nursery owners and two carers.

Eleanor Laing, the MP for Epping Forest and now Deputy Speaker in the House of Commons, also lead a parliamentary debate in which she slammed the nursery owners and Ofsted. She said Rhiya died in the care of a nursery which subsequently evaded an Ofsted inspection by re-registering the operation in a different name two months before their next inspection was due and were, therefore, able to wipe their record clean. Mrs Laing condemned a box-ticking culture at Ofsted which meant nurseries were not being properly regulated.

Mrs Laing told the Commons many complaints about the Eton Manor Nursery had been made before Rhiya died. "I have evidence of complaints or investigations in September 2004, April 2005, June 2005. September 2005 and September 2007. There may have been many more, but those are the ones of which I am aware. Yet nothing was done. "It is Ofsted's job to ensure a nursery is properly run and properly regulated," she said. "After five years I perceive that nothing has changed in that nursery."

"One of the most concerning issues is re-registration. Soon after little Rhiya died, the nursery in question was re-registered under a different company name. We all know about the ownership of companies and the corporate veil and so on, but it looks as if deliberate steps were taken to re-register the nursery under a different name so that the record was wiped clean, and so that prospective parents researching whether it was a suitable company and place to put their small children would not have been able to find out that a child had died."

She further alleged that in September 2008 a director of Casterbridge Care and Education Ltd applied to register the five nurseries in that company with another company, Casterbridge Nurseries Ltd. She said Casterbridge's history at Companies House showed numerous changes of names over the last five years. "The nursery is still in operation; the people who were in charge are still there; no one has been held responsible for the death; and nothing has been done to ensure that it never happens again," she said.

"In bringing the matter to the House, I pay tribute to Rhiya Malin's parents - her bereaved, heartbroken parents. They could have drawn a line under their tragedy, but they did not. They have continued to campaign and to do all they can to ensure that no other parents and little children suffer the tragedy they have suffered. I pay tribute to them for all they have done and continue to do."

A spokesman for Casterbridge said: "This re-registration with Ofsted was made as part of a conventional re-organisation of the various Casterbridge companies. It had absolutely nothing to do with Rhiya's death or with any attempt to cover up any issue."

Jay and Shatl Malin's relentless campaign and Elaine Laing's impassioned plea for justice in the House of Commons helped reform Ofsted's rules for regulating nurseries, who are now forced by law to keep their regulatory history until three years after they have closed no matter what name changes may occur. Parents are able to research that history in full with Ofsted to satisfy themselves that the people they are trusting to care for the lives of their children are capable of doing just that.

Casterbridge Care and Education Ltd and Casterbridge Nurseries Ltd admitted breaching health and safety rules and were fined a total of £150,000, plus £70,000 costs. Nursery assistant Kayley Murphy, 25, denied health and safety offences but was found guilty and fined £2,400. The nursery's manager, Karen Jacobs, was cleared by the jury. During the trial it emerged that Murphy still worked at the nursery and had been promoted three times by Casterbridge since Rhiya's death on 7 November 2007.

After the court case, Shatl Malin said: "We will never ever be at peace with what happened to Rhiya. Now I can start to remember her for all the good times without the dark cloud of the case hanging over us." She said they see a reminder of Rhiya every day - their 15 month old daughter Maya is the spitting image of her sister. "I couldn't have faced a life without a child. To me, having a child, was my purpose, you can't unknow being a mum. Having Maya has made a big difference to our lives. Of course she's not a replacement for Rhiya, but she has given us our hope back." Shatl put her successful career as a life coach on hold so that she could remain at home with Maya until she starts school.

Casterbridge are no longer a part of the investment portfolio of Lydian Capital Partners with its millionaires and billionaires. The company was sold to Bright Horizons, a leading nursery provider from the USA, in May 2012, nearly ten months before Casterbridge finally faced its day of reckoning at Chelmsford Crown Court.

One year earlier, on the morning of 30 April 2011, Aidan Purcell was found dead in a staff house on Coolmore Stud, Fethard. Four years later his family still don't know why a fit and perfectly healthy young man of twenty, with no medical history and everything to live for, decided to hang himself.

Chapter 8

CANCER BULLYING SUICIDE

CANCER BULLYING SUICIDE

"If you are going through hell,
keep going."

Winston Churchill

    I found out I had prostate cancer a couple of days after burying my mother in December 2012. She was 93 years old and I loved her dearly. She was the rock on which my family was built, enabling my father to dedicate his life to his beloved farm. If ever there was a competition for workaholics, he'd at least get to the final anywhere in the world. We had buried him only a month earlier, just short of his 92nd birthday. I had first been told I might have cancer just after I returned fom his funeral, but I had been in denial thinking there must be a mistake. I had absolutely no symptoms, I was as fit as a 62 year old flea had any right to be.

    I had been taking up Coolmore's offer for employees over fifty to have a free annual medical. If it had not been free I wouldn't have bothered as I felt fit and well and had no symptoms associated with prostate cancer. If I hadn't bothered to have those few medicals the cancer would almost certainly have been infinitely more serious by the time I felt there was something wrong with me and finally went to see a doctor. After all, at 62 time catches up with everyone and you expect to slow down a bit. My knees gave me trouble, but that was because I had played rugby every winter for twenty years and cricket every summer for thirty years, back in Cardiff. They say there is no gain without pain and the pain from the wear and tear in my knees would never overtake the joy I took away from playing those brilliant team sports for so many years.

I was a bit deaf, too, but I was always quick to tell people that wasn't because I was old and falling apart. I had been telling people that since my forties. I had first started to lose my hearing in my late teens and despite countless tests and examinations, even when my parents took me to a top expert in Harley Street in London, no one could say for sure why this was happening.

It appears the likeliest explanation goes back to when I was 13 years old and away at boarding school in Somerset. I had a chronic bout of tonsilitis which kept me in the school sick bay for nearly a month. I just couldn't shake it off and the medical staff kept shoving more and more penicilin into me. Penicilin was viewed as a wonder drug in those times and I had penicilin tablets, penicilin injections in my arse, which wasn't very nice at all, and I reckon they were putting penicilin powder on my cornflakes. I eventually recovered and forgot all about it.

Twenty years or more later the medical experts found out that too much penicilin can damage the nerve ends in the inner ear, and that's the best explanation they could ever give me. Other than that there was no explanation. I eventually became 85% deaf in both ears. It's been at that level for a long time now. Over the years it did cause a lot of frustration, but I kept reminding myself of the numerous times I went to a hospital to have tests done in the early days and saw kids there who had never been able to hear anything at all from the day they were born. And they were unlikely to ever hear anything for the rest of their lives.

They would never know what it was like to hear the first little whinny of a new foal who seconds earlier hadn't even been born; or the roar of the crowd at the Millenium Stadium when Shane Williams scored the final try of his illustrious rugby career; or Mark Knopfler's guitar soaring into the night sky at Wembley Stadium as Dire Straits paid homage to Nelson Mandela with Brothers In Arms.

I was always grateful for any mercies. In later years the unbelievable advances in digital technology has meant there are hearing aids readily available which can let you hear as if you don't have a problem at all. It's amazing, but it wasn't always like that. One thing I didn't let it stop me doing was playing sport to a decent standard.

One thing it did stop me from doing was pursuing my chosen career as a journalist. I spent six years as a reporter on the South Wales Argus in Newport, starting out as all youngsters did in those days as an indentured apprentice. By the time I left I was covering rugby internationals at Twickenham, high profile court cases and the visit of Prime Minister Harold Wilson to South Wales, a big event in those long gone days before wall-to-wall television and something called the internet. People really did rely on newspapers to tell them what was going on in the world in those distant times.

Two of my contemporaries were Michael Buerk, who went on to forge a huge career at the BBC, and Ken Follett, who became a best-selling thriller writer. I decided to go off to New Zealand, but pulled the plug on it because of my hearing difficulties. I was offered a job with the Wellington Post and wanted to spend at least a couple of years in the country who were the undisputed kings of the rugby world.

Not long before I was due to leave I was covering a murder trial involving an ex-nun (she was the murderer) and when I wrote my story up I wasn't a hundred per cent certain I had heard everything correctly. Did I hear what was said or did I imagine I'd heard it? I told my editor of the problem and he thought I was just messing him about because he knew I wanted to get off general reporting and concentrate on sport, which he didn't want me to do.

I only did sports reporting on weekends. Rather than just produce a straight report on rugby matches, I went behind the scenes and trained with the players, I wanted to know more about them as people and I thought those who read the newspaper would be interested in that too. The sports editor thought I was mad to want to do this and after one incident I thought he was probably right.

I went training one night with Cross Keys, a top level club then but not fashionable like Cardiff or Newport, who were the glamour clubs brim full with internationals and British Lions. This was the amateur era, completely different to today's professional game. They had a young player who had been on trial with Cardiff for a few weeks to see if he might make the grade in the big time. They sent him back to Cross Keys and said he didn't have what it takes. I was surprised as I'd been watching him for a while and he was often the best player on the field, even against far superior teams.

He hit me so bloody hard in a tackle in this one training session I could hardly walk for a week. When he came back from Cardiff, he played matches like a man possessed and and also trained like one. He wanted to prove everyone wrong. I went to interview him a few weeks later where he worked, in a big steel works in Newport. All he thought about was playing for Wales. The fire burning inside him was as fierce as those burning in the furnaces in the steel

221

works Newport was famous for. This guy was the complete package – he had the skills and the desire.

I told him at the end of the interview I was convinced he was good enough to play for Wales, it would come, and that's what I wrote in my column the following Saturday. I took a photograph of him at the steel works. The sports editor wasn't impressed. He said how could I, a mere twenty something, know for sure he was going to play for Wales when he wasn't even good enough for Cardiff. He didn't want to print the story so I told him to shove it and I wouldn't work for him again on weekends. He was a nice old fellow really, he just lived 20 years behind times which were changing so fast in the 70s and 80s. He ran the story in the end.

Two years later that young player was in the Welsh side, not just any Welsh side but the all-conquering team of the 1970s. Bobby Windsor scored a try on his debut as Australia were routed 24-0 at the old Cardiff Arms Park. I was there. He won 28 caps as the Welsh hooker when international teams only played four or five matches a year and played five tests for the British Lions, including the whole series in South Africa in 1974 which is still regarded as the greatest tour ever by any British rugby side.

Ireland's legendary Willie John McBride was the Lions' inspirational captain and, while everyone wholeheartedly played their part in an unbeaten series win against a brutally hard Springbok side on their home turf, it was often Windsor who was the catalyst who ensured no Lion ever took just one step back in the face of a ferocious and bloody onslaught. I have never met anyone who wanted something as much as Bobby Windsor did: to play for Wales. He is still regarded as one of the two best hookers ever to wear the Welsh shirt. He had one abiding memory of growing up in Newport as a youngster, apart from the trouble he often found himself in - he was always hungry. They were hard times for a working class family.

That hunger drove him on to make the most of himself when he found out he had ability as a rugby player. Two years older then me, I had enormous admiration for him. Later on my kids had a beautiful black labrador puppy. The deal was they could have a puppy as long as I chose the name. They weren't impressed with the name at all, but I didn't care. A deal's a deal. I called him Windsor.

While Windsor the rugby player had a reputation as being as tough as anyone the game had seen, Windsor the man was twice knocked to his knees by cancer, which put him on the slippery slope towards suicide. It doesn't matter how hard you are if cancer and depression come calling. First, cancer claimed the life of his wife, then later Windsor himself had prostate cancer. With the fight against the illness and the breakdown of his second marriage, he was in such despair he decided to end his life. But for his son coming home unexpectedly early from work one day, he would have succeeded.

Bobby Windsor in the middle of the Pontypool, Wales and British Lions front row.

Afterwards, as he dragged himself back from the abyss with the help of his family, he said he felt so much shame that he had chosen to give his life away while his first wife had fought with everything she had to hang on to hers. There are two very important lessons to be learned. Firstly, men need to be more proactive about the threat of prostate cancer and, secondly, suicide is never the answer, ever.

Ireland has the highest per centage rate of prostate cancer cases of any country in Europe. Over 3000 men are diagnosed with the disease in the country every year. It is the most common male cancer in the developed world and second only to lung cancer anywhere in the world. In Ireland, recent studies have shown it accounts for 30% of all diagnosed invasive cancers and 13% of deaths from cancer. While Ireland is ranked highest in Europe - the reason given is the unhealthy lifestyle of Irish men - its mortality rate is only 11th highest. The big difference is attributed to the use of prostate specific antigen (PSA) testing. This blood testing can help pick the problem up early so that action is taken sooner rather than later. While the medical profession in America and Canada have voiced doubts about the effectiveness of blood testing, the statisics in Ireland say the opposite. That's how it worked out for me.

When cancer is present in the prostate gland, a blood test can indicate that presence by the level of antigens produced by the cancer. Antigens are a substance which can stimulate the immune system and a high volume in the blood can indicate the possibility of cancer. Its not a definite diagnosis: that comes with an internal examination and a biopsy, but it can give an early warning signal that something might be wrong and further tests are recommended. The bottom line, as with any medical condition, is often how good the professionals are dealing with any individual case. In my story, which throughout concerned the country's general health service, the people who treated me were fantastic.

It started with the small town practice of Dr Molly Owen in Fethard. It's small, but personal. They carry out the medicals for Coolmore staff and took my blood samples for analysis at Waterford Hospital. The PSA readings for those samples over four years were low for any indication of prostate cancer. Without getting too technical, they were between 3.00 and 6.00 on the scale used to measure antigens in the blood.

Dr Owen called me in one day and said although there was absolutely no sign at all I had cancer, including after internal examination, the underlying trend was the readings had been creeping up, albeit at very small and outwardly insignificant amounts. She suggested I go down to the oncology department at Waterford and have them check me out "just to make sure." It would take 3 to 6 months to get an appointment, she said, so let's get started now rather than wait another year when our request for an appointment might be more urgent. I was at the vulnerable age for prostate cancer.

I was given an appointment within four months and just before I went to Waterford I had another blood test, which showed the PSA level had gone back down to 4.00. Was there really a need for me to go down to Waterford after that result, I asked the surgery? Absolutely, they said, keep the appointment. Then my father died and I went back to Wales for a week. While it was sad to lose him I was actually glad for him he'd gone. He was in very poor health the last few years and it was a blessing he was out of it.

I met oncologist Dr Frank O'Brien and his team at University Hospital Waterford. When he was asking me about my job working in Coolmore's foaling team, he turned to the nurse and said: "He's one of us, an obstetrician, look after him!" I told them I would be more like an assistant mid-wife, the one who smacked the baby on the bottom after all the difficult work had been done. Their genuine interest and sense of humour put me at ease for what was to follow. His assistant first examined me and said to stay where I was for a minute while she got Dr O'Brien to examine me, which was a little disconcerting.

The news was not what I had expected. They both could feel two very small lumps on my prostate and I needed to have a biopsy to find out whether they were malignant or benign. The staff were excellent to talk to, they said the lumps might not be cancerous but if they were there were several very effective treatment options available. We can sort this out, was their always positive mantra. If you are going to get cancer, Dr O'Brien said, the one you want is prostate cancer, which cheered me up for a few minutes.

I didn't really give it too much thought, though. I didn't have any of the usual symptoms they said I should have in a situation like this. I felt fit and well and didn't believe I had cancer at all; the biopsy would show that, I told myself. I received notice of an appointment for the biopsy one month ahead. I had told my mother I would go back and stay with her for Christmas week – I had worked every one since I started at Coolmore so that my younger colleagues with families could have a few days off instead. This one was going to be different and my mother was so happy I would be going back at that time when we had not long lost my father. Within a week we lost her, too. She had a kidney infection and, I think, with my father gone she just didn't have any fight left in her. I went home for the funeral and on the way back to Coolmore stopped over in Waterford for the night in readyness for my biopsy early the next morning.

I was told it wasn't painful, a feeling like tapping your finger on the back of your wrist. And it wasn't painful at all, just a bit uncomfortable is how

I would describe it. There were three or four in the team and one of them came and sat by me while the rest were going about their business behind me. She asked me about my work and she told me she lived close to Henry De Bromhead's training yard at Knockeen just outside Waterford and would often see his string of racehorses. I'd also get the occasional question or comment about Coolmore from someone in the team behind me. So there I was, lying in Waterford Hospital with a rod up my bottom chatting about Henry De Bromhead's racehorses. The time flew by. Thanks Henry!

I didn't have to wait long before going back down to UHW to get the results. Twelve samples had been taken and two were positive for cancer. I had been slowly coming around to the idea this was going to be the result, but it was still a shock. Dr O'Brien and his team knew what they were doing when they first found the two small lumps. They weren't surprised at the outcome, but they were very positive about dealing with it. We had got it very early, Dr O'Brien said, and the two positive samples showed the cancer was low grade. There was much they could do.

He explained all the options and was brilliant to talk to. He said he was going to refer me to an expert from the Whitfield Hospital in Waterford for my next consultation as they would be able to advise me best on the right treatment. I was in a bit of a daze for a day, but then told myself to just get on and deal with it. What else was there to do? I googled Whitfield and found out that here in Ireland we have a world class cancer clinic, something I didn't know before. That gave me a lot of encouragement.

The appointment with Dr Dayle Hacking was just what I needed. You realised immediately this fellow knew what he was talking about and in that way many South Africans seem to have he looked you in the eye and told you it straight, no bullshit. I had already done a lot of research on the internet and I knew the way I wanted to go with my treatment, as long as he thought it was the right way.

He explained the three main options; surgery to remove the prostate gland completely, external radiotherapy often combined with hormone treatment and brachytherapy, the insertion of up to 120 radioactive pellets into the prostate which would kill the cancer over 12 months or so.

Removing the prostate completely by surgery is a major operation and is more likely to be recommended for advanced cancer and if the patient is under

60 years old. It can make you impotent and incontinent, but you are assured the cancer has been eradicated. I told him, funnily enough, at 62 years of age I was thinking maybe it was time I was cutting down on the sex anyway. Perhaps I could get a dog and go for walks instead. He and his asistant laughed when I said I'd had a great time of it but maybe my best days were behind me. The one thing that really scared me at that age, which is still quite young really, was being incontinent. I was fit and active, I wanted to carry on with my job. I just had this vision of suddenly becoming very old. You learn to live with anything if you have to, but the mere thought of being incontinent made me shudder. It can be the same situation with the radiotherapy and hormone treatment, though it's less intrusive than the surgery and the nasty side effects should be less.

Brachytherapy is the least invasive of the lot and usually has the least side effects. It is only suitable for those with an early diagnosis and low grade cancer. I desperately wanted Dr Hacking to tell me this was the one for me. While consultants will express an opinion in these circumstances, it is the patient with the cancer who must ultimately decide which way he wants to go. I was in the grey area between 60 and 65; it was really up to me, surgery or brachytherapy. I said I would go the brachytherapy route and he agreed with me. He said it would cost E18,000 to have the procedure caried out privately at the Whitfield Clinic but they weren't able to do it through the public health service. The HSE have their own brachytherapy units in Ireland and have been providing this treatment for some years, particularly in Dublin. It was disappointmenting to hear I couldn't be treated at Whitfield.

Dr Hacking had been carrying out brachytherapy treatment for many years and he so impressed me I would have started the treatment there and then if I could. But he said the HSE had recently opened a new unit at Cork University Hospital specifically for this treatment, he had helped train the man runnng it, Dr Paul Kelly, and he would have no hesitation in recommending him. "He's a good man, he will look after you," he said. Within a few weeks, I was at CUH being assessed by Dr Kelly, who was everything Dr Hacking said he was. He told me I was well suited for the brachytherapy treatment and he could fit me in quickly.

I first had to have a digital outline of the size and shape of my prostate put on a computer so that Dr Kelly could work out where to insert the radioactive pellets to make sure it was all evenly covered. In particular, the area with the two lumps which had tested positive for cancer had to receive sufficient attention. It took quite a bit longer than he had said it was going to take - he told me he had done the procedure twice to make sure it was perfect. That made me feel really good. I asked him if I could just finish the foaling season at Ballintemple Farm. No problem he said, and we agreed on 30 May. Two days after we had our last foal I was on my way to Cork.

It all went very smoothly. There I was, chatting to the anaesthetist about racing, and the next thing I was waking up afterwards. It took a few hours to insert a hundred of the radioactive pellets into my prostate and at the end of the day I was ready to leave the hospital. When I said goodbye to Dr Kelly I said thanks so much for everything but, nothing personal, I hoped I would never see him again. They were a brilliant bunch at CUH. Looking around at the some of the chronically ill people going in and out of the hospital, I thought I was so lucky to be fit and healthy, even though I was there for cancer treatment. I just didn't see myself as being ill.

I took three weeks off and was ready to go back to work. I ached a bit here and there but the recuperation went according to plan. For the next two years I went back down to Cork every six months to be assessed and everything was perfect. I had next to no side effects and the PSA blood readings were around the 1.00 mark. I now need only go back once a year for a check-up. All the way along I was told I was the perfect blueprint for how the HSE wanted to deal with prostate cancer in Ireland. I didn't intend it to be that way, it just happened. You can, though, see what they mean.

I was having an annual PSA blood test; Dr Molly Owen said go and get checked out just to make sure; the specialist oncologist, Dr Frank O'Brien, found two small lumps when others said they couldn't find any; Dr Dayle Hacking was another expert in a world class cancer clinic who was able to advise and give you confidence; and Dr Paul Kelly's brachytherapy unit is there to give the least invasive treatment if only those diagnosed with prostate cancer can get to him early enough, before it takes a strong hold.

From the moment Dr O'Brien found those two small lumps to when Dr Kelly inserted the radioactive pellets to kill the cancer was six months. I know I have been very, very lucky to have everything fall into place like this. I also know, from my own personal point of view, you can never tell what is going to happen in the next five, ten or fifteen years. But whatever happens, happens.

There are many problems within the HSE, or the public health service in any country, and they will still, rightly, get plenty of bad publicity when they get it wrong. When they get it right, that story also needs to be told. All those involved got my story not just right, but spectacularly right. Thanks to each and every one of them.

Any story is better for a twist in the tale. When I was researching all I could find out on the internet about prostate cancer, I came across information which showed that the night work schedule I carried out at Coolmore for eight years could have been the cause of my cancer. Furthermore, the men and women still there working the hours I was doing are continuing to put themselves at serious risk. In December 2010, the World Health Organisation classified night work as a carcinogen, which is defined as anything which is capable of causing or promoting cancer. Cigarettes are probably the most infamous carcinogen, followed by pesticides.

An expert working group for the WHO examined numerous studies, including one carried out by a nursing college in America which found a high risk of cancer among nurses who worked nights, even a few shifts a month. Scientists in Denmark found a direct link between night work and breast cancer in women. Further studies reveal men who work nights have a significantly increased risk of developing prostate cancer.

The explanation for this is straightforward. Working at night alters normal sleep patterns and suppresses production of the hormone melatonin. As the sun goes down and it gets dark, melatonin levels normally increase in preparation for sleep, but the body does not generate as much of it if you are working at night and have the lights on. This vitally important hormone helps prevent cancer and the body is at far greater risk from this desperate disease when levels aren't high enough.

The scientists who prepared the report for the WHO said: "It's a concern. As generations continue to try and work 24 hours a day to provide services, we will need to find ways to protect people." Everyone has to take this more seriously, not least because the Danish government has started paying compensation, following a landmark ruling by the International Agency for Research on Cancer, to women who have developed breast cancer when working nights. Companies are going to get sued.

Munster MEP Kathy Sinnott also sounded the alarm in Ireland about the dangers of cancer on the night shift, saying research has shown it is vital to get the balance right between day and night. Cutting down the number of hours people work at night, getting enough sleep and seeing enough daylight on days off are critical to staying healthy, she said.

I was working 50 hours a week at night for six months every foaling season for eight years when the law states I should have been only doing 39 hours. The Organisation of Working Time Act 1997 states night workers must not work more than eight hours in a 24 hour period if the job involves working in a physically or mentally demanding environment. Working with mares before, during and after foaling is both physically and mentally demanding.

I didn't get very far when I gave all this information about the dangers of night work to three managers at Coolmore. The health and safety manager emailed me: "In relation to working hours for night staff, please note that the actual working night is 9 hours. Therefore when working 5 nights on and 2 nights off this results in a 45 hour working week. The risk assessment did not highlight any special hazards." The safety manager was knocking off one hour a night as break time and not working time. The break was still taken at night, the whole point of what I was saying. Even a 45 hour hour week at night is breaking the law.

The evidence at Coolmore is irrefutable. The three longest serving night men there in the last twenty years have all had serious health issues. Another man who had clocked up many hours in the foaling barn was diagnosed with cancer in 2015. In my own case, something then happened which surprised and pleased the staff at CUH and emphasised even more what I had been saying to Coolmore's managers. The first four PSA blood tests I took after my treatment were all around the 1.00 mark, which is good. Five months after I finished working nights and left Coolmore my next blood test revealed a reading of 0.49 – a 50% reduction. CUH were very surprised as they had previously told me it was unlikely to go any lower than 1.00; they put the change down to me not working nights any more.

Horses mostly foal at night and mares and foals need expert supervision during that time, particularly at a big farm like Coolmore where the four main foaling barns and yards foal around 450 mares a season and the stock coming through the barn where I was working every January to June would be worth over E100 million. The job is an essential part of stud farm work, but employers are required by law to make that work safe. Derek Bailey, the manager at

Ballintemple Farm, said in a meeting we had about safety: "You don't have to do this work. The girls aren't being forced to do nights." That sums up the attitude: if you don't do it we'll get somebody else who will. That's thirty years behind the times. I loved the job and wanted to keep doing it. All I wanted was to make it as safe as possible, for everyone's benefit. It's the law.

The law in Ireland was very important in my efforts to get Coolmore to adopt the correct bullying policy and to have a risk assessment for night work carried out. I was just standing up for my rights. I received an email from the Health & Safety Authority in November 2014 which said that Coolmore had finally produced a bullying policy the HSA was prepared to accept – seven months after I had first made a complaint I was being bullied by a senior manager, who is no longer employed by Coolmore. Their original bullying policy was a complete mess. They had been forced to re-write it twice before the HSA were prepared to gave it the green light.

By then my complaint had already been investigated. Coolmore Stud was exonerated of any wrongdoing and my behaviour in fighting for my and my workmates' rights was deemed to be unacceptable to any employer. I was doomed. The judge was putting on the black cap. When I first made a complaint, Coolmore wanted it to be invesitigated by David Gleeson, the stud's operations manager and a close working colleague of the man I had complained about. I said this wasn't fair at all and I had a right to have my complaint investigated by an independent outside expert.

They only agreed to this when I said I was going to take it up with the HSA and the Rights Commisioner Service. The expert they chose was Tommy Cummins, of Adare Human Resources Management, Dublin. I agreed to Mr Cummins because he showed me a letter from the Labour Relations Comission's chief executive, Mr Kieran Mulvey, which said Mr Cummins was suitably qualified and recommended for this role.

I was told he had written an article in the Irish Field warning employers that bullying was on the increase in the workplace and it was imperative they had the correct procedures in place for dealing with it and that they followed those procedures to the letter. Coolmore didn't have the correct procedures in place - they made it up as they went along.

I had nothing but trouble with Mr Cummins throughout his investigation, which went on for six long months. One month is the usual timeline for something like this. I twice had to get him to re-write his summary of the evidence I had given him because it bore little resemblance to what I had actually said. He reneged on the written agreement we had reached before his investigation started on how witnesses for both sides were to be interviewed. Not unreasonably, I wanted all interviews to be carried out in the same format and with the same rules for both sides. We agreed this before we started out, but it didn't happen. Two of the Coolmore witnesses, which included six senior managers lined up against me, were even present at the same interview.

He introduced what he said was confidential information from David Gleeson which I wasn't allowed to see. I discovered afterwards Mr Cummins kept two or three mares of his own and they would visit major studs to be covered by stallions. I also found out he described himself on a business website as a successful thoroughbred racehorse owner and breeder in the UK and Ireland with an "interest in the international bloodstock industry with a particular view of employment creation in Ireland." He clearly believed himself to be of some importance in the thoroughbred world and there was an obvious conflict of interest which he didn't declare at the outset. There was only ever going to be one outcome to this investigation.

I heard one other startling revelation at this time. I saw area manager Paraic Dolan one day and he said: "You are not alone. There are other similar complaints about bullying in." He wouldn't say any more. I then found out there had been at least four other complaints against the same manager, which I had known nothing about.

I told Mr Cummins he was not independent and had conducted my investigation in an unfair and totally biased way. I told him he should withdraw, which he refused to do. Instead, he supplied a verdict which said the manager I had complained about had no case to answer, Coolmore had complied with their duty of care at all times and my complaint had not been submitted in good faith. This was despite Coolmore not having an acceptable bullying policy in place until seven months after I first made my complaint and that they finally introduced a major re-write of the safety procedures for night work, the core of the bullying situation, 11 months after I had first raised concerns. Sixteen new rules for night work were eventually introduced with immediate effect – all because of the improvements I had campaigned for. But my complaint had not been submitted in good faith, Mr Cummins said.

So I took my case to the Rights Commissioners Service, who are part of the Labour Relations Commission, a government agency which is truly independent. Mr Jim O'Connell, the Rights Commissioner who heard my case, was a very firm investigator. More important than anything else, he showed throughout that he was a man of honesty and integrity and he brokered a deal between Coolmore and myself. I am restricted as to what I can say and am not allowed to disclose the details of the agreement we reached.

It had been an extremely stressful time. It was now nearly nine months from when I first made a complaint about management bullying to when the Rights Commissioner finalised an agreement. I had not gone into this exercise for money; just a bit of ordinary, every day respect for people who do a difficult job at night with real commitment and bags of skill. We wanted to go to work in a safe environment with a support structure in place so if we were ever in trouble we could get help quickly. I was bullied because I stood up for those rights.

I had six senior managers giving evidence against me in the so-called independent investigation. When I came to the two Rights Commissioner hearings, I was opposed by a senior partner in Arthur Cox solicitors, one of the top five law firms in Ireland with offices in Dublin, Belfast, London, New York and Silicon Valley. He charges €2000 an hour for his services. I continued to do my night job, researching and preparing my case for the investigation and the subsequent Rights Commissioner hearing around it. I could never have afforded a solicitor to assist me with all this, which is why I did everything myself right from the start. I only asked a solicitor one piece of advice - about my legal position because I didn't have a valid contract of employment, and that cost me €100. It's easy to see why people are reluctant to stand up for their rights as the potential costs are prohibitive. There really is one law for the rich and one for the poor.

There is no support system within Coolmore for these situations. Trade unions or any representative body aren't allowed. I was told I could take a work colleague along with me to any meetings, but I never asked anyone. To be associated with any kind of dispute or grievance like this inside the farm would have serious ramifications for anyone involved no matter what the outcome. Coolmore are in complete control.

My former colleague Josie is a perfect example of what can happen if you put your hand up to support a workmate. She eventually got her job back in November 2014 after she had been wrongly let go at the end of the foaling season the previous May, but she was then let go again at the end of the 2015 foaling season. Others who had been employed since she first started at Coolmore were kept on in her place. Manager Bailey admitted to her that the reason she was let go and was now only working seasonally instead of permanently was because she had been involved in the campaign to improve safety for night work. It was to teach her, and anyone else, a lesson: that's what happens if you stand up to Coolmore.

One of the safety procedures we had asked the managers to evaluate was a man down device. It's like a small mobile phone attached to a belt you wear. One quick click of a switch and a message would be immediately sent to the farm's 24 hour security office alerting them a night worker was in trouble and needed instant help. It could be because of an incident with a horse or with an intruder.

Farms and houses in the Fethard area are regularly broken into by thieves; in one case a gang came down from Dublin in the middle of the night and threatened to cut the fingers off the children of a family they terrorised and robbed in Killenaule. The gang of seven were eventually jailed for up to 20 years each for the horror attack. Night staff call regularly to Killenaule checking mares boarded for Coolmore at Demi O'Byrne's stud farm there.

We felt it was important to have a support system in place which could summon immediate help for any emergency, particularly for the six female staff who are out checking isolated farms on their own in the middle of the night during the foaling season. One of the other benefits of this device is that it sends an alert if it detects there is no movement from the worker for fifteen or twenty minutes. So, if that person has had an accident and is unconscious, he or she is not left lying there for hours - there's support always in place to check lone workers are safe.

Night work is tiring, particularly if you are on your own, it's easy to fall asleep. Security staff have written off two jeeps in the last few years because the drivers fell asleep at the wheel at night. At the end of the 2015 season, one man working on his own for 10 hours in a foaling barn fell asleep. Unfortunately, when he woke up he found a mare had foaled unattended and the foal had died. The foal was by Galileo and it belonged to John Magnier. If that man who had the misfortune to fall asleep had been wearing a man down device it would have detected there was no movement coming from him, that he wasn't out and about walking around the foaling barn, and an alert would have been sent to security. One phone call from security would have woken him up.

The man down device was Josie's idea. She could see how it could benefit the night staff at Coolmore in so many ways and

Josie and Secret Garden, dam of Classic winner Roderic O'Connor

give everyone peace of mind that help was never far away. They aren't expensive - they cost €7 a week each. It would come to just over €50 a week to cover the whole night operation for the horse staff. I gave managers all the facts but they weren't interested. I even arranged for a Canadian company, world leaders in this technology, to give us one device free of charge for a month to evaluate. I was told it was not about cost, the devices just weren't needed. They wouldn't even try one for free. If these devices had been in use when that Galileo foal was born it would likely be alive and well today. The stud fee for Galileo is at least €300,000. If the foal which died had survived and become a champion it would have been worth tens of millions.

That's what happens when you have accountants running the show: accountants with an inflated opinion of their own worth but who know next to nothing about life on the front line. They said the risk assessment carried out highlighted no special hazards at night. As this book was going to press, one of the night team was attacked and seriously assaulted in the middle of the night. It could have ended up much worse.

Josie has a new job and she won't be going back to Coolmore. We helped foal 12 Group 1 winners in the last couple of years, but it obviosuly wasn't enough. I agreed to leave in January 2015 and in the end, while I had a never-to-be-forgotten experience with the brilliant people and fantastic horses, I was happy to be driving out through the gate for the last time. In my view, the country of Ireland and its people are second to none. As you go down the ladder of life there, away from the double-dealing of the cynical politicians and the exploitation and greed of the super-rich corporate class, you find the real Ireland which enchants all visitors. People like the Purcells of Glengoole. Honest, genuine and hard working; a typical rural family just trying to make a bit of a life.

It was a moment Mary Purcell will never forget. The worst nightmare for any parent. Her son was dead. Mary was at work in the job she has done for the last 20 years, a carer at a nursing home in Killenaule. The moment she saw her parish priest, Father O'Rourke, and estranged husband, Eamon, walking towards her, she immediately knew something was badly wrong. She said to them: "Who is it? Brian?" Then she said: "Joseph? Then: "Nicola?" It was the one she never imagined getting into a scrape as serious as this. It was Aidan.

Twenty year old Aidan had been found dead not long before in the bungalow he shared with three others at a yard called Lakeview on the main farm at Coolmore Stud, just outside Fethard. It was Saturday, 30 April, 2011. He hadn't turned up for work that morning and one of his workmates had gone to give him a shout, thinking he had overslept. He was found dead in his bedroom. Lily Lawlor, the owner of the nursing home in Killenaule, immediately drove Mary to Coolmore. She couldn't go into the bungalow because the Garda were conducting an investigation. It was a crime scene until they were sure a crime hadn't been committed. An hour later she was able go and see Aidan and all she can remember is just holding him in her arms.

Four years later she and her family still don't know how or why it came to this. They have heard lots of rumours, but they need real answers. The longer it goes on without those answers the more it torments them. Mary calls every day into the cemetery in Glengoole, a small village a few miles from Thurles and a fifteen minute drive from Coolmore, to visit Aidan's grave. Every day, usually twice a day.

She won't go in there in the dark, so in the winter, with the light fading early in the afternoons, she will call in on her way to work in the mornings. She has the kind of smile which can light up a room, but it doesn't break out as often as it should. Nicola and Aidan were not only sister and brother but also best mates. They went everywhere together and did everything together. She used to jokingly call him her plus one. Whenever she was invited anywhere she would take Aidan. She keeps all his final belongings immaculately in her bedroom.

Losing someone close is bad enough for any family. To lose someone so young to suicide just seems to make it even worse. And worse again if it is totally unexpected and unexplained. Why on earth did it happen? He was in perfect health, hadn't seen a doctor for years, no physical or mental issues.

Mary had seen him three times in the week he died. Nicola and Aidan had been exchanging text messages, as they always did. He was in his usual good form, plans had been made. He last spoke with his mother two days before he was found dead. He and elder brother Brian had arranged to go to a rally at Killarney Lakes on that last Saturday in April.

It was nearly the end of the breeding season in Ireland. Aidan had made plans to go to Coolmore Australia for six months for the southern hemisphere season. His departure was still two months away and he was looking forward to it. He had already done this trip a couple of years earlier and loved it. He returned to tell his family dozens of stories of his time in Oz and had all the photographs as evidence. He wanted to be in Ireland for his own 21st birthday and Jason's First Holy Communion and then he hinted he might go back to Coolmore Australia and stay for longer.

As Nicola says – he left for Australia a boy and came back a man. He had first gone to Coolmore for work experience as a 16 year old. He progressed to working weekends on the farm and then did his first trip to their stud in the Hunter Valley, New South Wales. When he returned he became part of the furniture at Coolmore Tipperary. His grandfather still lives in Fethard.

The day before he died, Friday, Aidan had a half day off, finishing work at 12 noon. He was due to do a couple of hours work Saturday morning, then have the rest of the day off to go with Brian to Killarney. During the breeding season at this time, January to June, staff on the main farm worked every day for six months. Their time off consisted of two half days each week, usually one in the week and one on the weekend.

A typical weekend would be two or three hours work each morning from around 7am, when horses are fed, put out into paddocks and their stables mucked out. The afternoon work would consist of a couple of hours from about 2pm bringing horses back in to their stable to be fed and settled for the night. Staff would also have to be available throughout the week to take mares to be covered by the stallions from early in the morning to late in the evenings. The covering shed is open 7 days a week from 6am with the last covering in the evenings around 9pm. It's very busy during the six month breeding season: constant work.

Nothing more was seen or heard from Aidan from around the time he finished up just before 12 noon until he was found dead the following morning.

238

He had texted a couple of his friends earlier in the day to see if they could go to the beach that afternoon on his half day off, but no one was available. It was typical Aidan, always wanting to be doing something. Nicola texted him on numerous occasions that afternoon but she never received a reply. She didn't think too much of it because the plan for the weekend was written in stone; he had posted on Facebook how much he was looking forward to the trip to Killarney and she expected to see him at the family home shortly after 10am on the Saturday to see his youngest brother. It was Jason's seventh birthday. He didn't make it.

Aidan lived with three other stud staff in a bungalow adjoining Lakeview Yard on the main Coolmore Farm. Staff walked out of the bungalow into a courtyard surrounded by three lines of stables. It is typical of many similar yards dotted around the immaculately kept stud. Mares waiting to be covered by one of the Coolmore stallions are housed here during the breeding season. When he didn't turn up for work one of his colleagues went to the house to call him. She found him dead in his bedroom. As news of what happened spread staff around the barns and yards were shocked in disbelief. Very little information became available about what had happened.

But something had clearly happened to precipitate such a desperate course of action. Here was a fit and healthy young man who had made plans for the weekend; he had posted about it on Facebook; he had been trying to fix up a trip to the beach; he was looking forward to going to Australia in a couple of months; he was his usual chirpy self when last seen by his family and in the phone calls and texts he was always making all day and much of the night. None of his family had any inkling whatsoever that he might end his own life. And he didn't leave a note that might have explained it. Nothing. His life just disappeared into thin air.

It wasn't long before Mary's brother, Tony Maher, started to hear a few stories. People were telling him Aidan was being badly bullied at Coolmore. "We had to go to the coroner's office a couple of weeks later and he asked us if we wanted to say anything about what had happened to Aidan. I said we believed he was being bullied, that was why it happened. I told him what I had heard. He wrote it down and said he would look into it. I was told Coolmore keep pushing these young people to their limit, they are never satisfied with the amount of work they do," he said.

There was no follow-up. No garda ever went to the Purcell house in Glengoole and spoke to Mary. Not even to ask her how she was getting on. No questions were ever asked about what might have led Aidan to do what he did. No one from Coolmore has ever spoken to Mary about what happened, to offer any kind of explanation. The family were in deep shock and four years later they are still shocked.

"But for having Jason to think about - he was only seven then - I don't know how I would have managed," Mary said. She also had the job she loves – over twenty years working in the same nursing home in Killenaule. Some of the patients there have nothing and no one, she said. "I think about Aidan all the time every day. He's always on my mind. We want to know why it happened. We've heard rumours but that's no good. We want answers to our questions and no one has given us answers." Some of the rumours have been extremely hurtful and completely untrue, as Nicola painfully recalls:

"We heard it was being talked about in Coolmore he had a problem with drugs. That is rubbish. He was anti-drugs. That was just being said to try and put the blame somewhere else. He might have a couple of pints on a weekend but that's all he ever did. He never touched drugs. It hurt so much to hear what was being said."

She would know as she and Aidan spent much of their time together. She is fiercely protective of his memory and the post-mortem carried out on Aidan backs her up. No drugs or alcohol were detected in his blood samples. Every other test carried out showed him to be in perfect health.

The Purcell family believe the coroner, Mr Paul Morris, let them down very badly. The inquest into Aidan's death was held in Clonmel on 16 August 2011. It was over in ten minutes. The cause of death was "self-inflicted hanging." The family had made their feelings known to Mr Morris about the bullying they believed was behind this tragedy. Mr Morris said he would look into it. He asked Joe O'Dwyer, the barn foreman at Lakeview where Aidan had been working and the only person from Coolmore who provided any evidence for the inquest, if he knew anything about Aidan being bullied. He asked the same question of Aidan's father, Eamon, who had not lived in the family home for many years. They both said no. That was it. That was the sum total of the coroner "looking into" the concerns the Purcell family had previously raised.

No garda officer was asked about this. Plainly, Mr Morris had not asked the garda to investigate, the very least the Purcell family reasonably expected him to do when they told him about the bullying.

I went to meet Mr Morris at his office on behalf of the Purcell family on 8 May 2015. I had contacted them because a couple of people had approached me with information that Aidan was being bullied, including the day before he died. I had worked with him at Ballintemple Farm during the foaling season of 2010. I was, along with everyone else at Coolmore, shocked about what happened to him. I asked a lot of people a lot of questions at the time, but no one knew anything. When I was about to leave Coolmore's employment, I was approached with information I previously knew nothing about. I went up to Glengoole and met Mary and Nicola at their home to tell them about it. To tell them, according to the information I had been given, who had been bullying Aidan. My informants had emphasised I shouldn't just leave it, that it wasn't too late to do something about it.

I had requested a copy of the inquest file from the coroner's office, which they are obliged to provide by law. I told the coroner the inquest had not been told the full truth, that there were a number of inaccuracies. Important information appeared to have been deliberately withheld. In particular, no mention had been made that Aidan lived in the Coolmore bungalow with three other people. There was no mention of them anywhere in the inquest file. It appears the Garda did not know of them and, therefore, couldn't interview them as part of their investigation into an unexplained, sudden death. They either didn't know or they chose to ignore this information.

Mr Morris told me, after reviewing the file, he understood Aidan lived in the bungalow on his own. He said he believed he had been misled and if he had known in 2011 what I told him in 2015 he would have stopped the inquest and instructed the Garda to carry out a full investigation. But Tony, Mary and Nicola had told him in 2011 they believed Aidan was being bullied and that was the reason he took his own life. The Purcells believe the investigation and the inquest have been a cover-up.

After I had spoken to the coroner, Mary made a complaint directly to the Garda about the way they had investigated Aidan's death and received a reply from Superintendent William Leahy of Clonmel Station on 4

April 2015 saying he would look into what they said and get back to them. Two months went by without any word from either Mr Morris or Superintendent Leahy. Further letters were sent to them saying Mary expected the Garda to carry out a full review of the case and that Mr Morris should re-open the inquest because a serious crime may have been committed. "The grounds for doing this relate to perjury. We believe a false and untrue statement was deliberately given under oath to the coroner at the inquest," the letter stated. Another two months went by without any word from the coroner or the superintendent and Mary wrote to them yet again.

Two years after Aidan's death Mr Morris had plenty to say at a time when the suicide rate in south Co Tipperary had doubled from the previous year. Reflecting on the 18 suicides which had been recorded in his territory, he warned financial institutions and debt collectors they were breaking the law if they harass a person over debt repayment. The coroner advised people to complain to the Garda if they felt they were being harassed.

He said a number of factors contribute to suicide. "I think it's more the type of society we are living in. There is a distorted idea of what success is. I think we have to get away from the concept that the person with money is successful when that person may be living a life of desperation." As far as Aidan's suicide is concerned, the silence from Mr Morris has been deafening.

It is said those close to a suicide victim feel guilty about what happened, that they should have known there was a problem and if they did know they should have done more. Mary and Nicola didn't know Aidan had a problem with bullying at Coolmore. They are a close family and devoted to each other. It is inevitable they will think they should have known and done more, but the truth is they were doing all they could for their family, and more.

At the first anniversary of Aidan's death, Nicola paid a moving tribute to her younger brother. "There is not a lot you can't say about Aidan, he was kind and friendly, always had a big smile across his face for whoever he would meet, whether he was walking down the village, at work or cruising around in his car, you would always be greeted with a cheeky grin and a big salute." He was the baby of the family, but 13 years after him Jason came along and, as Aidan liked to put it, the baby became the babysitter.

Aidan loved kids and would often be playing with them around his home in Glengoole, especially his little brother Jason, who he doted on. From a young age he was known as 'Jacko' because of his dancing moves and took part in competitions just for the fun of it. "Many a night out we had, no matter what part of the country we hit with Aidan with us we were sure to have a laugh and a good time," Nicola said. "He went to primary school in Glengoole NS and secondary in Scoil Ruain where he made his name well known, sometimes for good reasons. With Coolmore he travelled to Australia for six months and had the time of his life, had loads of stories to tell us when he came home, all good of course."

"I have so many memories of my little brother I could stay writing for the day but I think it's safer if I stop now. The day Aidan left us he broke our hearts and although our lives will never be the same without him, looking back on all our memories and pictures, we wouldn't change any of it."

One of Aidan's workmates, Marie, came up with the idea of holding a charity walk in his memory and Nicola did much of the organising involved. The first one was held in 2014 and I mentioned it in a letter I wrote to John Magnier about staff concerns regarding safety and bullying.

"Yesterday, there was a charity walk from Coolmore in memory of Aidan Purcell, who tragically commited suicide when working here. That walk was really good, but shouldn't we be concentrating on doing more for people when they are alive rather than them have to go through this culture of oppression, bullying and victimisation."

I told him I knew some of what Aidan was going through in the months before he ended his life because I spoke with him. The last time I saw him he was exhausted from his work schedule - he didn't mention bullying - and I advised him to ask for a transfer away from the main farm, but he said he wouldn't be able to do that. I told Magnier the point I was making was if you are under so much pressure at work that might contribute to you making the kind of tragic choice that Aidan ended up with. I wrote this six months before I found out about the alleged bullying Aidan had been subjected to.

"How would the younger staff who are employed on the main farm hope to be able to deal with the kind of bullying and intimidation I have been put through if they chose to make a complaint? What would their reaction be if HR immediately told them they could be disciplined if their complaint was deemed by Coolmore to be malicious? They would walk away from it." Mr Magnier didn't reply personally though his son, MV, left a message on my mobile to say they would look into what I had said.

Like many people in Ireland, I found the story of a Kerry teenager called Donal Walsh both heartbreaking and inspirational. He was a sports mad 12 year old when a lump near his knee was diagnosed as cancerous. For the next four years he and his family fought the disease with incredible bravery. Three times it looked as if the treatment had worked, but the cancer kept coming back even stronger and it eventually claimed his precious life. In those four years he did many good things, including raising over €50,000 towards upgrading the cancer ward in the Crumlin Children's Hospital in Dublin. He stunned the audience and the rest of the country when, on the Saturday Night Show on TV, he described the archaic conditions he and other seriously sick children and their families had to endure.

He had come to national prominence when he wrote a letter about suicide and he struck a chord with Irish people of all ages as he described on live television his battle with cancer. "I wanted to live, to play for Munster, to travel the world, to raise children and die when I was 100, not 12," he said. He was angry that it seemed suicide was almost becoming accepted, particularly among young people. He and his close group of friends knew of three around their own age who had taken their lives. The South Kerry coroner said he had never before had to deal with such a spate of these tragic deaths. In 2012, Ireland had the fourth highest number of deaths by suicide in the EU among young people between the ages of fifteen and twenty four. In the year Aidan died, a total of 554 people took their own lives in the country, the highest number ever recorded. Donal wrote:

> "Yet I am here with no choice, trying as best I can to prepare my family and friends for what's about to come, and leave as little a mess as possible. I know that most of these people could be going through financial despair and have other problems in life, but I am at the depths of despair and, believe me, there is a long way to go before you get to where I am.

> For these people, no matter how bad life gets, there are no reasons bad enough to make them do this: if they slept on it or looked for help, they could find a solution, and they need to think of the consequences of what they are about to do. So please, as a 16 year old who has no say in his death sentence, who has no choice in the pain he is about to cause and who would take any chance at even a few more months on this planet, appreciate what you have, know that there are always other options and help is always there."

Donal's letter went all over the world. His remarkable composure and courage inspired a fresh debate about suicide, particularly among the younger generation, and his mother and father, Elma and Fionnbar, have carried that torch on since he passed away on 12 May 2013. Donal has made a difference in so many ways. His legacy lives on through the Donal Walsh Live Life Foundation, which runs events to raise awareness about suicide and funds for charity.

In 2013, just 38 young people attended the launch of the first Cycle Against Suicide ride organised by Kerry entrepreneur Jim Breen. One year later, Fionnbar addressed over 4,000 students at the start of the 2014 cycle ride. Pieta House, a crisis centre in Dublin for the prevention of suicide and self-harm, held its first Darkness into Light mental health awareness walk in 2009 with 400 participants. At 4.15am on Saturday, 9 May 2015, as dawn approached, more than 12,000 early risers set out from Phoenix Park to walk or run the latest version of the 5km event. Over 100,000 people took part in similar walks at 80 locations in Ireland and around the world to support Pieta House with funds to help prevent suicide.

Watch Donal's interview with Brendan O'Connor on Youtube – Donal Ryan – Saturday Night Live. This was a 16 year old who held the country in the palm of his hand. It is not just his family and friends who had their hearts broken when he died because Ireland lost a leader no matter what road in life he would have chosen to follow, if only he could have lived. And Ireland seriously needs all the leaders it can get.

Paul O'Connell, the captain of Munster, Ireland and the British Lions, is many people's idea of the ultimate inspirational leader, at least on the field of sport. He got to know Donal during his four year fight against the curse of cancer. He said: "It's not often you sit beside a 16 year old boy and feel in the presence of greatness, but that's what it was like for me with Donal Walsh."

You could also read Fionnbar's book, Donal's Mountain, but don't read it in public like I did. A few months ago I had a copy delivered in the post. It was a beautiful afternoon so I thought I'd make a start on it while having a pint in the beer garden of Mikey Ryan's pub in Cashel. The tears were soon flowing down my cheeks. The pollen count was very high that day, wasn't it?

When I mentioned to Coolmore managers my serious concerns about safety and bullying and warned that what happened to Aidan could happen again, I came up against a brick wall. David Gleeson, the operations manager, didn't want to discuss him. He said in a meeting we had on 17 July 2014: "At the end of the meeting I told Will that he had made references to a suicide in the workforce in 2011 in his various letters. I told Will that this was a very difficult chapter for the organisation to deal with and I said I felt he could make his points perfectly well without raising this painful matter and I asked Will to give some thought and consideration to this."

The pain Mr Gleeson said Coolmore felt about Aidan's death would not be a scratch on the surface of the heartbreak endured by his family, who still don't know why it happened. I said in a submission I subsequently made to the Rights Commissioner: "I ask the Commissioner to consider that Coolmore are in denial about these situations and instead of trying to cover them up they need to embrace a change of attitude so that more is done to try and ensure what happened to Aidan doesn't happen again."

This was, after all, the second time a young employee had hanged himself in this same part of Coolmore. I obtained the inquest file for that other young man, aged 25 and from Co Wexford, from the coroner's office. Two colleagues made short statements, both virtually identical. There was not one word of explanation in the file as to why he took this dreadful action. I have been told it was connected to work.

Two further tragedies involving cancer and suicide in Co Tipperary in February 2014 emphasised the desperate irony of one woman who would have given anything to live but couldn't and another who could have lived but didn't want to. Lucy Stack, the 28 year old wife of Fozzy Stack, son of trainer Tommy Stack, a close friend of John Magnier, left notes for her family and friends and planned the details of her funeral before taking her own life at her home in Golden, just down the road from Ballydoyle.

"No call could have changed this. No chats over wine. Sadly, this is just my fate. I know it's selfish and cowardly but for me it is my only option. I can't face this world any longer. I'm just not strong enough. Too much has happened," she wrote in a tragic note left for her friends.

In the same week, Tina Phelan, the 52 year old wife of Eamon, Magnier's former head stallion man since the early days of Coolmore Stud, had given her all in a desperate battle with cancer, which she finally lost. With her young family growing up and Eamon's own stud business doing well, she had everything to live for but, just like Donal Walsh, had no say in the death sentence she had been given.

It's a different kind of sentence for Aidan's family; a life sentence of heartbreak and unanswered questions. Why did it have to come to this? What happened? Why? Why?

Chapter 9

THE SOUND OF SILENCE

THE SOUND OF SILENCE

"Fools, said I, you do not know

silence like a cancer grow."

Paul Simon

Which is the better comic – The Racing Post or The Beano? It has to be The Beano, but The Racing Post is getting closer to it all the time. When my book was all but finished, I decided to place adverts in the racing press to give some advance notice about its upcoming publication. This is common practice in the industry. The Racing Post in Ireland agreed to run the advert on the first day of Royal Ascot and gave me all the details and costs involved. When I sent them an image of the advert I wanted they said they couldn't publish unless they could read and approve what was written in my book first. If they didn't like what I had written they wouldn't run the advert.

They gave a couple of reasons for this bizarre situation. One was that they published books themselves and they needed to make sure my book didn't conflict with one of their own. This was ridiculous, but when I pointed out they didn't have another book advertised on their website written by someone who had worked for nine years in Coolmore Stud, they came up with another equally silly reason for not running the advert.

I wrote to the editor, Bruce Millington, to complain that this was censorship and any real journalist wouldn't accept such a blatant abuse of freedom of speech. He didn't reply. I decided to make a complaint to the authority which regulates the press in the UK, the Independent Press Standards Organisation (IPSO). All the major newspapers and publishers volunteer to be governed by a strict code of conduct. Over 1400 print titles and over 1000 on line titles are signed up to IPSO. Anyone who is anyone in the UK publishing industry agree to uphold the highest standards. But not the Racing Post.

IPSO told me they would have been able to investigate my complaint if racing's leading newspaper was a member of their organisation. All the big papers like the Times, Mail, Telegraph and Sun are in; but not the Racing Post. Even the smallest and most obscure publications are members, such as Bob The Builder, Cross Stitch Crazy, Heating & Plumbing Monthly and Hair Ideas; but not the Racing Post. And The Beano is there, putting its hand up; but not the Racing Post. They are not bothered that much about regulation, they prefer to be a law unto themselves. It is my belief the Racing Post refused to print my advert because Coolmore Stud are a major advertiser with the paper and Magnier and his associates may even own the paper. I gave Mr Millington every opportunity to comment, but he didn't reply.

An investigation in 2013 by the data privacy watchdog Information Commission Office (ICO) also found that the Racing Post wasn't that bothered about protecting the personal data of over half a million of its customers when hackers were able to access the newspaper's supposedly secure website. Investigators discovered that the last time the Racing Post tested its website was six years before the attack, in which the names, addresses, passwords, date of birth and telephone numbers of 677,335 customers were stolen by the unidentified hackers. They had failed dismally to protect their customers' information by not keeping their IT systems up to date. They received a stern warning from the regulators but, surprisingly, escaped a fine.

The Post was set up by Sheikh Mohammed in 1986 as a rival to The Sporting Life and in 1998 the Trinity Mirror Group acquired the licence to operate the racing paper. That licence was purchased for £170 million in October 2007 by FL Partners, an Irish private equity firm. There was much speculation at the time that FL Partners were connected to Coolmore Stud.

I sent a recorded delivery letter to Mr Millington asking him who owns the Racing Post. He didn't reply. A quick check of a website connected to Companies House shows that it trades under the name of Centurycomm Ltd, which is owned by Stradbrook Holdings Ltd., which is owned by Stradbrook Acquisitions Ltd. I didn't bother to delve any deeper, it wasn't important any longer who really owns the Racing Post. I remembered what the report said into the abuse scandal at Winterbourne View in Bristol in 2011. The report's authors had tried to understand the complex ownership arrangement of the private equity firm of Irish tycoons, Lydian Capital Partners, which owned the company at the centre of the scandal. They were unable to unravel it.

As usual, it was a brilliant Royal Ascot, perhaps the best race meeting in the world. Thanks mostly to the class of jockey Ryan Moore, the Coolmore partners had five winners. Bruce Millington, this champion of freedom of speech, also enjoyed a few moments in the spotlight when presenting the trophies to the winning connections for one of the lesser races. One rule for the rich and another for the poor. He writes a column in his newspaper every thursday in which he gives his opinion on the important topics of the day. One of his articles was headlined **"Big money at the top but its tough at the bottom."** He was critical of how much the chief executive of the British Horseracing Authority earns. This from the editor of the Racing Post who dances to the tune of its rich and powerful owners.

I turned my attention to the upcoming Irish Derby, which celebrated the 150th running of the great race this year. Another good opportunity for me to publicise my book. The Irish Field's advertising department accepted the same advert I had put up to the Racing Post. They even took the money for it out of my bank account. Why wouldn't they? It was a perfectly legitimate advert, but when editor Leo Powell found out it was about Coolmore Stud he refused to run it unless he could read the book first. He needed to "verify" it, I was told. I sent him two emails over the next week remonstrating about this totally unacceptable censorship, but he didn't reply, so I made a complaint to the Press Ombudsman.

Unlike the Racing Post in the UK, the Irish Field is regulated in Ireland, but the Press Ombudsman declined to investigate my complaint because they said it didn't come under their remit. I argued back and for with them for a few days, just for a bit of fun, but they took the soft option and wriggled out of doing their job to police the press industry in Ireland. The Irish Field is a great newspaper for the country's varied equine pursuits, but they refused to run my advert in case it upset Coolmore Stud, who spend a considerable amount of money with them on advertising. They should rename it the Coolmore Irish Field, it would be a lot more honest. On page 5 of the edition for 27 June 2015, there was a report about Magnier receiving honorary life membership of the Royal Dublin Society. Written by the Coolmore Irish Field's editor, Leo Powell, Magnier was lavishly praised "for his outstanding contribution to Irish bloodstock and horse racing and his entrepreneurial spirit." Mr Powell had refused to run my advert in the same edition of the Coolmore Irish Field. That's called censorship. That's how it works in North Korea. Supreme Leader Kim Jong-un would have been impressed.

Times have changed and a stable hand's life has improved a bit in the last fifty years. But then it had a long way to come up. John Lowe became a top jockey in England, to where many Irish youngsters migrate, and he tells a story of what it was like in Newmarket when he first came down from the north to work as a young stable lad in the 1970s. "After three weeks three kids in the yard had died. One had hung himself, one got run away with when riding out and hit a tree and another was fooling around when someone threw a pitchfork that hit him in the head and killed him," he said. Lowe was just 15 years old and went back to his home city of Livepool double quick.

It's still the same old problem in Ireland in many respects, though. Stable staff, whether in racing yards or on stud farms, are often very young and with little formal education. Add in that many are foreign and a long way from home and the mix makes them soft, easy targets: ripe to be bullied and exploited. Not only is there no worthwhile organisation to look out for them, to offer them some form of protection, but racing's ruling authority, Horse Racing Ireland (HRI), seem happy to stand over this obscenity. They even appear to control it.

When I left Coolmore I decided to contact the Irish Stable Staff Association (ISSA) to find out a bit more about what they actually do. They seem to be a bit secretive. There had been a splash in the press about the Godolphin sponsored Irish Stud and Stable Staff awards. Godolphin, the racing arm of Sheikh Mohammed's empire, which does so much to support education and training in the horse industry throughout the world, had come on board for the first time, supporting the awards with hard cash – €70,000.

However, this is an empty public relations exercise which gives a completely false impression of what it's like for many stable staff in Ireland. The ISSA doesn't represent stud staff, only those who work in racing yards. Stud staff in Ireland have no one to represent them. The ISSA proclaims on its website:

"Our specific aim is to protect, advise, educate and promote the basic rights of all staff that work within the racing sector of the Irish Equine Industry."

Its a sham, a front. They only hold a couple of meetings a year, always in Kildare. They only had one meeting in the first ten months of 2015. Their archaic website said they held their latest AGM in April 2015. When I requested the minutes for that meeting I found out it never actually took place.

Bernard Caldwell has the grand title of chief executive officer and chairman of the ISSA. He also sits on the board of HRI, where he serves on four committees, which is a clear conflict of interest with his prime duty of looking after stable staff. He earned €13,000 as a director of HRI and when I asked him for details of his salary at ISSA he refused to supply them. He also refused to provide me with a copy of the associations last available accounts, for 2013.

HRI, because they receive government funding as a state body, are required to publish all their financial information and they provide excellent reports for anyone to view on their website. But the ISSA, who are also funded by the Irish taxpayer through HRI, do not believe this applies to them. Mr Caldwell says their financial information is their own little secret.

I took this up with Margaret Davin, HRI's finance director. She said the ISSA should put their annual accounts up on their website for all to see and she obtained a copy of their 2013 accounts for me. They show there were directors' salaries for the year of over €33,000 and expenses and subsistence payments of a staggering €23,089. There are just two employees, Mr Caldwell and a secretary who works one day a week. The other notable amount in their accounts was €4655 for attending a soccer tournament in England.

There are no details available of what they actually do to protect the interests of stable staff. They do not keep an office register of any issues raised by stable staff, the action taken and eventual outcome. I was told Mr Caldwell attends over 90% of all Ireland's race meetings every year, where he is available for any staff to approach him with an employment problem – except most staff aren't there because they are hard at work back at the training yards. He is not allowed to go into a training yard to talk to staff. I have been repeatedly told that staff have no confidence in the ISSA; if they went to them with a problem the chances are they would end up losing their job.

I asked Mr Caldwell for three months for a breakdown of the directors' salaries and expenses. He refused to provide them and eventually said: "We have received legal advice that we don't have to give out the information you have requested. It's sensitive information and we don't have to give it out." This is nonsense. The ISSA is funded by the Irish taxpayer and how they operate should be totally transparent. The ISSA are legally and morally required to disclose their financial information in exactly the same way as HRI. Margaret Davin said governance is a very important issue at HRI; that should be the same at the ISSA.

Why is there so much secrecy about such a routine matter? This financial information should be readily available – full transparency is vitally important to maintain integrity. In the circumstances there is a perfectly fair question to ask. Is there something in the financial information Mr Caldwell does not wish to reveal? He doesn't seem to do transparency and integrity.

I have learned he owns a number of racehorses, which his son Garry trains for him. I have also been told he acts as a de facto assistant trainer to Pat Martin and regularly represents the Co Meath trainer at race meetings, saddling runners amongst other duties. When I asked him about this, he said: "I'm not going to answer that. You find out for yourself." I did. As of 1 October 2015 he is listed on the Irish Turf Club's website as the authorised representative for both Pat Martin and Garry Caldwell – he's an assistant trainer in all but name.

In November 2014, Mr Martin appeared before a disciplinary committee of the Turf Club, who have been responsible for the integrity and reputation of Irish racing for over 200 years, as a result of a random inspection at his training yard. Turf Club officials found six "anomalies" during their inspection. Crucially, as far as stable staff in Ireland are concerned, they said they could find no evidence that employee bonuses won by the yard at the races had been paid to staff despite Mr Martin informing the Turf Club they were paid. Investigators were also unable to confirm that employees named as having received bonuses were even employed by the trainer. He had kept the bonus money due to his staff for himself, which is a serious breach of Turf Club rules. Actually, you might even call it stealing. This is a problem which continually haunts racing.

The workers who had not been paid their bonus payments confirmed in writing at the disciplinary meeting that the trainer had now paid them the money they were owed. He was fined a total of €780 for all six "anomalies," which is the term the Turf Club quaintly uses to describe breaking the rules. He also failed to produce the medicines register for inspection. How can stable staff in Ireland have any confidence whatsoever that Mr Caldwell is looking after their interests in a fair and honest manner when the trainer for whom he acts as an assistant has been found in breach of such serious charges. Or doesn't HRI believe this is serious enough? After all, he is also an HRI director.

It gets much worse. In 2013, a qualified rider employed by Garry Caldwell sent a letter of complaint to the ISSA that he had been sacked for raising issues about his pay. Garry Caldwell had only been paying Jason Delaney €200 per week, less than €5 an hour, when he had been promised much more. He had been working more than 40 hours over six days every week for six months and Garry Caldwell was always making excuses for not paying him the full amount. Jason stuck with it, but when he was sacked he wrote to the ISSA to ask for help to get over €2000 in back pay the trainer had withheld from him. Bernard Caldwell tore the letter up and ignored Jason's complaint.

This is the chief executive officer and chairman of the Irish Stable Staff Association, who are supposed to protect the basic rights of racing's workforce. Jason told me: "Mick Maher was very helpful, but Bernard Caldwell swore at me on the phone and said they did me a favour giving me a job and they wouldn't be giving the money they owed me."

Then there is the story of the young woman who worked in one of the biggest National Hunt yards in the country which shows exactly the problems people in the industry face day in and day out; the ISSA is a watchdog without bark or bite and there is a constant fear of losing your job if you step out of line. She raised a number of issues with the ISSA, including having to work excessive hours, having no mid-morning break, no canteen and just one toilet shared by a huge number of people. She gave all the details in several emails to the ISSA, including her name, but they wouldn't act.

This was Bernard Caldwell's reply: "Following your last email, I would like to point out that it is not ISSA policy to respond to accusations without proof of identity; the ISSA will not leave ourselves open to liable (sic)." You could not make that up in your wildest dreams. Every story about him shows he is on the wrong team; he is doing more to support the Irish Racehorse Trainers Association than stable staff. He didn't want to get involved in a complaint against a major figure in Irish racing, so yet again he did nothing.

In her final email to the ISSA, she said she was incredibly disappointed nothing had been done. "I was always led to believe that the ISSA stood up for stable staff rights in the workplace. Why is it that in this country those at the top are untouchable? I have left the yard and I've left a lot of friends there who deserve better."

All the while HRI turn a blind eye to what is going on at the ISSA and, more importantly, what is not going on to help look after those who work in an industry which has a sad history of exploiting and abusing vulnerable young people.

When I emailed HRI with a list of 17 points I wanted to raise, Margaret Davin said: "Mr Caldwell is better placed to respond to this. I will forward a hard copy to Mr Caldwell to allow him to respond as he sees appropriate." I heard nothing more. No one wants to give a straight answer to a straight question; it's obviously difficult to defend the indefensible so the best way out is to say nothing at all.

The Irish horse industry is flying. HRI chief executive, Brian Kavanagh, said in his 2013 report: "The horse racing and breeding sector is an industry which contributes about €1 billion annually to the Irish economy, employs in excess of 16,000 people and is responsible for exports worth €205 million." Everything has gone up another level since then. Exports of Irish bred horses increased to €229 million in 2014. Ireland is the largest producer of thoroughbred foals in Europe and fourth in the world, but no one at HRI cares enough about the the workforce which contributes so much to this success story. A few stable staff awards and best turned out prizes are just a bit of gloss to make the picture look pretty.

M/s Davin said the ISSA is independent of HRI. It's not: it's a puppet totally controlled by Horse Racing Ireland. Worst of all, its a puppet riddled with infighting and with some of those involved only interested in what they can get out of it. The ISSA needs a complete overhaul so the interests of the brilliant staff working in the horse industry in Ireland are cared for as you would expect and it should include those from both the racing and stud sides.

HRI, which is ruled by rich trainers and millionaire stud owners, do not see any need for change, but they are about to be forced to take some belated action. The Irish Government's Department of Agriculture commissioned a review by independent experts and one of their findings released in 2012 said HRI were not adequately representing the interests of employees in the industry.

New legislation is to be introduced in the autumn of 2015 which compels racing's hierarchy to set up an Industry Services Committee to represent jockeys, stable staff in racing yards and others employed directly in the industry, which should include stud staff although they are not specifically named. Brendan Gleeson of the Department of Agriculture said the legislation being introduced is intended to strengthen governance and transparency and "improve accountability and control over state spending." This is not an initiative volunteered by HRI, they are being forced into this action and if they don't comply their government funding could be withheld. The Horse Racing Ireland Bill 2015 says: "HRI shall establish a committee to identify and improve the requirements of those employed in the industry and represent the interests of such workers."

The Irish horse world needs to sit up, take notice and make sure HRI acts. When I asked them what was being done about this they were unable to give any firm details. It also appears the ISSA will need to be forced into change. Look at the website of the National Association of Stable Staff and check out the support available to horse staff in the UK. It's embarassing to look at the ISSA website, which is at least three years out of date for most of its information and light years behind its UK counterpart for the services and help it provides to those who graft so hard in yards all over Ireland. Mr Caldwell is, though, very good at posting photographs of himself on Facebook.

The board of directors at ISSA sum up the very serious concerns about the way the organisation is run. It is dominated by Mr Caldwell, who also had his brother as a director in 2013/2014; travelling head lads Ger Flynn and Patrick O'Brien from the yards of Jim Bolger and Dermot Weld; and Shane Lyons, the brother and assistant trainer of Ger Lyons. Why is an assistant trainer on the board of an association which represents stable staff? When I asked Mr Caldwell about this, he replied: "I'm not going to get involved in that." Is it right that three of the main directors at ISSA hold influential positions with three of the biggest trainers in Ireland? Isn't there an obvious conflict of interest?

This same conflict of interest applies to Mr Caldwell, who not only acts as an assistant trainer but is also on the board of directors of HRI, the industry's governing body. You couldn't make this astonishing situation up.

There is no representation at grass roots level. I attended the annual general meeting of the association when it was finally held on 12 October 2015. There were 16 people there – 12 of them were directors on the board of ISSA, two were accountants representing the auditors and there were just two people from the thousands employed in racing throughout Ireland. It's some laugh that this organisation with no full time employees has a board of directors of 12 people.

Take a close look at the winners of the Irish Stud and Stable Staff Awards for 2015, so generously sponsored by Godolphin. The four main categories for racing were won by a member of staff from the Bolger, Weld and Lyons yards. A total of €37,000 of Godolphin's money went to these three yards each of which is represented by a director on the board of the ISSA, who organised the awards along with HRI. Those directors received a share of the Godolphin prize money allocated to the winning yards. That's some coincidence in an industry which has so many yards and thousands of staff all over Ireland to choose from. Not one employee from the country's brilliant National Hunt yards was deemed worthy of winning an award. I was told Noel Meade, in particular, was very angry about this.

Three of the remaining four categories for horse workers were won by two staff from Coolmore and one from Islanmore Stud in Limerick, a magnificent 400 acre estate bought by JP McManus for over €10 million in 2009 as a home for his daughter Sue Ann. The only award winner on the list who appears independent was an employee of Jockey Hall Stud, which is based just up the road from the ISSA at the Curragh.

> **No criticism is intended of the trainers mentioned and none at all is implied of the winners of these awards. They are all fine individuals who serve the racing and bloodstock industries well, but doesn't all this look like a private feast organised by a select few who are pursuing their own agenda with no consideration at all for the thousands of top class racing and stud staff outside their grubby little clique?**

Until now, Coolmore have never put anyone forward for the awards in the 11 years they have been running. In their first year, with all that Godolphin money up for grabs, they walk away with two winners. The awards were decided, apparently, by a committee comprising representatives of the Irish Thoroughbred Breeders Association (ITBA), the Irish Racehorse Trainers Association (IRTA), the ISSA and HRI. The ITBA have five senior Coolmore managers sitting on their management committee. No one at all was put forward from Ballydoyle for the racing staff awards, which is a story in itself. Wouldn't you say this inner circle, who had control over the awards and then won virtually all the awards, are just a little too cosy for comfort?

While Coolmore were happy to nominate staff for the ISSA awards, and win two of them, no one there belongs to the association. They won't accept a trade union, any association or any gathering however described to represent staff inside Coolmore. I'm told the same applies at Ballydoyle. You are on your own. Isn't this just a bit hypocritical?

In 1946, the Irish government set up the Labour Court which subsequently brought in Joint Labour Committees (JLCs). They have since played a significant role in establishing conditions of employment and minimum rates of pay for up to 200,000 people working in the lowest paid jobs in the country, the ones who are at the greatest risk of exploitation. In 2011, a group of fast food retailers faced with prosecution over pay and conditions for their staff mounted a successful challenge in the High Court which ruled JLCs were operating against the law. Coolmore Stud had also made a similar consitutional challenge when they appeared in court in Clonmel in May 2011 charged by the National Employment Rights Authority (NERA) with not paying their staff properly. As JLCs were deemed illegal by the High Court the charges against Coolmore and the others were dropped. They, effectively, escaped prosecution on a technicality.

The government subsequently carried out an extensive review of the system, which led to JLCs being reformed. All stakeholders were invited to take part and make submissions. Seven organisations attended a meeting to review the Agriculture JLC, including IRTA, ITBA, IBEC, who represented employers, SIPTU, representing trade unions, and the Irish Farmers Association (IFA).

According to the report into the review, which was published in October 2013, the ISSA were not present. Those actually working in the horse industry had no voice; the ISSA didn't turn up.

The IRTA, ITBA and the IFA either wanted the Agriculture JLC abolished altogether or the horse industry removed from it. The IRTA said the Irish racing industry could not operate within the restrictive confines which are imposed by law through the Agriculture JLC. "Thoroughbred horse racing is a hugely competitive industry and the Irish industry faces significant threats from abroad, in particular France and the UK, countries with less stringent work practices. Any system which has the potential to change or alter established work practices could jeopardise the industry's competitiveness, which ultimately could lead to owners moving horses abroad with the consequent loss of employment," the IRTA submitted.

Much the same drivel on changing established work practices was said about sending children sweeps up chimneys until it was finally made illegal in 1875. The Agriculture JLC requires that all workers are given Saturday and Sunday off every third week. The IRTA doesn't like this at all and that's why it wanted the horse industry removed from the system. They said trainers shouldn't have to give any of their staff every third weekend off because weekends are one of the key times in a training yard.

"It would mean that trainers would not be able to match the same horse with the same exercise rider/handler, which is recognised as best practice by trainers and works best for the handler and the horse from a health and safety point of view."

There was no mention of the physical safety and mental health of an employee having to work every weekend without even having one per month off. Taking the horse industry out of the JLC system would give trainers the right to force staff to work every weekend.

Both the IRTA and the ITBA told the review there was no history of employee unrest in the horse industry, which is not surprising considering stud and racing staff have next to no rights and no worthwhile association to stand up for them. The ITBA said: "There has been no evidence, anecdotal or otherwise, of any deterioration of pay and conditions for those working in the industry." But SIPTU, although not representing people in the horse industry, said there was widespread evidence of employers knocking pay and conditions down since 2010. The latest employment figures for the agriculture sector in late 2012 showed there were 19,000 employees in the agriculture, forestry and fishing industries of which 4300 were directly employed as stable staff in the horse racing and thoroughbred industries, they said.

If the horse industry was removed from the Agriculture JLC, trainers and stud owners in Ireland would have the power to decide what hours their staff worked and when they worked them. One hundred per cent control. And that's what has happened. In the face of such a one sided argument, with absolutely no input from those supposedly representing the staff involved, it is no surprise the review recommended taking the horse industry out of the JLC system. The government signed the review off and it will become law in due course.

It needs to be emphasised again how much Coolmore dominates the ITBA, who advocated strongly for the complete abolition of the Agriculture JLC. There are five senior managers from the stud on the ITBA Council and several others with close ties, including Eimear Mulhern, the daughter of Magnier's close friend Charlie Haughey; Joe Foley, who once worked at Coolmore and now stands a couple of stallions which were top racehorses at Ballydoyle; and Cathy Grassick, niece of Coolmore's Christy Grassick. The ITBA is a home from home for the Coolmore managers.

Compliance with employment law is ensured through regular inspections by NERA. That's how Coolmore ended up in court in Clonmel in May 2011. With the horse sector now out of the Agriculture JLC this will mean significantly less regulation of employers in the racing and bloodstock industries. As an example of this serious situation, in just the first six months of 2011, NERA carried out 33 inspections in the agriculture division and 58% did not meet minimum employment terms and conditions, which amounted to E87,771 in unpaid wages. This is just the tip of the iceberg. Compliance with the law is a major issue.

In July 2015, the Irish Field carried a story reminding trainers they have to make payments of winning bonuses allocated to staff by racing's administrators according to strict rules and trainers do not have a right to take a share or decide how the bonus is distributed. Compliance with HRI's and the Turf Club's own rules is a major issue. Any way you care to look at it, stable staff have even less rights now horse workers have been removed from the JLC system. Employers have tightened their already fierce grip around the throats of the racing and bloodstock industries and workers are at a growing risk of exploitation

The Racing Academy and Centre of Education (RACE) based in Kildare do a great job training a new crop of potential jockeys each year. Twenty eight young men and women graduated in 2015 after a 10 month residential course. Johnny Murtagh and Cathy Gannon are just two professional jockeys to have come through the system. Keith Rowe, the director of RACE, has warned the Irish racing industry that more must be done to develop properly structured careers for young people going through RACE so they can branch off into other areas if their initial aspirations to become a jockey are unsuccessful.

"After all the initial groundwork, it seems a shame that capable individuals sometimes feel compelled to leave the country or depart the industry due to the absence of any suitable framework for advancement. As the class of 2015 finish up their programme, we wish them well and hope they meet a greater level of support from the industry along their career pathway than many of their predecessors have enjoyed," he said.

That sums up the situation for all young people coming into the horse industry. Wheel them in, wheel them out. There's always someone else looking for a job, but that will change. With the country starting to prosper again there will be alternatives for Ireland's young people, as one trainer pointed out in the Irish Field: "Young people are leaving the industry and something needs to be done about it," he said. And what about all those young people who left when jobs evaporated as the financial apocalypse exploded in 2009? Will they want to return to Ireland and an industry where you are exploited by being forced to work excessive hours for low pay? What do they think of an industry where some trainers steal staff bonus payments? Will they need the hassle and be, as one long standing horseman in the Kildare area told me "treated like dirt?" Look at what happened to Jason Delaney. He has gone back to college to further his education – he has finished with the horse industry.

The racing authorities in the UK have committed £3 million to fund a campaign to attract young people into their industry. It is estimated there are up to a thousand jobs which trainers are unable to fill because of a lack of available staff. What happens in England happens in Ireland and vice versa. It has been said even top trainers with the most successful yards are struggling to fill vacancies. Jockey Tom Cannon supplied the perfect answer to that when he tweeted: "Stable staff just want to be treated with decency and respect half the time regardless of how successful the yard is."

Since I raised all these staff issues with HRI, the Racing Post has published a story headlined **Applications for stud staff positions drop**. Katherine Fidler's excellent article on 24 August 2015 said this: "The Racing Post recently highlighted the growing crisis among British stable staff – the crisis being there simply aren't enough. Estimates suggest there could be between 500 to 1,000 vacancies waiting to be filled at a time when the BHA is striving to increase the number of horses in training.

"A large proportion of the proposed extra runners will likely come from the domestic markets the British and Irish bloodstock industries, which themselves require a large fleet of skilled and dedicated workers to keep producing the horses without which racing could not survive." She pointed out that while racing staff had the support of the National Association of Stud Staff in Britain "stud employees are without a dedicated representative body." Ted Voute, a leading breeder and consignor to sales around the world, said he has noticed a big change in the quality and numbers of people looking for work in the stud business.

"It's a lot more difficult, but I don't know why. People seem to think it might be the working hours, or younger people like to work Monday to Friday. I wonder whether we're doing enough as an industry to get kids in schools interested in what we're doing."

What has happened at Coolmore as a followup to the health issues faced by its night work schedules? Nothing much, except another man who worked long hours at night for many years was diagnosed with cancer. Night staff are still working the same illegal, risky hours.

Marcy Borders died from stomach cancer on 25 August 2015, aged just 41. She had been covered from head to toe in the maelstrom of dust which enveloped everyone trying to flee the collapse of the Twin Towers in New York on 11 September 2001. As of May 2015, it has been reported that over 4000 first responders, rescue workers and survivors have been diagnosed with cancer linked to the terrorist attack on the World Trade Centre.

Not every case of cancer anywhere in the world can be fully explained. There are still many unknowns even now, but explanations can be found in people's lifestyles and environment. It is criminal not to act when those potential explanations have been highlighted. Doing nothing is not an option. How many people have to get cancer before Coolmore will act?

Nearly seven months after Mary Purcell raised issues about the death of her son Aidan in 2011, she has received no answers to the questions she has asked. She followed up the original complaint made through a local garda with two letters to Supt William Leahy at Clonmel Garda Station.

Other than to say he is looking into the matter, Mary has heard nothing back. I last spoke with the coroner who conducted the inquest into Aidan's death, Mr Paul Morris, on 10 July 2015, when he told me he would write to Mary about the case within the next week. Mary has received no letter from Mr Morris. There is now another cover-up on top of the cover-up that plainly happened when Aidan died in 2011. I am going to spell it out once more.

Aidan, a twenty year old who was in perfect health, was found dead at Coolmore Stud on 30 April 2011. The coroner's verdict four months later said it was suicide by hanging. Soon after his death, his heartbroken family were told he had been badly bullied at Coolmore. They raised their concerns with the coroner, who said he would look into it. He didn't look into it. Gardai were either misled or didn't bother to carry out a thorough investigation. They never once visited Mary at her home in Glengoole and she was never asked one single question about what might have happened. Just one colleague, a barn foreman at the yard where Aidan worked, gave evidence at the inquest, when important information was withheld and the coroner misled. The evidence given at the inquest did not give the full story and a new investigation needs to be carried out to discover the truth.

All of this was put in writing to Supt Leahy. He has not replied other than to say he is looking into it. That was nearly seven long months ago. Mary Purcell put her trust yet again in the authorities and waited patiently. Yet again she has been let down. How long does Supt Leahy need? If there are problems, why hasn't he contacted Mary to brief her on what he is doing about her complaint. It is reasonable to assume in the circumstances that he is having trouble defending the wholly inadequate investigation carried out by his officers and that is why he has told Mary absolutely nothing.

Perhaps he is going to say and do nothing in the hope the Purcells will give up and go away.

Why didn't gardai investigate this case in an acceptable way? Were they influenced by anyone to hush this matter up, because that's what it looks like. A cloak of secrecy was thrown over what happened to Aidan on 30 April 2011. The Irish Mail reported that John Magnier gave England's Queen Elizabeth a private tour of Coolmore shortly after Aidan's tragic death. Was this the reason for the wall of silence at the time?

Mary is not giving up. She is now going to contact the Attorney General, Maire Whelan, to request the inquest be reopened because she believes the serious crime of perjury was committed at the original one in 2011. She is also making a formal complaint to the Garda Ombudsman about the investigation into her son's death and, as this book goes to print, Supt Leahy's reluctance to give her any answers this past six months and more. It's a disgrace. And a scandal.

I wrote to Coolmore in June 2015 and told them I would like to ask them some questions. I said I wanted to do this to give them every opportunity to tell their side of what I had written in my book, in the interests of fairness and balance. I received a reply from solicitors Arthur Cox, of Dublin, Belfast, London, New York and Silicon Valley. The details of that reply, they said, are top secret. What reply? Three months later I had another reason to write to Arthur Cox.

"This is now the third letter I have received from your firm written by three different solicitors and all saying the same

thing. I have already given you my answer. I have previously told you that I consider you are trying to harass and intimidate me. You should know that it is not about what you think is acceptable behaviour but more about what effect this is having on the person being harassed and intimidated. I have had enough of it. Are you listening?"

The rich are getting richer and the poor are getting poorer. An Oxfam report has revealed the richest 1% of people own more than half the world's wealth. By comparison, 80% of the world's population own only 5% of the world's wealth. Rich tycoons can never be rich enough and don't they just love the power and control that go with it.

The Volkswagen scandal has shown that there is a crisis in capitalism. Paul Mason of Channel 4 news said this in his book, **PostCapitalism**: "Capitalism is creating bullshit jobs. We have nothing better for people to do, so we are going to create jobs to which you can't apply technology – jobs for minimum wages." That's if you are lucky enough to even get minimum wages. The problem for those working in the horse industry is not about improving pay and conditions; it's about ensuring you actually get what has already been agreed and is the law – not being forced to work excessive hours, paying correct overtime rates, getting proper rest periods, working in a safe environment, being aware of mental health issues.

In England in 1972, three years before John Magnier, Vincent O'Brien and Robert Sangster combined to set Coolmore on its way, the industrial conglomerate Lonrho, headed by another driven tycoon, Tiny Rowland, was famously described by Prime Minister Edward Heath as "the unpleasant and unacceptable face of capitalism." There are many who would say Coolmore, who set the standard in Ireland, have become the unpleasant and unacceptable face of racing and bloodstock.

Everyone has the right to freedom of speech; it says so in the Irish Constitution and the European Convention on Human Rights. I must have asked a lot of good questions along the way, which is my right, because no one has wanted to answer them. Everyone has the right to silence and everyone has the right to draw their own conclusions about that silence.

"First they ignore you
Then they laugh at you
Then they fight you
Then you win."

Mahatma Gandhi

ACKNOWLEDGEMENTS

Muriel Lennox's brilliant book, **Northern Dancer – The Legend and His Legacy,** provided the foundations for my story. Muriel's painstaking research over many years means that her book will be an even more important record of the great Northern Dancer a hundred years from now.

Patrick and Nick Robinson's **Horsetrader – Robert Sangster and the Rise and Fall of the Sport of Kings** was another fascinating read which gave an insight into the larger than life existence of Sangster, Vincent O'Brien and John Magnier in the early years of Coolmore.

Vincent O'Brien - The Official Biography, by Jacqueline O'Brien and Ivor Herbert, is a classic from the racing world which will last forever, which is entirely appropriate considering who the book is about.

Life's Too Short to Cry is a compelling story of the life of Battle of Britain hero Tim Vigors, who laid the foundations for Coolmore Stud.

Conor Ryan's book, **Stallions & Power – The Scandals of the Irish National Stud,** is another notable for it's exhaustive research. When will the racing industry in Ireland accept that bullying by those who hold all the power is just not acceptable?

Donal's Mountain – How One Son Inspired a Nation must have been so tough for Fionnbar Walsh to write, but every page was worth the pain.

The national newspapers in Ireland and the UK and the journalists and photographers involved in reporting on racing set a very high standard. Those Irish newspapers include the Times, Independent, Mail and Examiner for the stories I was able to draw on over time and the same goes for the Guardian, Telegraph and Mail in the UK.

In my view, Donn McLean is always worth reading in the Sunday Times and David Ashforth at the Racing Post will always be a hero of mine. Those interested in the racing and bloodstock industries are lucky to have the Irish Field there for them week in and week out.